Building Up Self-Confidence

A Fundamental Way of Conquering Fear

Chinedum Joachim Konye Nwadike
(Roseann Nkechinyere), HFSN.

This is a work of fiction. Names, characters, places, and incidents either are the product of the author's imagination or are used fictitiously. Any resemblance to actual persons, living or dead, events, or locales is entirely coincidental.

Copyright © 2021 by Chinedum Joachim Konye Nwadike

All rights reserved. No part of this book may be reproduced or used in any manner without written permission of the copyright owner except for the use of quotations in a book review.

ISBNs:
Paperback: 978-1-914078-77-4
eBook: 978-1-914078-78-1

Published by PublishingPush.com

Dedication

I dedicate this book firstly to the memory of my elderly brother, Mr. Ikechi Sylvester Konye Nwadike, for the agony and fear he sustained from his estranged marriage and as a result of which he died. Dede'm Ikechi, Jeremiah, Ofojiogu, Ikejiofor, Oganampa-VC-10, remember that, "death comes to every individual. There is an amazing democracy about death. It is not an aristocracy for some of the people, but a democracy for all of the people. Kings die and beggars die; rich men die and poor men die; old people die and young people die; death comes to innocent and it comes to the guilty. Death is the irreducible common denominator of all men." I hope you can find some consolation from Christianity's affirmation that death is not the end. Death is not a period that ends the great sentence of life, but a comma that punctuates it to more lofty significance. Death is not a blind alley that leads the human race into a state of nothingness, but an open door which leads man into life eternal. Thanks for your contribution to this book. Our light will never turn off. You are my inspiration, my role model, and my hero. Remember, Dede'm, as Mahatma Gandhi rightly put it, "Death is the appointed end of all life;" so you are not alone.

I also dedicate this book to my parents, Mr. Mmuoegbulem Konyezuruyahu John Nwadike and Mrs. Ojukwu Agim Monica Konye Nwadike, and to my late sister, Mrs. Clementina Konye Alisigwe, and our late little brother, Onyemaechi Konye Nwadike.

This is also dedicated to Mr. Simeon Basil Nwadike, a fearless fighter of justice; a truth speaker. You're noble as Nelson Mandela, Mahatma Gandhi and Martin Luther King Jr. God is on your side. Keep up your good work.

Mr. Ikechi Sylvester Konye
A Gentle Great Teacher,
A Man of Integrity, Rest in Peace.

Acknowledgements

With God, all things are possible and with the mystery of possibilities, one can always conquer impossibilities. Glory be to God Almighty for His blessings, wisdom, and good health bestowed on me all these years of hard labour and struggling. All these years I spent in the USA and Britain, I have been enjoying the grace and privilege of sound health of both mind and body. I sincerely thank God for such a special show of love to me. Your love, oh Lord, sustains me in the midst of all my troubles; your consolation gladdens my soul" Psalm 94:18-19 (p. 761) Jerusalem Bible. Surely, His goodness and kindness shall follow me all the days of my life (Psalm 23:6 (p. 693) Jerusalem Bible.

It is with great pride that I give special reverence to my parents, Papa Konye Mmuoegbulem John and Mama Ojukwu Monica (Agim) Konye Nwadike, who gave me the privilege of acquiring both primary and secondary education in spite of the fact that they were uneducated. My parents showed me the true pathway to life.

Huge thanks, Mama, for using proverbs, idiomatic expressions, figurative expressions, and body language to direct and instruct me and all your children. You gave me the best of informal education which aided me greatly in coping with the demands of formal education. May the Lord reward you abundantly in heaven for the wonderful work you did in my life and for making me what I am today. I am pleased and proud of my parents.

I thank you in a special way, all my Religious Sisters in the United Kingdom who gave me every co-operation being their Zonal Superior, which created a peaceful atmosphere and successful mission in Britain. Thanks for your team efforts and may God reward you splendidly. Keep it up, wherever you may be.

No author ever writes a book alone. For this reason, I am deeply grateful to all individuals whose expert ideas and wonderful creative inputs contributed towards this production. I am profoundly grateful to you - many thanks. My heartfelt gratitude and appreciation also go to all who directed and guided me when putting this work together. Your motivational encouragement inspired and sustained my ardent efforts towards the completion of this book. You were hugely resourceful and insightful for the success of this book. I am proud of all – God bless you.

I give many thanks to my late elderly brother, Ikechi Sylvester Konye, (VC-10), for his contribution on the fear aspects. Your death left a huge hole in my mind; rest in peace. God is in control.

I don't have adequate words to express my sincere gratitude to Rev. Fr. Dr. Eberechukwu Cyprian Adibe for agreeing to write the foreword to this book. Father, thanks immensely for your brilliant inspiration.

I must not forget to extend my enormous appreciation to my brother in-law, Engineer Declan and his wife, Mrs. Livina

Onyeajuwu, for your great vision and influence to this project.

I also give many thanks to Sir Fabian Nnodim for taking the pain to edit this work. Thanks so much.

I must recognize all my Primary, Secondary, and University Teachers for educating me. You are all great; you made significant impacts towards my intellectual enhancement, so many, many thanks.

Many thanks to the Marist Brothers of the Schools for the important role played in my life's journey. You are role models. May God abundantly reward all of you who are still living and grant eternal repose to the souls of the departed ones. Brother Andrew S. Iwuagwu and the late Brother Bernard Okafor; your predictions concerning my academic pursuit were exact. Brother Andrew, thanks a lot for your efforts in seeing that this production is edited well. I am thrilled.

In a special way, I doff my hat to my motherland -Igboland in southeastern Nigeria, to my naturalized country, the United States of America, and my residential country, Great Britain, where I got the inspiration for writing this book. Long life to these great nations that have contributed a lot in molding my life. These great countries have proved to me the wise saying- "Endurance is a mighty power and patience gives many good things," for they have fortified and encouraged me to attain my highest goal and enable me to be where I am now and what I am today. I pray God to guide the leaders of these great Nations and to grant to them more wisdom and discretion to rule and to guide the people entrusted to them.

I will never forget the late Mr. Aloysius Roland Clarke, my former USA Manager, who made my academic pursuit possible by granting me an opportunity to work in his company and allowing me to use some of my work periods to complete my class assignments. Your legacy will never fade away from my heart and I pray God to reveal your killer; rest in peace, Mr. Al.

I owe great appreciation to Dave and Tony Connelly and their families, Mary Best and her family, as well as their prayer groups for their tremendous support for our mission in the UK. God bless you all. Dave and Carol, the two books you gave me – Feel the Fear and Do It Anyway and Panic Attacks – had an incredible impact on this work. I appreciate you very much; your books were very helpful for my research.

Thanks to all the staff of the Good Counsel Network United Kingdom for assisting the ladies in pregnancy crisis and the needy. Thanks for allowing our congregation – The Holy Family Sister of the Needy - to work with you. Knowing you is a great inspiration.

I am most grateful to brilliant authors such as Oprah Winfrey - *What I know for Sure,* Og Mandino - *The Greatest Salesman in the World,* and Stephen R. Covey - The 7 Habits of Highly Effective People, Dr. Viktor E. Frankl - Man's Search for Meaning, Margaret Dureke - Words and Phrases of Wisdom for Spiritual and Emotional Upliftment, Sarah Litvinoff – The Confidence Plan and others I could not mention here. Your wisdom gave huge enlightenment to my research. I thank you all.

What of Jack Canfield? I must acknowledge you, Jack, in a special way for your most magnificent inspiring book –

"*The Success Principle: How to Get from Where You Are to Where You Want to Be.*" Jack, I am glad to be where I want to be at this moment. Your book had a remarkable influence on my research. I lack the words to express my thoughts about your book. It made me wish to go back to teenage life to begin afresh. Since it is impossible for me to do so, I will endeavour to enhance the life of the younger generation who are ready to extract your wisdom. Your book is a piece of gold. Thanks so much, Jack. You're highly recommended. And I recommend all to read this book to obtain enlightenment in your journey towards success. Jack, I re-titled your book as a "Book of Wisdom and Enlightenment." God bless you, Jack -you are a fabulous author.

To all individuals who will find this book – **"Building Up Self-Confidence: A Fundamental Way of Conquering Fear"** - useful and will be able to improve your quality of life, especially those living in fear, I wish all of you good luck and I urge you to say, "I will resist until I succeed." Do not be afraid; rather, stand firm and keep striving. Enlarge your vision and your knowledge by reading this book. Set your goal now to reach where you want to be. Hence, you will be on the right trail to enjoy a fruitful labour.

To all who supported me and all who challenged me in life, you all contributed hugely in making me what I am right now. I am very grateful to you all. I have succeeded by making my dream of writing this book a reality. "To die is to rust and to resurrect." God bless you all. "If I should walk in the valley of darkness, no evil would I fear." Psalm 23:4, Jerusalem Bible (p.693).

Farewell Fear! "Those who put their trust in the Lord are like Mount Zion that cannot be shaken; that stands firm forever." Psalm 125:1, Jerusalem Bible (p.793). Thank you, Good Lord, for enabling me to resist until I succeeded. "Near restful waters He leads me to revive my drooping spirit." Psalm 23:2-3, Jerusalem Bible (p. 693).

Reverend Sister Chinedum Joachim
Konye Nwadike, HFSN.

Foreword

With God all things are possible and with the mystery of possibilities one can always conquer impossibilities.

I am pleased to contribute a foreword to this book- *Building Up Self Confidence - A Fundamental Way of Conquering Fear.* This is a unique book which will enhance, uplift, enlighten, empower, and motivate anybody who reads it. This book will enable you to fill up that "psychological crack" created in you by fear and lack of self-confidence. This book is a well thought out writing put together through years of experiences working with pathological situations in America. Fear is a negative crumbling situation in one's life that can run down and ruin the person's potentialities in life. For those who want to come out of fear in their life, this book – Building Up Self-Confidence and Conquering Fear- is a must-read. The book has three chapters, each dealing with how to handle fear in different circumstances. The author, an indigenous daughter of Ndiowerri Village in Orlu Imo State, Nigeria, is a Reverend Sister of The Holy Family Sisters of the Needy. Chinedum Joachim Konye Nwadike, HFSN is holder of an Associate Degree in Medical Secretarial Diploma with honour-roll, Lackawanna Collage, Pennsylvania USA; Bachelor of Science in Computer Information Systems,

Strayer University, Washington DC, USA; Master of Science Degree in Business Administration, with honour-roll, Strayer University, Washington DC, USA and Doctorate Degree of Philosophy/Psychology, with honour-roll, Lacrosse University, Louisiana, USA. She has been in association with many people through various experiences.

The book she put together is a book for humanity and for the work of God.

Rev. Fr. Dr. Eberechukwu C. Adibe
Rector St. Paul's Catholic Parish Okwudor-Njaba

Preface

Having been in association with many people with various experiences, coupled with my varied knowledge in academic fields, this book on fear and building self-confidence is detailed because fear, as a universal emotion, exists in different forms. As such, I have endeavoured to incorporate in its entirety the practical experiences of many business people, executives, sales people, engineers, bankers, accountants, students, ministers, psychologists, psychotherapists and philosophers, as well as physicians, who had applied the principles being illustrated here to achieve the remedial solutions of problems resulting from lack of self-confidence and fear. This book will be an essential role model that plays in your journey towards self-development and growth. This book will provide positive ideas that may enhance your aspiration towards building self-confidence and conquering your fear. It will provide you with the avenue of self-prestige that uplifts your total being. In this book, I intend to help you develop within yourselves the skills of getting into the habit of building self-confidence and getting rid of fear. Therefore, it is not something difficult to do. It requires you to be hardworking, paying attention, listening attentively to people's talks and performances, bench-marking role models, reading inspirational books like

The 7 Habits of Highly Effective People: Powerful Lessons in Personal Change by Covey, Stephen R., Feel, The Fear And Do It Anyway by Susan Jeffers, The Autobiography of Martin Luther King, Jr., role models like Nelson Mandela, Mahatma Gandhi, Pride Of Black British Women by Deborah King, and a host of others. It also involves reading novels, listening to tapes, speeches, and sermons, paying attention to famous quotes, reading Newspapers, especially the encouraging and motivational articles of the papers, joining assertive clubs, debating clubs, and being observant and keen to learn. You have a fabulous opportunity and resources to awaken self-confidence. Positive thinking offers a power boost to help you handle whatever life offers to you. Be mindful that a lack of self-confidence and fear is universal, so, you are not alone with your experience; many others do experience them too. Why are you hesitating? Work on it and free yourself. Structuring self-confidence and overcoming fear takes an awful lot of courage and laborious efforts. Perseverance is the key. For this reason, muster courage and exhibit your true potential power. In this way, little by little, your previous obstacles will eventually vanish immediately and automatically, you will begin to have a new self which results in self-esteem. Once you're ready to build up your self-confidence, try as much as you can to avoid all distressing thoughts which are misleading your reasoning.

You have the ultimate power to shape your self-confidence and conquer your pressing fear now; it is you who will put all your potential power into freeing yourself from low self-esteem. It is your sole responsibility to seek guidance on how to go about it. Keep reading motivational books and asking questions of those who know better than you but do not ask arrogant fellows otherwise they could put you off. Follow the directions as I have stated above. Once you do this, you're on the path towards your self-assurance. You're the master who holds the balance of power in your hands. Therefore, do this to feel the tremendous progress of your will and power. If you have a desire for something, you must have a time for it. For this reason, be focused and never let your mind roam about. Rather, focus your mind in order to identify your desired goal. Let it be what you would like and enjoy. I desired to be a reverend sister; I worked hard to reach this level and I am happy to have achieved it, and I am enjoying it. Don't look back and feel regretful. I enjoyed studying psychology and I am still enjoying reading psychology books because they enhance my knowledge and personality. Anything that would be a roadblock to you, just push it aside and say, "next." Then, ask yourself, where do I go from here? The answer is, once you follow the next step, you walk through doors of golden opportunities that lead to self-actualization.

This book will give you an incredible insight and light that lead to enlightenment that awakens your vision. This enables you to make a new start with powerful encouragement and inspiration that brings about coping with and surmounting fear. I am convinced that you will ultimately find this book very helpful. Start building your self-confidence as soon as you get hold of this book. "It is never too late to go after your dreams. Always remind yourself that dreams do not come marked with expiration dates on them. Even if you have been putting them off all this while, it is time to take action. Stop talking about it. Just do it! So, what if you "failed" before? You have just become a stronger and wiser person and would definitely be more optimistic to take the next step because you can now apply what you learned from the not so-successful ones to your next venture…" "It does not matter what was or hasn't been; the sun will rise again and the sun will shine again. No condition is permanent. In fact, the only thing that is permanent is change itself. Everything else is evolving. Therefore, never give up hope that your condition will change. It is never over until it is over. And it's only over when you die; for as long as you are alive and doing your best, your day will come!" Be sure you engage in a career that you desire and you can handle. "Every thousand –mile journey begins with the first step." This development was merely the first step in a long journey towards self-confidence.

The future of your new self begins with your bold effort to free yourself from fear and lack of self-confidence. You have to face challenges so that you who are fearful become fearless and more powerful. I am advocating and encouraging you never to allow the cold hand of fear to ruin your destiny. No matter how long and difficult it will be to reinstate your self-confidence, just begin now to work on it. Once upon a time begins a story. As you begin, shine a light of hope towards achieving your crucial goal. I advise you to take forthright action to overturn your fear and establish your self-assurance. Never dwell on the past; rather, move on with the future.

Here, we have many people from all walks of life telling real stories of life-saving events that made them feel restored and whole because they applied the right principles for building self-confidence and fighting fear. Our trouble is not that we do not know these principles, but that we often neglect to use them.

The purpose of this book is to highlight, restate, illustrate, streamline, revitalize, and vindicate the use of ancient and basic truths and the resulting profound and proficient rewards in order to inspire and make you apply them to your lives. Pick up this book and go through it and discover that you have been lucky enough to have found a treasure. This book gives guidelines and direction, also the assistance you need to improve yourself and to empower you to come out of your phobic fear and to uplift the self. I believe and I have the confidence that once you finish reading this book, you will begin to have a new self and overcome low self-esteem. Good luck on your adventures.

> *"Believe in yourself, get lots of experience, be confident about putting yourself forward and look for ways of creating opportunities for yourself."*
> -Sharron Wallace
> Pride of Black British Women
> By Deborah King 1995, (p. 69).

Table of Contents

Dedication   iii
Acknowledgements   v
Foreword   xi
Preface   xiii

Introduction   1

Chapter One
Building Up Confidence in Oneself without
Inhibition of Fear   19
    Section I: What is Fear?   34
    Section II: Individual Views on Fear   40
    Section III: Management of Fear   57
    Section IV: Overcoming Fear that Invades
       Your Self-Confidence   62
    Section V: Fear is a Quality of a Virtue in a
       Modest Person   71
    Section VI: Fear is a Preprogrammed
       Genetic Aspect of Life   77
    Section VII: Fear: Pathological Aspect of a
       Neurotic Person   81
    Section VIII: Fear: Biological Function of
       Emotions of a Person   84

Section IX: Instances of Fear	86
Section X: All Power to Your Elbow Hang Tough	92

Chapter Two

Section I: How to Treat Fear in Case of Pathological Situations	99
Section II: Fear Breeds Stress	106
Section III: Factors Affecting Confidence	139
Section IV: Relaxation is Needed	156
Section V: Help Yourself to Adjust to Change and Get Organized	160
Section VI: Be Assertive: Passive and Aggressive	162

Chapter Three

Section I: Take 100 Percent Responsibility for Your Life; Total Commitment	169
Section II: Release the Brakes Avoid Fencing Yourself in at Times	194
Section III: Act As If	210
Section IV: Acting, Being More Confident, Achieve Your Full Potential	221
Section V: Experience Your Fear and Act Anyway; Replace the Physical Sensations Fear Brings	234
Section VI: Reject Rejection - Just Say Next	238
Section VII: Commit to Constant and Never-Ending Improvement	243
Section VIII: Be Confident in Asking for What You Need	250
Section IX: When Your Fear is Really a Phobia	253
Section X : The Challenge	258
Section XI: Practice – Practice - Practice	262

Section XII: Exceeding Expectations ... 273
Section XIII: Time Schedule in Planning as You Search for Self-Confidence that Dismantles Your Fear ... 278
Section XIV: Education Schedule for Under-Achievement and Under-Privileged Students from 2 Years - 40 Years Instils Confidence into Under-Privileged ... 284
Section XV: Transcend Your Limiting Beliefs ... 299
Section XVI: Fuel Your Success with Passion and Enthusiasm ... 310
Section XVII: Just Say No to the Things that Would Inhibit Your Self-Confidence ... 313
Section XVIII: Transform Your Inner Critic into Your Inner Coach ... 326
Section XIX: Create Successful Relationships ... 341

Conclusion ... 355
Bibliography ... 373
About the Author ... 381

Introduction

This book will assist you to master the fundamental way of building self-confidence. The main focus of this book is all about self-enhancement through gaining self-confidence and self-assertion, avoiding negative self-image and taking a positive stance.

To gain self-confidence, first of all, you ought to value yourself and accept yourself. Then, develop personal techniques, skills, strategies, and methodology for it to transpire. Maintain positive control of the methodology you choose to use. Stay with the struggle till you realize your objective and arm yourself with greater readiness to win. You must stand with a greater determination and willingness to conquer. And you have to move on with powerful conviction to make your dream goal a reality. To achieve your objective, uphold a healthy frame of mind and body by uplifting your self-worth. Avoid self-doubt. If you're constantly ill, your self-confidence is at stake. Subsequently, you have to be healthy and happy first and in good relations with self. Your efforts will never be in vain. Explore various ways to achieve this ultimate desire. These various ways can give you a compendium of ideals and knowledge on how to employ self-confidence.

Many people have misunderstood self-confidence or achieving self-confidence. They think that attaining self-confidence is achieved by getting intoxicated with rum or taking hard drugs in order to feel high. No, it is absolutely the wrong way. Self-confidence is not being over-pompous, arrogant, sarcastic, or proud. A self-confident person doesn't put people down, or make them feel low. A self-confidence fellow is always humble and inspiring. You have to read, research, and always keep your eyes on your dream goal as Josephine Melville has rightly stated here,

"Never lose sight of your dreams. But make sure you are equipped to carry them through."
-Josephine Melville
Pride of Black British Women
By Deborah King 1995, (pp. 24-25).

You need to work extensively to actualize your goal. You need to accelerate the transformation of your self-confidence by working harder in Educating yourself.

This book is a role-play model for our entire young generation. It is a book of choice. If you choose to live a better way, read this book to enhance your self-confidence. To gain your self-confidence means hard work and self-reliance. No one can solve your problem except you.

Acquiring self-confidence is your total responsibility for your needs.

Barack Obama, in his book entitled "Change We Can Believe In", on page three of the foreword, advised his readers, especially Americans, on how to meet their ultimate goals. He stated,

> *"It will require new ways of thinking and a new spirit of cooperation. We will need to work harder, and study more, and teach our children to replace the remote controls and video games with books and homework. And most of all, we will need the kind of politics and policies in Washington that finally reflect the best values of America. It won't be easy. It won't happen overnight. But I am running for President because I believe that it is possible. I believe that if we seize this moment to look beyond our differences and focus on the challenges that affect us all, we can meet them. It's our choice."*

Barack Obama, USA No. 44 President
Autobiography Change We Can Believe In (P. 3).

I am asking you, my readers, what are you running for? What is your choice?

Therefore, I urge you to follow the same advice from President Barack Obama, to obtain your fundamental objective. Drop everything that will inhibit you from accomplishing genuine aspirations that would heighten your self-esteem, a purpose that earns your life prestige and pride, and an ambition that would cause people to doff off their hats for you. Not a goal that commits you and your beloved ones into shame. Today, engage in those things that can bring value into your life. As Gillian Butler, Ph.D., and Tony Hope,

MD. rightly stated, "Valuing yourself will help you to build your life on a secure foundation" (p.18).

This book is based on collective years of personal thoughts and experiences. There is an ever-growing lack of confidence and a life cycle of fear in each individual on a daily basis. For these reasons, lack of confidence and fear are inevitable in our lives. All we are is what the brain knows, feels, and does. The brain refines itself in response to its genes in the womb environment, early care-givers, friends, experiences, and cultures in the outside world. The mother provides her own emotional climate and sensory world where the child learns what to expect and models the self to interpret self, others, and the world.

In life, there are three obstacles to success which we must avoid in order to find the way forward. They are considerations, fears, and roadblocks. Considerations as a result of a lack of self-confidence may impose a series of suggestions that would set back your aspirations. For instance, you say you are going to enrol in a computer skills class. Suggestions like this would fill up your vision immediately; do you have enough money? Would you be able to do the C++ and its programs? Would you be able to attend all the classes and do your assignments? On and on, questions like these could emerge. The solution is not to give in to these thoughts but to use them as bases for analysing your chances and developing how you would approach the promotion success. Lack of self-worth and fear are feelings that might be psychologically and emotionally disturbing. Have you ever had a time when you wanted to ask your boss a favour? Fears of rejection, failure, or the consequence may cause you to panic or even withdraw. The fear is meant to be your advisory guard to fine-tune your action so as to have a pleasurable result even though there is a failure. Anyone who aspires to an office position experiences roadblocks; a roadblock is always in opposition to one's desires. Roadblocks are not thoughts and feelings. They are real situations or persons or rules that you must overcome to be what you want to be.

1. Is it that you do not have money for a project?
2. Is it that you are unable to present facts?
3. Or are there rules that prohibit your action?

A good effort should be made to locate the real roadblocks and a well-thought plan can be put up to combat the obstacles. Many have succeeded by confronting the unyielding obstacle at its roots and so, daringly, win over it. In more notes, we have learnt that fear is a natural emotion for safeguarding our existence but it could become a nightmare, a curse to our survival in a pathological circumstance.

According to Dr. Seuss,

"You have brains in your heads.
You have feet in your shoes.
You can steer yourself
Any direction you choose."

-Dr. Seuss
It Takes A Village 1996, (p. 146)
By Rodham Clinton.

Dr. Seuss encourages us to be responsible for building our strong self-confidence. Whether you're confident or not depends on you. If you steer yourself in the right direction, you will definitely become a successful confident fellow. But if you steer yourself in the wrong direction, you will be full of low self-esteem. It is your duty to work harder to gain your self-assurance. I agree with Dr. Seuss; one could steer herself to be noble, and one could steer herself to be bogus (counterfeit). Here, steering yourself is making effective decisions.

I write this book not because I am a genius or more intelligent than others, rather, with a determined effort in order to share with you my experience on the effect of fear in my life. This is also to help you to combat basic psychological fear in yourself if you are having the same problem as I have. Fear is psychological weakness in human life. It is an unpleasant emotional feeling that undermines reasonable thinking. Fear always inhibits one's progress. For this reason, one has to work harder to get rid of it. It has both positive and negative effects on each individual. Fear is what we instil in ourselves, or what others implant in us. Consequently, I intend to treat in this book, **Building Up Self-Confidence A Fundamental Way of Conquering Fear** that restricts each individual from achieving his/her dream goals. This book will assist you dismantle and remove the fear that could disrupt your future progress, whether it is man-made or self-made. I want you to join me today in saying goodbye, farewell, rest in peace, and be gone, fear in your life.

"Do not live-in fear of the future because of the past.
Rather, be strengthened by it for a better, stronger

*you! Do not live in fear. It can paralyze your life
and dreams. If you walk toward the truth, fear will
dissipate!"*
-Margaret Dureke
*Words and Phrases of Wisdom
For Spiritual and Emotional Upliftment 2002,
(p. 37).*

For instance, I cite myself here as an example. I am always afraid of standing in a pulpit reading. Fear always overwhelms me and I begin to have reservations and reasons for not proceeding. One of the considerations will always be fear of making mistakes and fear of failure, rejection from people and their remedial critics, and what they would say and think about me. After thinking this way, the next action is stepping down. Once I step down, I start to feel sad, depressed, and upset within myself. Psychologically, no one feels good when they are not doing well. I hope you feel the same way. For this reason, be mindful of your fear, consideration, and roadblocks. Consideration is one of the main roadblocks in your progress. One has to be alert. This awful experience motivated me to embark on writing this book in order to get rid of this fear in myself and help you to do the same too. Fear could have stopped me carrying out many of my major life goals. Success depends on personal thinking; if you think positively, your mind will give you successful results, but if you think negatively, the mind will equally issue negative results. When you form the habit of thinking positively at all times, you will only do positive things. I believe this because, since I said no to fear, I perceive myself progressing effectively in all aspects. Once you say no to your fear, your ("chi") that is, your God, will affirm you. As you are developing your confidence and conquering fear, be mindful of the roadblocks which could be individuals, your boss, parents, best friends, financial problems, the state of your health, diabolical individuals, natural calamities, and other possible external circumstances that place obstacles on your pathway. Hence, the worst obstacle is you, if you think and reason negatively. You can overcome this if you work harder and adopt an operative strategy. As you read through this book, you will realize how others overcame their fears and achieved self-confidence. Be yourself, and never blame anybody for your failure. If you fail, you're the cause. Remodel your negative thinking into positive thinking in order to attain your objective. Success relies on a positive manner and thinking. Positive thinking is the answer to self-empowerment.

Self-trusting is another way of getting rid of fear. Once you trust yourself, you will triumph over your terror. Self-development is always accompanied by consideration, panic, and roadblocks. It is left for you to handle them to succeed because, they are potential hazards on our objective aim. Most importantly, try to discover the sources of your fear, and obstacles in order to face and process them so as to undertake your ambition successfully. Always ask yourself these questions:

1. What am I afraid of?
2. Am I afraid of making decisions?
3. Am I afraid of speaking publicly?

4. Am I afraid of asserting my opinion?
5. Am I afraid of commitment or responsibility?
6. Am I afraid of competition?
7. Am I afraid of being judged or criticized?
8. Am I afraid of taking a risk?
9. Or am I afraid of making mistakes, etcetera?

Then, as you proceed, apply an effective methodology to disarm your fear. No medication for the cure of the fear; rather, you are the cure through positive action and commitment. Immediately you complete recognizing your dread factor, it will gradually disappear from you and you will be freed. Just work harder on it; you will be alright.

I was delighted when I came across Jack Canfield's wonderful book, The Success Principles, and I said to myself, I have found meaning for my research. I was interested in researching fear and lack of self-confidence as this is a chronic disease I suffer daily. Fear has besieged me since my teenage years. It prevented me from doing the things I love to do. For instance, I love to be a lay reader in my local church but I couldn't as a result of being afraid of standing before the crowd and of making mistakes. Consequently, fear makes me develop stage fright that thwarts me from reading or speaking to among people. I always consider making mistakes in everything I embark on. Most often, I discontinue with what I intended to do as well as withdrawing from airing my views to avoid challenges from anybody even though I have a good point to make. Each time this happened, I regretted it within me. Today, I decided to contest fear of this kind by doing research on it. I am counselling you, dear reader, to join me to fight a war against fear. I have numerous stories to narrate about the effect of fear on me, hence, if I begin my tale, it is going to take up much space and time, thus, I will make it concise.

Fear prevents one from forming one's self-esteem, self-worth, self-reliance, and self-fulfilment. I urge you never to allow any negative thoughts to overshadow your mind. If you allow it, you ruin your career.

Try to erect your self-esteem by ignoring fear and self-critics, roadblocks, and considerations. Try to disarm them. I tell you, never to say no to yourself. Instead, let someone else say no to you. However, you can equally object to someone's no to you. Only God Almighty is the ultimate yes or no. If God says yes, no one says no, etcetera.

"The self-criticism becomes one of the main factors that differentiate human beings from other creatures and is the awareness of self and ability to form an identity and then attach a value to it. "In other words, you have the capacity to define who you are and then decide if you like that identity or not. "The problem of self-esteem is this human capacity for judgment. It's one thing to dislike certain colours, noises, shapes, or sensation. "But when you reject parts of yourself, you greatly damage the psychological structures that literally keep you alive. "It seems that self-esteem grows out of your circumstances in life, and your circumstances in life are influenced strongly by your self-esteem. Self-esteem determines circumstances, this means that

if you improve your self-esteem, your circumstances will improve. So, just stop hating yourself, and you'll improve.
- *Matthew McKay, Ph.D.*

It is your duty to shun chronic self-criticism and forge ahead. Apply positive reinforcement to reward yourself. Never feel dismayed. Hence, self-criticism results in fear. Therefore, it is better that you balance your self-criticism, criticize your weaknesses and rate your strengths. I want you to know, dear reader, that someone can put fear in you make you feel bad or to unbalance you. He or she does it out of envy. It is your duty to spurn it, resent it, throw it away, and move on. I am talking to you based on my personal experiences. Fear engulfed me and I found myself lagging behind in all aspects until one day, something struck me and I wakened and said to myself, I must stand tall against the threat of fear and its agents without wasting time. I began immediately dealing with it; and gradually, I started freeing myself from this chronic cancer that was consuming me. How did I do it? I did it by doing the things that are difficult for me. Once I started freeing myself, I began to feel relieved, happier, and enthusiastic within myself. I believed that nothing was impossible.

"When self-empowerment is acquired, coupled with aspirations, inspirations and one's core beliefs, it can really move mountains! The impossible becomes possible. The "I can't dos" become "I can dos." It restores ones' self-esteem, self-confidence and self-

worth irrespective of how others may perceive one's actions or views."
- Margaret Dureke
Words and Phrases of Wisdom for Spiritual
and Emotional Upliftment 2002, (p. 80).

Throughout this process, anything that inflicted fear in me, I chased it away and frowned at it. I was aggressive towards it. I hope it will work for you if you strive harder. When some people tried to infuse fear in me by putting across nasty suggestions on my career goal, I resented it strongly. People will make you feel and look inferior as well as stupid but don't accept it; instead, press on and keep trying. If you fall along the way, get up and dust yourself off and keep rolling on. I dwell in striving and paving my way and it works for me. "It is better to fail sooner so that you can succeed later!"

"Do not be afraid to pursue your passion or calling because of the possibility of failure. Anytime your undertakings did not go as planned, consider yourself as being closer to getting to where you were going and not see it as a failure. Just press on
- Margaret Dureke
Words and Phrases of Wisdom for
Spiritual and Emotional Upliftment 2002, (P. 94).

Remember, not all of us were born with silver spoons in our mouths. In the academic fields, some are geniuses, some are average, and others mediocre. For this reason, wherever you find yourself, just bloom. The only requirement is that you do all you can to exceed.

If you're a genius, give us your intuition, and if you're an average, show us your ability, etcetera. There is an Igbo" proverb, "ibughi onye oku, iburu onye oru." This means you are either a craft person or a farmer. Always bear in mind that we are not equals and our fingers are not equal either; some are bigger and taller than the others but all are performing important tasks. We are not equal in all aspects; in life, some are tall, short, white, black, big, thin, beautiful, and ugly, wealthy, and poor. God made it that way to beautify his creation. We should be grateful for whatever one we have and blossom where we are planted. You should never use your talent to block others or pull them down. Remember, God gives and God takes. Your gifts are neither yours nor mine, but God's, thus, make proper use of them. If you are less privileged, never mind and never shy away and or let yourself be paralyzed. As Margaret Dureke again stated,

"Fear is one of life's nuisances that everyone must face at one time or the other! However, if fear paralyzes you, then you are in trouble. To dispel fear, you face the thing that you are afraid of squarely and deal with it once and for all. If you face it and do not shy away from it, fear becomes a thing of the past."

-Margaret Dureke
Words and Phrases of Wisdom for Spiritual and Emotional Upliftment 2002, (p. 95).

One day, a demeaning fellow said something that just struck me and I wakened and said to myself, I must stand tall and commence to fight against fear tirelessly. And I said, fear shall not win. Then I started gradually fighting it. I began to involve myself in church readings, giving talks to a small group of people. Anytime I want to do something positive and someone comes to discourage me, I harden my resolve, ignore the person and move on without minding. What the heck! I don't believe that God created me and infused psychological fear in me. So, right now, I have "81 Nos" for fear. As from that day on, I started paying close attention to phobias, especially their causes and consequences.

I was an eye witness of fear in a gathering where some members were taking an oath to be full-fledged members of their association. One of them couldn't stand in front of the others reciting her promise. She was gripped with fear, sweat filled her body, her voice cracked, she was shaking, and panicking till one of her members helped her sit down. Also, she was given a glass of water to cool herself. This was a display of anxiety. After that, on one occasion, she met me and told me of her life's ordeal and why she was panicking. According to her, her husband was a perfectionist and too analytical. No matter what she did, he condemned it. As a result, this woman had a nervous breakdown. To avoid that situation again, she separated from her husband.

Beware for fear could threaten your life, even make you lose your job, or enable you to make a big mistake. Fear, as you know, can make you lose control of yourself. You better guard against it. Avoid over-recounting of your past difficult experiences; these can hold you back from moving forward.

Though, St. Ignatius suggested; "we use the past to provide guidance for the future," for this instance, I advise you not to dwell on your past, rather, use it as guidance for the future as I did and succeeded. Remember, your mistakes are part and parcel of life; without them, you cannot learn. We all learn through our mistakes or from the mistakes of others. No one is faultless. Therefore, do not be afraid of making mistakes. An American musician sings, "When we fall, we get up..." It is not taboo for one to fall but what is taboo is to remain down without getting up. If you fall, get up and dust yourself down and keep moving. According to Margaret Dureke, "Allow yourself to fall from time to time if that is to be, but never, ever remain down." The problem lies not in the falling down but in not finding ways to get right back up. Always keep thinking positively towards your success, no matter the odds. Never sleep on your mistakes; always have solution to your problems.

An alternative solution is a key to success. As you strive to succeed, never be afraid of any difficult situation. No matter the odds, you must not panic under pressure, or uncomfortable conditions, even when there is an immense problem. Never shrink away from pressing on. Always keep fear behind you and take your steps one by one, as I did, to prosper. Don't feel ashamed of asking questions of wise people to assist you in the struggle. Remember, the proof of wisdom is to learn even from little children. Be ready to learn. No one is insignificant; everybody is valuable in one way or the other. As long as one lives, one has ample opportunities to improve the self. The essential thing is first to accept yourself and work on your limitations, then you will be fine.

Once you make daily efforts to upgrade yourself, you will be attracting fear, worries, deprecating individuals, and anxieties; but don't mind; all shall come to past. Maintain your stand, and work hard to affirm your authentic self.

"Affirm your authentic self-every day you wake up by saying nice things about yourself and those around you! By doing this, you do not allow people to talk you down. When you talk yourself up, you empower your self-esteem! Don't wait for others to validate you if you are to define self authentically. If you did, you will have to wait for a lifetime, as many people out there would rather prefer not to validate you. Remember, not everyone would like to see you happy or successful. That is why you owe it to yourself to succeed or be happy against all odds!"

-Margaret Dureke
Words and Phrases of Wisdom
for Spiritual and Emotional Upliftment 2002,
(p. 39).

According to Anthony De Meuo, fear is the root of violence. Ignorance and fear; ignorance caused by fear, that's where all the evil comes from; that's where your violence comes from. The person who is truly nonviolent, who is incapable of violence, is the person who is fearless. "It's only when you're afraid that you become angry." Go ahead, think of the last time you were angry and search for the fear behind it. What were you afraid of? Were you afraid of making mistakes? Are you afraid of crowds or have a fear of failure? Are you afraid of your opponent...? Fear will make you lose your balance, so you better watch it and begin now to work on it. A new driver doesn't look behind while driving to see how all other cars are following her, for if she does, she must surely crash out of fear.

Then, it is advisable for you to put fear behind you. "Strong self-esteem depends on two things; (1) learning to think in a healthy way about yourself, and (2) ability to make things happen, to see what you want and go for it." A lot depends on you. If you lead the way, you will surely make it. Develop positive rational thoughts of self-affirming and responses; say to oneself I will do this or I will carry out this goal successfully without any inhibitions. Remove fear completely from your mind. Next, demonstrate your ability and willingness to perform the goal you set. Irrational or self-defeating thoughts draw you back. Thus, avoid applying a negative image of self; instead, encourage yourself always. Positive self-thinking facilitates healthy growth and increases success. The critic is always with you - judging, blaming, finding faults etc. It is your duty to shun it and keep pressing on. Apply positive reinforcement to reward yourself. An insight from "My Daily Bread" - "I must see what virtues I need most consider, how Jesus would practice these virtues in my place, and then make a determined effort to imitate Him. He expects a continued effort in spite of repeated failure and constant difficulties.

"I promise that I will refuse to be discouraged by my failures. I am determined to begin over

> *again no matter how often I may fall down in my resolutions."*
>
> Anthony, Paone S.J.
> My Daily Bread 1954, (P. 227).

Extreme criticism leads to fear; avoid it because it is deadly. Advise yourself, forward - ever, backward - never. Never wait for someone else to get you up; you are the self-boss and captain of yourself, so if you fall, pull yourself up and shake off the dust and ride on. No one is ready to shake it off for you. You take the lead. When agama lizard fell from a tall tree, he looked right and left and nobody was there to cheer him up, so, he nodded his head and cheered himself up and kept going; this is the reason why agama lizard often nods his head. People can easily talk you down instead of cheering you up, so, cheer yourself up and keep moving on. I can recommend a tremendous book from a great author – **The 7 Habits of Highly Effective People. Powerful Lessons in Personal Change A wonderful book that could change your life – Tom Peters, bestselling author of In Search of Excellence by Stephen R. Covey.** Please, if you have the opportunity, read this book; you must have absolute transformation of self. Thus, endeavour to read it for your self-enchantment.

"There is nothing I cannot master with the help of the one who gives me strength." (Philippians 4:13). With God, all these are possible and with the mystery of possibilities, one can always conquer impossibilities. No one is born insignificant. Persist until you succeed; never give up. Keep running until you triumph.

Chapter One

Building Up Confidence in Oneself without Inhibition of Fear

Confidence is belief in one's own or another's ability. This book is all about "Building up confidence in oneself." Now that you are keen to build your confidence, your success depends on the amount of effort you put in. You must cultivate self-belief; that is, you must believe in yourself and trust yourself that you can do it. You must cultivate self-motivation; that is, you must encourage yourself to strive higher. You must foster self-conviction, that you have the power to carry out your daily obligations. Be an action fellow like Gandhi: "He was the doer, and he grew and gained knowledge through action. "Gandhi 2010 Calendar). Once you begin achieving self-confidence, you're on the road to conquering your fear and gaining absolute control over all those things that set you back. You have a long walk to make it happen and you must navigate the course. To attain confidence, first, you ought to value yourself and accept yourself and avoid those mental blocks that hinder your progress. What are those mental blocks? They are self-doubts such as pessimism, apprehension, self-defense, negative self-assuming, and lack of self-confidence among others.

Here are some explanations of self-doubts:

Do not doubt your capabilities or become apprehensive; that is, being fearful that you cannot do it. Sure you can. Self–assurance is necessary, assuring yourself that you are capable of conquering great heights in life. The three brilliant ways of encouraging self-confidence are being enthusiastic, passionate, and optimistic. Negative self-talk is when you tell yourself, "I cannot do it. I cannot perform. I am scared to stand up among the crowd to speak." Once you stop voicing negativity of yourself, you will start to feel more positive about yourself. Negative self-thoughts are a huge obstacle to one's advancement. Choose to have positive self-talk and select good role models to help you improve on your career. When you empower yourself, then you will appreciate the effectiveness of your performance. Maintain the principle of constant self-improvement and self-reassurance. Motivate the self, be positive and optimistic, feel enthusiastic and be confident. Set your goal ahead of you and pursue it to the end; that way, you will be triumphant over your dream goal. Develop personal techniques, strategies, or methodologies for it to happen. Set your standards and maintain positive control of the maneuver you choose to work on. Be focused, determined, and hard working. There are a lot of techniques that could help you boost your confidence; modelling is one of them. You must choose a role model that you would imitate or copy. But never long to be that person; rather be you. Stay with the struggle till you realize your objective;

that is, stay in control to ensure you get the effective result that you are expecting. Abide with self-discipline and so, arm yourself with greater readiness to win. You must maintain self-improvement skills that will enable you to develop your potential in an applicable manner, by encouraging and acknowledging your efforts towards success. Increase your mental strength and willingness to take action. You must dwell with greater determination and self-sacrifice to conquer, moreover, engage in the things that could inspire you to prevail. You have to challenge yourself to make it happen; after all, 'it won't happen unless you make it happen. To make it happen, you must move on with powerful conviction to actualize it. Make use of your time properly and schedule yourself. When you schedule yourself, you must devote time to make it effective.

"Your vision will become clear only when you can look into your own heart. Who looks outside, dreams, who looks inside, awakes."
- Carl Jung

To achieve your objective, maintain a healthy frame of mind and body through increasing self-worth, no self-doubt. If you are constantly ill, your self-confidence is at stake. For this reason, you must keep fit and maintain a happy frame of mind within you to be in a good relationship with yourself. Your efforts will never be in vain. Explore various ways to achieve this. These various ways would give you a compendium of ideal knowledge on how to gain self-confidence. Many people have misunderstood being self-confident or achieving self-assurance. They think that achieving it is getting intoxicated with strong wine or taking hard drugs to get high. No, it is absolutely the wrong way. Rather, that is the quick way to self-destruction.

You must read and research and always keep your eyes on your career goals. Josephine Melville rightly put it,

> *"Never lose sight of your dreams. But make sure you are equipped to carry them through."*
> -Josephine Melville
> Pride of Black British Women
> By Deborah King 1995, (p. 25).

You need to work extensively to achieve your ultimate heart's desire. You need to accelerate the transformation of your self-confidence by working harder in self-education. What is self-education? It is laying your hand on anything that is educative to uplift self-esteem. The future lies before you, so, you must make exceptional and unique efforts to uphold its treasure. You must embrace endurance and patience. Remember, endurance is a mighty power and patience gives many good things. Thus, work towards greatness to achieve your potential. For this to be effective, you have to create the space; a good environment enables you to realize this crucial target. You must be around role models to empower you; you cannot do it alone. One of the famous confidence builders – Steve Miller - advises you and I to "copycat" the role models but we should not wish to be them. By "copycat" he means mimic, mirror, and imitate them. Hence, we should imitate them (good role models) to be successful.

This book is a role-play model for everyone who wants to improve his or her confidence. It is a book of choice. If you want to conquer your fear and regain confidence, read this book. Gaining confidence can lift you from grass to grace. Once you form your confidence, you are then the proud and confident master. Above, I suggested that you should be an action-doer. Here I must reinforce this by quoting Steve Miller in his 7 Secrets of Confidence in the preface section of the book:

> *"This book was written because I feel that many people around the world need to restore their confidence, which has been knocked down by the slings and arrows that we all must face. There are so many big problems that are out of our control these days, from economic bubbles bursting to natural disasters brought on by climate change. Never have there been so many daily tests of confidence for people. I want to offer people who need to build or rebuild their confidence a tool that is practical, action-based, and immediate. For too long, we have simply listened to the theory from head-in-the-clouds, head-up-their-backside therapists and life coaches. I am all about delivering a product that offers real-world, here-and-now solutions to building and maintaining confidence."*
>
> Steve Miller
> 7Secrets of Confidence
> Straight Advice on How to Become More
> Confident 2010, (p. 1).

I hereby quote Miller to inspire you today to shape your self-confidence. To gain confidence, you ought to work harder and develop practical means and deep self-reliance for self-transformation. No one can solve your problem except you. How do you achieve your goals? I urge you to take 100% responsibility for your goal. Take full responsibility, then ask yourself: How can I take responsibility for my aim? I am here to help by suggesting that you should, first and foremost, ask yourself these questions:

1. What do I want to do?
2. I am okay with what I want to do.
3. Plan well how to go about it.
4. Develop workable skills.
5. Start working on it.
6. Always do checks and balances to keep track of your performance,
7. Ask yourself, am I getting it right?
8. If not, then amend where necessary and try harder.

Gaining self-confidence is your absolute responsibility. Barack Obama, in his book "Change We Can Believe In", advised readers, especially Americans, on how to meet their ultimate goals. He said,

> *"It will require new ways of thinking and a new spirit of cooperation. We'll need to work harder and study more, and teach our children to replace the remote controls and video games with books and homework. And most of all, we'll need the*

kind of politics and policies in Washington that finally reflect the best values of America. It won't be easy. It won't happen overnight. But I'm running for President because I believe that it's possible. I believe that if we seize this moment to look beyond our differences and focus on the challenges that affect us all, we can meet them. It's our choice."

Barack Obama (2006).

I ask the reader, what are you running for? What is your choice? What is your target goal? I commend you to follow the advice of Barack Obama to choose, set, plan, work harder, and achieve your aspiration. Bin things that don't matter to achieve a genuine career; a goal that earns your life prestige and pride, a goal that would enable people to doff their hats for you and a career that would uplift your life from grass to grace. Not a goal that puts you and your beloved ones to shame. Today, involve in those noble careers that would bring value to your life and the life of others. Gillian Butler, Ph.D., and Tony Hope, MD, rightly said, "Valuing yourself will help you to build your life on a secure foundation" (2007).

Begin today to devise a means to uplift your confidence. Once you start doing this, it will register automatically.

"Without confidence, approaching anything in life is a challenge. Without the right level of confidence, you are doomed to be a loser. Confidence makes us feel good about ourselves; it helps us shape positive

behaviors and supports us to be the best we can in everything that we do."
Steve Miller
7Secrets of Confidence
Straight-Talking Advice on How to Become
More Confident 2010, (p. 7).

I encourage you, keep striving tirelessly even if the road is tough. Keep moving. Adhere to this inspiration from Martin Luther King Jr. during his Civil Rights movement in the 1960s when his supporters were in despair.

"If you can't fly, run; if you can't run, walk; if you can't walk, crawl, but by all means keep moving."
- Martin Luther King Jr.
https://www.bing.com/videos/search?

I implore you to keep striving according to your own strength.

"Your goal is to speak to the unconscious mind and instruct it to become confidence."
Steve Miller
7Secrets of Confidence
Straight-Talking Advice on How to Become
More Confident 2010, (p. 67).

What is Confidence?

In this book, I treat two main things: Building Self-confidence, and Conquering Fear. Thus, the question is how do you build your confidence? And how do you conquer the fear that inhibits you from confidence? Here I must explore what confidence and fear are all about.

At this point, I am going to give you a wide definition of self-confidence. According to Wikipedia,

> **"The socio-psychological concept of self-confidence relates to self-assuredness in one's personal judgment, ability, power, etc., sometimes manifested excessively. Being confident in yourself is infectious. If you present yourself well, others will want to follow in your footsteps towards success. Promise yourself that no matter how difficult the problem life throws at you, that you will try as hard as you can to help yourself. You acknowledge that sometimes your efforts to help yourself may not result in success, as often being properly rewarded is not in your control.**
> **(http://en.Wikipedia.ord/wiki.Goggles)**

Jan Ferguson gave her definition of what confidence is all about. According to her,

> *"True confidence is a happy, comfortable state of being which doesn't rely on putting others down or measuring ourselves against other people. It involves respecting yourself and other people. It is possible to be 'overconfident' and that might have all sorts of results. When we are among other*

people, it's important to be sensitive to the effect we are having on them" (2009).

Sarah Litvinoff, the author of "The Confidence Plan", defines confidence as:

"A much-desired quality but it is difficult to measure. Since becoming a coach, I haven't worked with anyone who didn't suffer from a lack of confidence to some extent. Even the most outwardly poised people are racked with self-doubt on occasion. Confidence doesn't relate to what you have achieved, but to how you feel. I approached one new client with awe, having read through her CV showing page after page about her successes. She was as bold and forthright as I expected and yet, scratching the surface, I found another woman, one who was fearful of making decisions, who felt that her impressive track record had been a fluke." (2009).

Dave Connelly, a psychotherapist, defined self-confidence thus:

(1) psychologically: It is the adult in you confirming the true goodness of the self to the inner child. There can be no lies or deceit in this process. It needs no confirmation from outside. The inner child needs constant reassurance, encouragement, praise, and affirmation for self-confidence to prosper. (2). Spiritually: Self-confidence comes from existential

experience of what God says He has made us. The spirit convinces us of our status as children of the father, royalty in the kingdom. The psalm says we are awesomely made. Oral interview by Dave Connelly- a British Psychotherapist.

Robert H. Schuller, in his book, "Discover Your Possibilities", stated:

"It is the God-power within you! There is a tremendous verse in the Bible which J.B Phillips translates: "For it is God working in you giving you the will and the power to achieve His purpose." The good news I have for you is this: The Eternal Creative Force of the universe we call God can surge within your being to give you self-belief, self-esteem, self-love, self-confidence! Without it-you're sunk, with it-you're invincible! At this point, "Eliminate the unholy triad of negative emotions-inferiority, inadequacy, insignificance-wipe these destructive devils out of your mind with the positive power of self-confidence!"

-Robert H. Schuller
Discover Your Possibilities
Positive, Inspirational Guidelines that will
Enrich Your Life as You Reach for Your Highest
Potential 1978, (p. 3).

In my own opinion, self-confidence is the safest way to conquer fear. It is a means of getting from where you are now to where you desire to be. It is stripping off your childish self and putting on the authentic adulthood. Self-confidence is doing things out of being convinced. You become the master and the captain of yourself in handling your affairs, responsibilities, making daily decisions with conviction, taking challenges that effect positive results, surmounting ups and downs, trusting, applying positive self-talk, affirming, encouraging, motivating, empowering, believing, assuring, being self-reliant, uplifting, validating, cheering, making the right judgement, living out your dreams and potentials, pushing self forward to make a difference, and asserting self positively without being aggressive. Besides, it means being able to motivate others to achieve their potential. The power of self-confidence gives you belief in yourself and, with the articulation of these virtues above, enables you to respond to new situations with self-assurance instead of dread, with self-belief instead of doubt.

The power of belief is key to self-enhancement, self-empowerment, self-affirmation, and they are the sources of achieving your self-actualization. Without them, it will be impossible to believe in yourself and when you do not believe in yourself, you cannot be empowered to reach your ultimate goal. If you intend to achieve self-confidence and conquer fear, first of all, you must believe in your dream and strive towards it with determined effort and a willingness to obtain your dream. Believing without action yields no good result. Be an action-doer and always affirm yourself by saying, "I can do it and I am doing it right now." Try to build strong trust within yourself and always encourage yourself to press on. And add to it, "I am willing and ready to move on and I am equal to the task." You must be up and doing to gain self-confidence. Self-confidence is the way you shape your life, that is, replacing your old primitive self with the new self which gives you a clear self-image. To achieve self-confidence, you must read and practice. What you think of yourself is what you will be. "As a man thinketh in his heart, so is he." If you rate yourself lazy, ugly, good for nothing, etcetera, then that is what you will be. Anytime you intend to take on a responsibility, your mind will automatically trigger and tell you, you cannot do it, you're good for nothing. Begin now to sow a seed of self-confidence to reap a healthy harvest. How do you sow the seed? Start by saying to yourself, "I am able, I can do it, and I am achieving it already."

Once you embrace positive view of yourself, you're progressing. Picture yourself as beautiful, smart, happy, loving calm and able. Marian Harrison, a British high-class fashion designer who is proud of her skills said,

"I enjoy the freedom and self-satisfaction that comes from being your own boss."
-Harrison Marian
Pride of Black British Women
By Deborah King 1995, (p. 42).

I agree with Marian Harrison because once you are responsible and skilful, you will feel joyous and fulfilled. Many individuals do not feel fulfilled unless they are in a high-ranking job but that is not true. Even if you are a carpenter, a driver, a gardener, etcetera, if you are skilful at it and make your living from it and help others with it, you are somebody and master of your responsibility. Somebody must be something and what matters is that, whatever you are, you are in control and can develop it well. Marian Harrison is proud of her skill. Are you proud of your skill? If not, why? Be proud and have the self –conviction that you can develop what you already have. This self-conviction can aid you achieve confidence and can help you to alter your fear. Be self-assured and always motivate yourself by saying, I am able, and I am doing well. Love yourself and cherish your capability. Kick off now to remove fear and negative thought from your vocabulary. Remember, fear is always out there and is already doing those things you are afraid of, but you must do them anyway.

> *"If everybody feels fear when approaching something totally new in life, yet so many are out there "doing it" despite the fear, then we must conclude that fear is not the problem."*
> - Susan Jeffers
> Feel the Fear and Do it Anyway
> How to Turn Your Fear and Indecision into
> Confidence and Action 1987, (p. 33).

Nonetheless, never shrink as a result of fear. Move on, go out, and do it. In spite of air crashes, people still do fly every day knowing that life is full of taking risks. Here one needs strong self-conviction to move on. *As Robert H. Schuller stated,*

> *"What **you see is what you'll be**. There is need for **self-confidence; without it, you can't go anyplace,***

do anything or be what God wants you to be. If you have a negative self-image of yourself, don't harbour it or hold on to it. Throw it away! Begin to see yourself as what you want to be, aggressive and enthusiastic; picture yourself being enthusiastic. If you want to be a good student, picture yourself as a very scholarly student, poring through your books, working hard, and you'll be that person! If you want to be slim and trim, picture yourself slim and trim, and keep holding that picture of yourself in front of you. What you see is what you'll be! "As a man thinketh in his heart, so is he..."

Mayer & Salovey, 1997; as cited in Passer et al., 2005, (p. 7).

Go on board now to sow the seed of self-confidence with a strong belief. Hold those positive pictures firm in your heart and nurture them. Feel buoyant in your relations with people, feel confident in socializing, moving about, carrying on your work, doing your assignment, in reading your book, taking your exam, in caring for your baby, in dancing, in driving, in running, in playing, in giving a speech or in doing your presentation, in handling your crisis, etcetera. So, feel confident in anything positive you can think about; this is the way to build successful self-confidence. *According to Sarah Litvinoff:*

"Confidence is an attitude of mind." "Confident people believe they can succeed. They are convinced they have the ability to tackle whatever comes up

and they aren't put off by setbacks..." "People who feel confident at work will take on a difficult new project with a sense of excitement: 'I have no idea how I'm going to do this, but I always rise to a challenge.' When they make mistakes and come up against problems, they learn and try different methods, secure in the belief that they will crack it eventually. When you honestly think you can, you do" (2004).

Section I: What is Fear?

According to the Dictionary of Psychology, fear is an emotional state in the presence or anticipation of a dangerous or noxious stimulus. Fear is usually characterized by an internal, subjective experience of extreme agitation, a desire to flee or to attack, and a variety of sympathetic reactions. (See Autonomic Nervous System). Fear is often differentiated from anxiety on one (or both) of two grounds: (a) fear is treated as involving specific objects or events while anxiety is regarded as a more general emotional state; (b) fear is considered a reaction to a present danger, anxiety to an anticipated or imagined one. See also PHOBIA, a specific, persistent, irrational fear." Fear hinders the development of self-confidence; subsequently, we must explore its sources to eradicate it.

Definition of the Fear

Fear is a fundamentally emotional human faculty that is ingrained in beings for their safe existence. It is also a handicap in persons having malfunctioning bodily systems which misbehave in an out of the ordinary way. It helps you key into the right value and keeps reminding you of that value and keeps reminding you to adjust, modify, and actuate to the right standard. This normal procedure is upset when the motivators of fear are not in good working form.

In this case, fear becomes diseased and pathological. To expose human emotions, fear, being one of them, is generated by hormonal chemicals which must function with high fidelity in normal persons. Since fear is characterized by a mood of run-or-attack, any mishap in the molecules triggering fear will either be a permanent run away or attack episode. So, here I am talking of the crippling fear that deters you from daring to do your utmost but not about that which helps you to save yourself.

Malfunctioning fear is a vast obstacle that keeps you and me from experiencing life the way we intend to live it. This fear is that diabolical voice within you impeding your ability to act positively. It always puts across your negative thoughts and suggestions. Here is exactly how Susan Jeffers highlighted such *fear:*

> *"Part of my problem was the nonstop little voice inside my head that kept telling me, "YOU'D BETTER NOT CHANGE YOUR SITUATION. THERE'S NOTHING ELSE OUT THERE FOR YOU. YOU'LL NEVER MAKE IT ON YOUR OWN."*
> *You know the one I'm talking about - the one that keeps reminding you, "DON'T TAKE A CHANCE. YOU MIGHT MAKE A MISTAKE. BOY, WILL*

YOU BE SORRY!" My fear never seemed to abate, and I didn't have a moment's peace. Even my doctorate in Psychology didn't seem to do me much good. Then, one day, as I was dressing for work, I reached the turning point. I happened to glance in the mirror, and I saw an all-too-familiar sight - eyes red and puffy from tears of self-pity. Suddenly, rage welled up inside me, and I began shouting at my reflection, "ENOUGH ... ENOUGH ...!" I shouted until I had no more energy (or voice) left."
Susan Jeffers
Feel the Fear And Do It Anyway! How To Turn Your Fear And Indecision Into Confidence And Action 1987, (p. 4).

Fear is an inhibitor and you need to put more efforts and travel a bit further before you can get rid of it. You have to be mindful of your threat source to be able to combat it. Then ask yourself, what is your fear? For instance, my own fear is that of making mistakes. I am afraid of crowds, afraid of airing my view and asserting myself, afraid of being criticized, afraid of being punished for speaking the truth, afraid of being a dropout from school, afraid of the unknown, afraid of not achieving my career. Outline your own fears and work on them. We have millions of fear factors around us and we cannot do without them. They're inevitable. What you might fear might not be what I fear. Just take it to heart that fear is all around us and it is unavoidable because it is there from the beginning till the end. Today, ask yourself this question, "What am I afraid of, and why am I afraid of it?" So, feel your fear and work out the solution to sort yourself out. Fear has no cure. You, yourself, are the cure. How? By knowing what you are afraid of and working on it. I am working on my own fear by researching and writing this book. By the time I finish researching and writing, I must surely have conquered that fear which obstructs my development. By saying this, it is a self-affirmation of getting rid of my fear. Once you get rid of the "doubting Thomas" out of your mind, you are a free human being. However, fear does not go away completely. For example, when you conquer the fear within you, what of the unknown fear like wars, Boko Haram of Nigeria, Fulani Herdsmen, earthquake, Mother Nature, unknown enemy, and so on? Be mindful that fear is inevitable, potent, and an incredibly strong emotion in ones' life. Hence, if you work harder, by and by, you can overcome those fears that inhibit you from functioning well - Amen. You have to put a lot of strength into building your self-confidence as you are overcoming your fear. On the way to establishing confidence, you must definitely face difficulties but never mind, just keep hoping and strive to make it.

Here is a word of encouragement from Martin Luther King Jr. to his people and all of us who are the builders of confidence.

> "**Whenever you set out to build a creative temple, whatever it may be,** *you must face the fact that there is a tension at the heart of the universe between good and evil. Hinduism refers to this as a struggle between illusion and reality. Platonic philosophy used to refer to it as a tension between body and*

soul. Zoroastrianism, a religion of old, used to refer to it as a tension between the god of light and the god of darkness. Traditional Judaism and Christianity refer to it as a tension between God and Satan. Whatever you call it, there is a struggle in the universe between good and evil. Now, not only is that struggle structured out somewhere in the external forces of the universe, it's also structured in our own lives. Psychologists have tried to grapple with it in their way, and so they say various things. Sigmund Freud used to say that this tension is a tension between what he called the id and the superego. Some of us feel that it's a tension between God and man. And in every one of us, there's a war going on..."

Martin Luther King Jr., (1998).
https://www.awakin.org/read/view.php?tid=725

In this book, we are not discussing physical war or other forms, however, we are deliberating on the war against the low self-esteem which results in a lack of self-confidence. Fight harder, then you must definitely become the winner.

In another note, Susan Jeffers is asking you and me this question:

"What is it for you? Fear of...
public speaking,
asserting yourself,
making decisions,
intimacy,

changing jobs,
being alone,
aging,
driving, and
losing a loved one or ending a relationship?
Is it some of the above? All of the above? Perhaps you could add a few more to the list. Never mind... join the crowd! Fear seems to be epidemic in our society. We fear the beginnings; we fear the endings. We fear changing; we fear "staying stuck." We fear success; we fear failures. We fear living; we fear dying."

Susan Jeffers
Feel the Fear And Do It Any Way
How to Turn Your Fear and Indecision into
Confidence and Action 1987, (p. 3).

"Fear creates what is feared.
Fear is another emotion that nips efficiency in the bud."
J. Maurus
How to Win Personal Efficiency 1988, (p. 49).

"Mrs Eleanor Roosevelt was afraid of being afraid, because, she said, she might be influenced in her actions by fear rather than by honest convictions."
J. Maurus
How to Win Personal Efficiency 1988, (p. 48).

Now ask yourself the question, what am I afraid of? Then ask yourself again, how would I sort myself out? To be realistic, once you are able to detect your sources of fear, your problems have already been solved. Once you have located these sources, you know where to begin the chase. The only way to get rid of the fear of doing something is to go out and do it. You have to change course, that is, changing your old ways of life and failure by moving towards a hopeful future with optimism; hope that can enable you to overcome setbacks and challenges. If you work hard, you will definitely achieve your vision.

Section II: Individual Views on Fear

Fear is a virtue that is incorporated in the bodily constitution of a normal civic person. To be respectful and respected, to obey the laws of God and man, one has to have fear as a necessary check and balance to ensure that the desired expected behaviour is expressed and spiteful conduct avoided. Some people, by fearing what could happen if they failed to rear their children properly, dared to work ceaselessly even in helpless situations. Jesus Christ trembled three times in prayer, asking his Father to let go his commission to suffer and die: *"Father, if you wish, remove this cup from me. Nevertheless, let not my will but yours take place" (Luke 22:42),* New World Translation of the Holy Scriptures. He feared and died as a man. Legislators and parliamentarians, in fear of bringing dishonour to themselves and showing a disregard for the public trust, law, and order, play their part with caution even though they are on the top rung of the socio-cultural and socioeconomic ladder.

According to Blaise Pascal, "There is a virtuous fear which is the effect of faith, and a vicious fear which is the product of doubt and distrust. The former leads to hope as relying on God, in whom we believe; the latter inclines to despair as not relying upon God, in whom we do not believe. Persons of the one character fear to lose God; those of the other character fear to find him."

Blaise Pascal
J. Maurus
How to Win Personal Efficiency 1988, (pp. 48-49).

On another occasion, a psychologist wrote,

"Fears send them hurrying to their palmist; and some foolish remark by the palmist inoculates them with a fear which falsifies all their reactions: "You will come to a tragic and horrible end."

"I cannot of course enumerate all the fears which beset men and women and dominate them to such an extent that they are afraid to acknowledge them. They range from a vague anxiety which is all the more persistent because it has no precise object, and involves a hopeless struggle against an invisible enemy to those more specific fears which derive from an association of ideas which may or may not be conscious."

- Paul Tournier

Read Wisdom that is Contained in Fear from the Following Maxims

1. Cowards die many times before their death. The valiant never taste of death but once (Shakespeare).
2. There is no speculation in those eyes; it is the eye of childhood that fears a painted devil (Shakespeare).
3. "That the best way to manage some kinds of painful thoughts is to dare them to do their worst, to let them lie and gnaw at your heart till they are tired and you find you still have a residue of life they cannot kill" George MacDonald in Phantasies (p.176) An Alchemy of Mind.
4. Adversity-sweet are the uses of adversity, which, like the toad, ugly and venomous, wears yet a precious jewel in his head (Shakespeare, As you like it, ii)
5. What we have to fear is fear itself. Fear begets fear (Franklin D. Roosevelt 1933-45, 32nd President of USA).
6. The fear of God is the beginning of wisdom. All those doing them have a good insight (Psalm 111:10) New World Translation of the Holy Scriptures.
7. Who now is the man fearful of God? He will instruct him in the way (that) he will choose. His soul will lodge in goodness itself. And his offspring will take possession of the earth. The intimacy with God belongs to those fearful of him. Also his covenant causes them to know it. New World Translation of the Holy Scriptures (Psalm 25:12-14).
8. God is my Light and my Salvation; of whom shall I be in fear? God is the stronghold of my life; of

whom shall I be in dread? (Psalm 27:1) New World Translation of the Holy Scriptures.

9. You will not be afraid of anything dreadful by night. Nor of the arrow that flies by day. Nor of the pestilence that walks in the gloom. A thousand will fall at your very side. And ten thousand at your right hand. To you it will not come near (Psalm 91:5-7) New World Translation of the Holy Scriptures.

10. The only active force that arises out of possession is fear of losing the object of possession. If you defy an enemy, doubting his courage, you double it. By knowing, one reaches belief. By doing, one gains conviction. When you know dare. (Aldokkan Ancient Egyptian Proverbs, www.aldokkam.com/art/proverbs).

11. Have the wisdom to abandon the values of a time that has passed and pick out the constituents of the future. An environment must be suited to the age and men to their environment. (Ancient Egyptian Proverbs).

12. Organization is impossible unless those who know the laws of harmony lay the foundation (Proverbs from the Ancient Egyptian Temples, www.duboislc.org/html/proverbs).

13. Believe in yourself; you were not an accident. You were not mass-produced. You are not an assembly-line product. You were deliberately planned, specifically gifted and lovingly positioned on earth by the Master Craftsman-by Max Lucado from The Success Principles by Jack Canfield (p. 40).

14. Experience your Fear and Take Action Anyway. "We come this way but once. We can either tiptoe through life and hope that we get to death without being too badly bruised or we can live a full complete life achieving our goals and realizing our wildest dreams-Bob Proctor. The Success Principles by Jack Canfield (p. 114.)
15. When the evildoers approached against me to eat up my flesh; they being my adversaries and my enemies personally. They themselves stumbled and fell. Though against me an encampment should pitch tent, my heart will not fear.
16. Though, against me war should rise. Even then I shall be trusting, New World Translation of the Holy Scriptures (Psalm 27:2-3).
17. Let those fearing God now say for his loving-kindness is to time indefinite.
18. Out of the distressing circumstances I called upon God. God answered me and put me into a roomy place. God is on my side, I shall not fear. New World Translation of the Holy Scriptures (Psalm 118:4-6).
19. "On the other hand, the fruitage of the spirit is love, joy, peace, long-suffering, fear, kindness, goodness, faith, mildness, self-control" (Gal 5:22).
20. Shakespeare said: "Life is but a walking shadow - a poor player. That struts and frets his hour upon the stage, and then is heard no more. It is a tale told by idiots, full of sound and fury signifying nothing."
21. Shakespeare: "To live long, it is necessary to live slowly."

22. Cicero: "We must inculcate in our lives the principle of allowing for others' ways of living because variety is the spice of life." The seven gifts of the Spirit are wisdom, understanding, counsel, fortitude, knowledge, piety, and fear. Here we see that the noble attributes of fear and long-suffering are in the composite attributes of God, the creator. We are advised to incorporate fear and long-suffering in the activities of our lives (Gal 5:22) and Catholic Prayer Book (p. 46-147).

    For Robert H. Schuller, fear is a negative dynamic thought, and it can dominate you (p.203).

23. *"The world cares very little about what a man or woman knows; it is what a man or woman is able to do that counts." (Booker T. Washington.).*

Before I started putting my writing together, I asked my elderly brother, Mr. Ikechi Sylvester Konye, about his views on fear and he said,

"Fear is a feeling caused by the nearness or possibility of danger or evil. This is equally fright, apprehension, and uneasy feeling." Fear can equally be defined as heat inflammation, anxiety, ignorance, error, desire, and caution; all of these are states of being afraid. This is a situation where one becomes apprehensive of the unknown. For example, sickness may cause death, blindness, deafness, dumbness, certain bodily losses, and deformities." "To cure fear, remove the error

governing fear by telling yourself that there is nothing like fear. Remove fear from your mind. For instance, if you are walking at night, do not think about a snake biting you or think about meeting a ghost on the way. The moment this comes into your mind, all other evil thoughts will come into you. At this point, you will start seeing phantoms, hiding animals, and spirits all around you. Next you start shivering and become sick. Always say to yourself nothing will happen. Always remove all anxiety from your mind in all your endeavours. Imagination is another serious cause of fear. Negative imagination unleashes fear tendencies. Let your mind be free of anything that can make you shudder. Being self-conscious, we are always afraid of what might happen next. Since I know that I will die, why should the fear of death be in me? No, I would rather choose to die than to continue being afraid of death. Therefore, fear, as a matter of fact, should never exist. In whatever you are doing, remove fear for it is a figment of the imagination."

Ikechi Sylvester Konye Nwadike
"Oganankp-VC10, 2010
Author's elder brother.

Thanks, Dede'm, the late Mr. Ikechi S. Konye for this wonderful insight about fear. I am highly motivated by this word - in whatever you are doing, remove fear for it is a figment of the imagination. I am glad because my writing is based *on combating fear that undermines an individual's progress*. The late Mr. Ikechi S. Konye urged all of us to "roll back the stone of fear," if we are to succeed in our goals. 'Dede'm Ikechi, I knew you as being fearless and that is the reason why you could not escape from your murderer because you were not afraid of him; take heart. However, rest in peace. God is in control!

In my own little knowledge as an author of this book, fear is a negative emotional state of mind that emerges as lack of strong will by an individual, lack of self-confidence, lack of self-trust, feeling of guilt, when there is anticipation of an unpleasant threat such as insults, those who talk down to us, fear of unforeseen danger, insecurity, making mistakes, etc. When I was growing up, I developed stage-fright and each time I intended to appear before the public to read, to make a speech, or perform, I would start panicking and then I would discourage myself from appearing. I would rate myself a failure and withdraw. One of my limitations was a ***lack of self-confidence and lack of self-trust***. As a result, each time I wanted to do something, my mind would tell me I would not do it right; people would laugh at me and criticise me. Then, I would begin to consider a lot of things. Consideration was one of my biggest obstacles. Anyhow, you shall know more about consideration as we proceed. Another instance is that I used to be afraid of graves. Anytime I passed a graveyard I would see something like a ghost standing there and I would begin to panic, fret, and my heart would be pounding as fear would grip me. This happened for many years until, one day, I resolved with a firm conviction and determination to free myself from this virus – fear. In accepting this firm conviction with arduous commitment and determination,

I began to overcome it and I finally did. Nowadays, I can pass through graveyards at night without being afraid of ghosts. For example, on the 24th of November, 2009, I went to see my mother's remains in our local mortuary. The mortuary attendant felt for me and asked me again and again, "Would you still want to go in and see her?" And I answered yes each time. Then he let me in. I passed through different sections of the mortuary before I reached where my mother was being kept. I saw rows of corpses laying on their counters and some on the floor. I was courageous enough to walk through and look around to the front and back, right and left to see many corpses lying and waiting for their burial dates. This did not bother me. In the past, I would have suffered a tremendous mental torture. Seeing those individual corpses of different sizes would have given me nightmares. I thank God for giving me the fortitude to restore my self-confidence and get rid of fear. I accepted it as a challenge imposed on me to combat and restrain fear from blocking my way to actualization. I was able to achieve a whole lot in my life, academically, religiously, and otherwise, by taking risks and challenges. Now I can stand and address a large group of people without panicking. You can do so too. I want you to be aware that fear is *a giant roadblock, a stumbling block* to your life's desired goals. Subsequently, beware of it, then be firm, strong, and never succumb. Start now to dismantle it. Never allow fear of any kind to influence and overwhelm you. Remember, people can be equally the sources of fear to you; ignore them and press on. I did the same and succeeded and someone who knew me commented, "she is smart but not intelligent." Behold, this comment empowered me and made me smarter.

I implore you to be smart by improving yourself. Smartness is a desirable quality so uphold it if it can assist you towards your enhancement. Let your voice be heard louder and louder, never shrink, and never hide. Develop strategies to cope with your fear and shock and amaze people when they hear of your huge improvement and success. Be the little pot of boiling liquid that "foams off" the fire; the slow running stream that runs deep. Be like Gandhi who was the doer and action taker.

Dr. Robert Anthony described overcoming fear and worry in this way:

"Fear has been around for thousands of years that we know of. Our primitive ancestors feared thunder and lightning, feared the wild beast and feared each other. Fear was present when Noah launched his Ark. The word appears in the Bible over four hundred times. When nations are at war, the world fears an expanded conflict. When there isn't a war, we fear the war that might be. In between, we fear a thousand and one things, large and small, involving ourselves, other people and situations in our daily lives. We were born with only two fears: the fear of falling and the fear of loud noises. The rest we developed ourselves, through our own efforts. Fear takes many forms. There is claustrophobia which is the fear of confined spaces; agoraphobia, the fear of open spaces; ailurophobia, the fear of cats; astraphobia, the fear of thunder and lightning; hydrophobia, the fear of water; nyctophobia, the

fear of darkness; and the worst phobia of all, the fear of failure. Fear is a destructive emotion which deals a fatal blow to any attempt on your part to build total self-confidence. If you are afraid, it is impossible to have the positive mental attitude essential for successful living."

Dr. Robert Anthony
The Ultimate Secrets of Total Self-Confidence
Bestselling Author of THINK and THINK
AGAIN 1979, (p. 167).

Thus, I ask you to have abiding faith to lead you towards your successful destiny that can model you into a powerful affluent individual.

One can observe that fear is all around us; it is inevitable. Henceforth, we have to manage it as we manage our time and never allow it to envelop us. Overcoming fear and worry can be accomplished by living a day at a time or, better yet, a moment at a time, by making more efforts and being positive and keeping our promise to struggle harder to help to attain our goals. We can only do this one small bit at a time. Instantly, you achieve a lot as long as you keep fear from your mind. Self-motivation is a crucial part of attaining this ultimate goal. You have to believe in yourself that you're capable of making things happen; commitment and focus are the keys.

On June 8, 2010, I gave a talk to a group of vulnerable mothers on the fear aspects. Before I began, I asked them to air their views concerning fear. I could see that each mother had a different notion about fear, though, quite a good number had similar opinions. Some were afraid of dying while delivered a child, afraid of not being alive to raise their children, afraid of their husband or boyfriend abandoning them, afraid of getting HIV (human immunodeficiency virus), afraid of giving birth to a deformed child, afraid of the unknown, afraid of being a victim of a bomb blast, afraid of an attack by an enemy country on their homeland, afraid of dying a sudden death, afraid of addressing the crowd, afraid of losing a job, afraid of their own child killing them, afraid of giving birth to a bad child who drops out of school, afraid of being rejected by everybody. After all these brainstorming exercises, I asked them to suggest a remedy to all of these fears. One person said that we should rely on "faith" and maintain positive thinking. She went on to say, 'We have to tackle the unknown to move ahead in order to succeed.' I was impressed to hear these suggestions. Yes, once we maintain positive thinking and embark on it with faith, we must certainly undermine our fears. After that talk, one of my clients promised to put her views down in writing. Here is her contribution.

> *"Fear is something that holds you back. Usually, people's fear has a negative nature. As we are scared and moving along doing things that we classify as fear by ourselves, others around us impose more threats on us. For example, most of us were instilled with the spirit of fear during our childhood. Our parents, siblings, relatives and friends called us funny names that implanted fear in us. For example, they called me "good for nothing" and this*

entered my brain such that, each time I tried to do something, I found myself incapable of handling that task. Your childhood background and environment have significant roles to play in your life as you grow. So, things that happened to us in childhood or as teenagers created fears in us. Fear can make a person choose to remain in one job for a long time even if she is unhappy there. This is as a result of fear of uncertainty or the unknown in the new job place. Sometimes, our destiny is controlled by fear. For example, staying with your husband even though he has cheated so many times and you still choose to stay with that person because of fear of being without a partner. If you are suffering from fear, you cannot move forward on the things you propose to do. It is advisable to develop a strategy to cope with your fears. Try to abandon anything that can lead you into fear; because fear could cause emotional anger, frustration, sadness, sleepless nights, guilt, even death. Avoid diabolical critics because they have negative influences on your ultimate progress and self-esteem as well as your self-confidence. **Then, fill your life with a dynamic positive thought and fear will ultimately disappear. Embrace positive thinking with faith and this can paralyze and wipe away your fear.** *Your ultimate solution is to focus not on how fearful you are now, but on how fulfilled you will be after you take the right action. No matter how little your action is, the result is tremendous success.*

From Lola

Case Study 1

A young girl, Lola, grew up with four sisters. She was the middle child of the four sisters. She was underprivileged and the ugliest girl in the family. Her parents used to mock her and call her an idiot – 'good for nothing' - each time. They reminded her of her poor performance in school as a result of lack of confidence. At school, her classmates used to make funny jokes about her ugly face. These names registered in her mind and, as an adult, she still remembered them as they were still influencing her behaviour and affecting her performance. But she had a dark secret that none of her friends knew about. She had been sexually abused by her uncle. All her life, she always felt uncomfortable around men and was always sad.

Let us examine Lola's background and the reason why she was not doing well at school. Here, one could infer that she had been battling with a lot of issues in her mind such as being underprivileged, her ugliness, her parents' nasty comments, as well as mockery by her peers, and psychological trauma of her uncle's sexual abuse. Lola has been struggling with all these challenges in her that led to a lack of self-esteem. She was unable to focus at school because there were many things going on within her. Negative words said to people, especially to a child, create a lot of fears in the individuals. She had to hide the fact that she was sexually abused; keeping this within herself created a roadblock in her life. It would be harder for her to make friends or have a partner as a result of fear. In other words, fear can control one's destiny. What we think makes us who we are. Lola grew up thinking that no one loved her. This made her vulnerable to the wrong man. Feeling disliked enabled her to accept any man who came to her.

The point I want to bring to this case study is that a significant event that happened in one's life can always instil incurable fear and low self-esteem in that person. Unless we make ardent efforts to deal with all the pessimism of the past, we cannot move forward. To eradicate the fear, first, you must trace all those factors that make you fear and deal with them. In a nutshell, anxiety is something that we need to challenge in our mindset. If your mind is telling you that you are not good enough to do a kind of job, just tell yourself that you can do it, you are able and equal to the task. If your mind says you are a loser, or not worthy, tell yourself that you are very much worthy of getting that promotion; I am not a loser. Or if it means I must try again in order to get what I needed, I must try harder to obtain it and put fear behind me. The most essential thing is being positive in your endeavours. Being positive is having good thoughts of yourself and your goal. Make it your responsibility to be motivated and positive. One of the salesmen said: **"When you walk, don't hold your face down but hold it up and keep up."**

The summary of the whole thing is to encourage yourself through the power of positive self-talk. We all need our internal voice to help us navigate our way through the world. It's useful to be able to say things to oneself like, 'I must remember to call Frank' or 'Umm, I like the look of her' or 'Get out of the way-car coming!' Paul McKenna Instant Confidence (2006).

At this juncture, let us reflect on what Mohandas Karamchand Gandhi said:

> *"If we are to make progress, we must not repeat history but make new history. We must add to the inheritance left by our ancestors."*
> *- Mahatma Gandhi*
> *https://www.azquotes.com/quote/508540*

Here, Gandhi would like us to take a new look at our lives for adjustment in certain situations which enable us to attain self-confidence. We should not focus on our past experiences; alternatively, they should be our point of contact for future improvement. In other words, we must move along with the times. Some people keep on recounting what held or holds them back. What we need to do is to move forward positively and programme ourselves towards success in order to achieve a new desired goal. Successful people who are confident about their future make it their mission to learn. It is necessary to learn new things and forget the past. That is the reason why Gandhi advised us to put behind the past to create new history that would enhance our lives. Say to yourself, "change is on the way" as the American politicians, John Kerry and John Edward said during their political era and that change really manifested itself when President Barack Obama came to power. Mahatma Gandhi believed in faith and action, and that prompted him to quote, *"What is faith worth, if it is not translated into action?"* Subsequently, when you have faith, try to effect it in action that will lead you to change, progress, and success you wish to attain. *"Be the change that you wish to see in the world" (Mahatma Gandhi).* As you want to have a new look in your life, you must transform your frame of mind from fear into strong will. You must empower self, and invoke the Holy Spirit to instil in you that will-power to affect your wish. According to Mahatma Gandhi again,

"Strength does not come from physical capacity; it comes from an indomitable will. This means that your will should be unconquerable, so determined, and deep spirited; not feeble." (From the wisdom of Mahatma Gandhi 210 Calendar).

Here is another insight concerning fear from Engineer Declan Onyeajuwu, the author's brother-in-law. According to Engr. Onyeajuwu, positive fear is as follows:

Everyone, during life circumstances, experiences various forms of fear till death. One may ask where this fear originates. What causes fear? How does one manage it? Does fear have any benefit? To be alive is to be vulnerable. Fear is a burden of insecurity thrust in the mind of the individual due to life challenges at various stages of development. A child expresses fear by crying out and fretting because he is helpless. An indolent student often fears not making good grades in his subjects and succeeding in life. An adult may be afraid of securing a good job; the kind of partner he or she may get and avoid disappointment later, the kind of children one will get, rape, political posts, business failure, job insecurity, being molested by the people of the underworld, forceful retirement, feeling of anger, being involved in various types of accidents and sin. The reasons for some of the above may or may not be justified and realistic. Through other people's testimonies, news, and circumstances, one begins to brood over these ideas which may develop into debilitating anxiety or phobias if left unchecked. The sudden feelings of terror associated with panic attacks often trigger chest pain, heart palpitations, shortness of breath, dizziness, abdominal discomfort and even fear of sudden death.

Results of Fear

In Proverbs 17:22, it is written: "A merry heart does well like a medicine, but a broken spirit dries the bones." Medical practitioners have identified that heart attacks, ulcers, etc. are triggered by fear and anxiety more than any other cause.

Fear brings sickness, insomnia, bondage, torments, failure, and death. Therefore, avoid unnecessary fear and anxiety.

Section III: Management of Fear

"From the above, we know where fear is coming from and its consequences, so we acknowledge it, then take it on. Fear is a form of suffering and *we sometimes must accept that, but we should not indulge in it. We should try to muscle it gently aside with our trust, thinking less of what may come to us and our loved ones but more of who God is and what God wants. Then, we turn ourselves over to the love and care of God. Fear being spiritual attack, our weapons of warfare are not carnal, but mighty through God to the pulling down of strongholds, casting down imaginations and every high thing that exalts itself against the knowledge of God; and bringing into captivity every thought to the obedience of Christ (2Corinthians 10:4-5). Abide in the truth of God. In John 8:32, it is written, "And you shall know the truth and the truth shall set you free." There is nothing more powerful than the word of God, which is the sword of the Spirit. Remember, our Lord Jesus Christ scolded Satan during his temptations by using the words of the Scriptures. (1) Have faith in the Word of God; as you abide in the Word, freedom from fear develops and brings you into full control of every situation. Even if the symptoms persist, start singing and rejoicing and worshipping the Lord. Fear cannot withstand a victory spirit rooted and grounded in the word of God; it must leave (Nehemiah 8:10), (Matthew 17:20), and in Psalm 56:11, it is written, "In God have I put my trust; I will not be afraid what man can do unto me." (2) Paul and Silas prayed and sang praises unto God and victory came; (Acts 16:25). (3) Fear is a weak spirit out of hell; refuse it, press the joy button, (Isaiah 12:3), with the following passages (Philippians 4:13, Romans 8:37) sing praises to the Lord and rejoice. (4) Make sure you are righteous (Isaiah 54:14);* **the seed bed for fear is wickedness.** *A righteous life will eventually destroy all fears. (5) Seek God. Confess all known sins and forgive others that may be involved in either the present or the past problems. In Psalm 34:4, it is written, "I sought the Lord and he heard me and delivered me from all fears." (6) Love others (1 John 4:18). There is no fear in love, but perfect love casts out fear, because fear has torment. He that fears are not made perfect in love. (7) Identify with Jesus' nature (Ephesians 2:5-6), (Luke 10:19), (Jeremiah 42:10-11). (8) Fear is overcome by direct deliverance (Mark 16:17), (Acts 10:38). (9) Do not entertain bad news. We can do much to allay our fears if we wrap ourselves tightly in a network of believers. (10) Do not react carnally with worry, frustration, fear, confusion, or other sinful attitudes. Let God be true and every experience a lie. Stand on what God says; experience and fact may declare that you are going under; ignore it. As you confess God's spirit Word, it becomes a protective shield warding off the enemy. Your tongue creates life around you. You can speak victory into being. (11) Through Jesus and His Living Word, you become creative. Your tongue becomes a tree of life."*

Engineer Declan Onyeajuwu
Author's Brother-in-law

Anne R. Lastman gave another instance of fear when she stated:

> *"Fear is a highly aversive, negative emotion, uncomfortable, unpleasant, and requiring urgent attention and elimination of its cause. Fear is aroused when a threat or perceived threat or danger to oneself or a significant other is confronted. Fear results from the notion that pain may be experienced.*
>
> Anne R. Lastman
> Redeeming Grief
> Abortion and Its Pain 2007, (p. 78).

Bear in mind that once you have something to fear, you remain in a state of confusion; every progress folds and reasoning remains shallow. Try as much as you can in time of fear to revive your spirit and move on. Always say next.

Theresa Burke with David C. Reardon says, "Make a commitment to resist your fears." Fear is your greatest enemy. Perhaps you are afraid of losing control, going crazy, or opening a wound that is so excruciating, it can never be healed. Remember, however, that your fears are just an expression of unresolved emotions arising from your trauma. Fear is normal. But if you keep your eyes fixed on your goal, you will do fine, just as Hanna did; "I was terrified to take that first step forward and participate in Rachel's Vineyard. It seemed safer to remain hiding in the darkness, keeping the pain locked up deep inside rather than to risk exposing my shame to another soul. Now I'm grateful to have experienced God's healing and forgiveness with other women in an atmosphere of complete acceptance and trust. Rachel's Vineyard has been a blessing to me."

In your striving towards success as well as getting rid of fear, you must remind self that you have a major task ahead to accomplish. Therefore, you must cultivate a well committed, determined effort to achieve the goal. Once you are committed, fear will gradually move away. One can see that a lot of things impose fear on us. Most often, we create the fear in ourselves and, at times, other people do.

When does fear upgrade to terror? The answer is when an unpredictable unavoidable element of violence, danger, death, or threatening object is inevitable. Sometimes, imagination reshapes and redefines horror by convincing us that it is a must in the affairs of life, such as when soldiers' activities are termed heroic feats. But when fear, a mild apprehension necessary for normal existence, grows in a continuum, neurotic anxiety ensues. Maintain positive thinking; it checks your fear and earns you success. Fear leaves you to struggle in the "Babel" of confusion and hopelessness. **Positive thinking is the killer of fear and restorer of self-confidence**. Many people engage in taking medications and alcohol, drinking much coffee, and smoking packs of cigarettes when they are afraid. I commend you to limit taking these drinks and cigarettes but stick to positive thinking and self-commitment.

Research studies have shown that substances such as cigarettes, alcohol and caffeine have the power to ruin our hormones, thus creating a hormonal imbalance. Smoking drains women's store of hormones, especially oestrogen, both the natural and the supplemental oestrogens. Even when taking therapeutic glandular supplements for helping the endocrine glands like thyroid, adrenals, ovaries, and testicles while smoking, we run the risk of taking in toxic chemicals like pesticides, fertilizers, and antibiotics which are contained in them and which build up in the brain and cause dementia, and other neurological disorders. Whenever you are afraid, *consult your psychotherapist and your counsellor. Reduce your caffeine intake. T*ea is recommended as a relaxing beverage and, in fact, a hot cup of tea is psychologically calming. Truly, low doses of caffeine make us joyful, energetic, and self-confident but high doses drain the B vitamins and so render us anxious, irritable, and sleepless. If you find it difficult to quit, *go for counselling. Drink lightly or not at all.* "Alcohol," according to Shakespeare, "provokes the desire but takes away the performance." Alcohol causes the loss of water-soluble nutrients, especially B vitamins, potassium, and vitamin C, thereby causing deficiencies. B-vitamin deficiencies are attributed to nervousness and irritability, fatigue, aches, and pains, loss of appetite, itching, burning eyes, shakiness, mental depression, and impaired thinking. But moderate drinking is defined as a drink per day, a drink meaning 12 ounces of beer or 5 ounces of wine or a mixed drink such as 1.5 ounces of whisky.

Section IV: Overcoming Fear that Invades Your Self-Confidence

"We are generally afraid to become that which we can glimpse in our most perfect moments
Abraham Maslow
https://www.artofmanliness.com2020

From the Holy Scriptures, precisely 2 Timothy 1:7, *we read, "For God has not given us the spirit of fear, but of power, and of love and of a sound mind."* Fear is a spirit and is the nature of the devil. Regardless of the problem, fear comes from the devil. Because it comes from the devil, one must reject it or rightly put it this way, **resist it till it flees away**. In the book of James 4:7, it is written, "Submit yourselves therefore to God. Resist the devil and he will flee from you." The Holy Scriptures abound with statements like; "Fear not," and "Do not be afraid." In the Gospel according to Mathew 10:28, it is written; "Do not be afraid of those who kill the body but cannot kill the soul; fear him rather who can destroy both body and soul in hell." When we rebel and sin against God, we begin to chart our way on our own, full of darkness, uncertainties, and insecurities. We move away from God's plan. In Jeremiah 29:11, it is written: "Yes I know what plans I have in mind for you, Yahweh declares, plans for peace, not disaster, to give you a future and a hope." In 2 Chronicles 20:15, it is written, "Be not afraid, nor dismayed by reason of this great multitude; for the battle is not yours, but God's." In Deuteronomy 3:22, it is written, "You shall not fear them; for the Lord your God, He shall fight for you."

To overcome fear, you must keep striving till you reach your destiny. All you need to do to dismantle your fear is to develop more self-resilience, self-trust, and willingness to handle any task that comes your way. Try as much as you can to understand your strengths and limitations. You need to accept self; self-acceptance and believing in oneself matter a lot towards this struggle. Once you know these, self-motivation and self-improvement should emerge. Once you realize it, you will become a new you. Just keep pressing on till you attain positive self-esteem. Getting rid of fear is doing the things that are difficult repeatedly until you master them. Mastering them, you gain self-confidence, self-love, self-fulfilment, and self-actualization. Right now, you are a whole being. The only way to get rid of the fear and acquire self-confidence is to go out and do what you want to do. Never be afraid to make the move first; meet with whatever it is; touch it; feel it and handle it. By so doing, you acquire the ultimate power to conquer your fear. Arise now to cultivate the skill of problem-solving to challenge the obstacle. A simple way to do this is to do the things which you fear the most as mentioned above. Practice makes perfect. To emphasize on previous suggestions, I advise you to read novels, join debate clubs, read the books by famous authors like Susan Jeffers and others to uplift and enhance your self-confidence. Traders, research on your businesses; mothers, go to experienced mothers and learn how to handle family affairs. This book is for all walks of life. As you work on this, try to disband the primitive beliefs that imprison your self-confidence and push you towards fear. Apply a method that can assist you to handle your phobia. You need to start this race well to progress successfully and satisfactorily. Self-motivation and empowerment are much needed to combat fear. Let your key approach be self-motivation, self-empowerment, and self-discipline as you try to build self-confidence. Let one of your methodologies of fighting fear be constant reading of motivational books which can earn you self-discipline. Beverley Michaels, a black British woman, stated:

> *"Studying has allowed me to be more disciplined in getting closer to my aspirations in life. It has also helped me to develop and enhance skills I already had but didn't quite know how to utilize. It is my own personal achievement in life that no-one can ever take away from me because I have earned and worked hard for it."*
> *- Beverley Michaels*
> *Pride of Black British Women 1995, (p.25).*

Each person has a tremendous talent that God implanted in them which, most often, one never knows how to develop. Subsequently, try to develop yours and be proud of it. Ask yourself, what can I boast of? Yes, you have something to boast of; it is in you; you just need to find it out and uphold it. Another black British woman, Cheryl Burden said:

> *"I am proud to be a police officer and can see this being my career for life. I hope to achieve the highest rank possible during my time in the service..."*
> Cheryl Burden
> Pride of Black British Women 1995, (p. 29).

I encourage you today to bloom wherever you are planted. Always update yourself because no one can upgrade you; rather they will undermine you.

Be Careful of the Company You Keep

I recommend you to stay away from *negative* individuals because they will poison your mind and ruin your success. Negative-minded individuals are like roadblocks and disparaging people. They have the same goal of ruining your career. They would weaken your ability to strive towards self-enhancement. If you want to succeed, avoid dealing with them because n*egative thoughts wear away your strength*. Always be in touch and in love with positive-minded individuals, that is, good role models. Be first to approach them; never hesitate –**they are treasures**. Benchmark them. Practice positive thinking to gain self-confidence. How do I practice positive thinking? By projecting positive-self, positive self-concept, positive self-control, positive self-esteem, positive self-love, positive self-fulfilment, positive self-worth, and positive self-actualization. I call them positive. I presume that you have not yet acquired them but you have already claimed them. Remember, if you say yes, your mind will consent to it. A friend of mine said to me, "Sister, please pray for my trip to be successful." I responded to her, telling her to claim that the trip is already successful, and she said, "Amen, I claim it" and it was successful. Practising positive thinking is prerequisite for powerful self–improvement and powerful self-confidence. Positive action is the key to your self-actualization. Avoid anything that badly affects it. It is crucial you give up your old way of negative thinking. According to Susan Jeffers,

> *"All you have to do to diminish your fear is to develop more trust in your ability to handle whatever comes your way."*
>
> Susan Jeffers
> Feel the Fear and Do It Anyway, 1987, (p.16).

Bear in mind that as long as you are advancing in age and still in this world, fear will never leave you alone. It is always there with you. Have it in mind that once you have a goal to achieve and a brand new risk to take, you must confront it. The best option for you is to ignore fear and move on with your desired goal otherwise you are heading nowhere. The only way you can feel better about yourself is to go out and do what you are afraid of. The "doing it" comes before the feeling better about yourself. When you make something happen, not only does the fear of the situation go away, but also you get a big bonus: You do a lot towards upgrading your self-worth. It is fairly predictable, however, that when you have finally mastered something and gotten rid of the fear, you will feel so good you will decide there is something else out there you want to accomplish, and ... guess what?! The fear begins again as you prepare to meet a new challenge. You have to be aggressive with fear before you will be able to conquer it. You can only overcome it by being an 'actor' that is, action-doer. "Pushing through fear is less frightening than living with the underlying fear that comes from a feeling of helplessness." There are five ultimate truths about fear according to Jeffers:

1. The fear will never go away as long as I continue to grow.
2. The only way to get rid of the fear of doing something is to go out ... and do it.
3. The only way to feel better about myself is to go out ... and do it.
4. Not only am I going to experience fear whenever I'm on unfamiliar territory, but so is everyone else.

5. Pushing through fear is less frightening than living with the underlying fear that comes from a feeling of helplessness.

Susan Jeffers 1987 (p. 30).

Self-conviction is the key factor to self-confidence and conquering the fear. Convince yourself then you can be in charge. Right now, begin to hit your target goal; never hesitate. Remember, time waits for nobody. Again, start now to envisage your bright future success.

To Prevent Mood Disturbances, Meditate to Cleanse Your Mind. Maintain Good Mental Health

Our bodies are equipped with the necessary tools and techniques to keep us alive for maybe a hundred years, but it is the environment, the food we eat, the way we think, and the way we live that cut down our lifespan. For this reason, it is advisable for us to practice meditation, and self-regulation, coupled with routines of a good diet, exercise, and nutritional supplements every day. Before you go to bed and before you do meditation, you have to do a breathing exercise holding your breath for 38 seconds and then slowly exhale. Dr. Herbert Benson, M.D, Founding President of the Mind/Body Institute at Beth Israel Deaconess Medical Centre in Boston recommends some of this setup:

1. Sit erect comfortably on a chair, relaxed, free from fear, and stress.

2. With eyes closed, massage your muscles, beginning from your feet and moving up to your legs, thighs, trunk, arms, neck, and head.
3. While relaxed, breathe in slowly and naturally, holding your breath for thirty-eight seconds, then breathe out through the nose slowly.
4. While doing your breathing exercise, recite your keyword. You can choose your keyword or a phrase taken from your prayer. Just say: "Hail Mary or "Rosary," if you are a Catholic, "Om Tat" or "Hare Krsna," if you are an Indian Hindi, "Our Father", if you are a Protestant Christian, "Salam Allah", if you are a Muslim, "Shilom Yisrael," if you are a Jew, chant "Mantra," if you are a Buddhist, or "Ogunalo, Orusa gbawata," if you are a Nigerian Ibo Orusa worshipper. Do these as many times as you wish to.

In any case, after the breathing exercise, you have to fill the vacuum you created in your mind with your happiest event. Meanwhile, while sitting in front of a lit candle or a lamp, concentrate on your happy event, reciting your keyword or phrase and looking at the lit candle. It takes about 20 minutes. Then relax and go to sleep. You can also do it while lying on your bed. This attitude of removing stress-ridden overload from the mind and ushering in good feelings gives the body calmness and freedom from fear. Fear is a fundamental biological necessity of a normal person. Ingrained in our genes is an instruction of how to feel fear for whatever situation or condition that may arise in one's life. Biologically, all emotions, positive ones like love and negative ones like anger, and fear originate from the limbic system (a ring of brain structure of the inner wall of the cerebral cortex) of the brain. In the centre of this brain system are the nucleus of locus coeruleus and the amygdala from where flow the hormones and neurotransmitters such as dopamine, ACTH (adrenocorticotrophic), noradrenaline (norepinephrine,) serotonin, adrenaline (epinephrine,) gamma-amino butyric acid (GABA), monoamine oxidase (MAO) and melatonin. There are predators and prey created in our brains' chromosomes (cellular structure in the nucleus containing DNA-deoxyribonucleic acid which transmits genetic information). These senses, smell, taste, sight, touch, and hearing, authorise our bodies to monitor the environment and prepare the individual for an action or a retreat. In the brain, different sections are delegated to functions as follows: thalamus to co-ordinate the senses; amygdala for emotions; the hippocampus for memory, and the hypothalamus for regulating the body's basic needs and appetites. All these are grouped together as the limbic system, which is the seat of moods and emotions.

Surrounded in the landscape by hazards of different sorts, the brain developed, with experience and intelligence, what to do under stress for survival. Our brain learnt to co-operate, to judge, to act, to laugh, to love, to fear, and to ignore the irrelevant. By changing our physical, social, and psychological environments, we remove the element of fear and become confident in daring to deal with our daily tasks. Our brain has an intelligence that is capable of extracting information from within and without through the senses, storing it, processing it, and developing strategies to cope with what the information calls for. Our life has survived for ages, correcting itself after a barrage of several stimuli, good, bad, and neutral.

Section V: Fear is a Quality of a Virtue in a Modest Person

In the early changing and foreboding environments of the past, our forebears acquired a sense of survival by quickly examining new experiments, cross-checking opinions, making decisions, and learning from the results of their choices. This flexibility has been the guideline of how to sample, analyse, and make choices. We can change our minds when pressured by restraints in order to avoid danger. We can persuade others to dare or retreat. It is also said in Psalm 25:12-13, "Who now is the man fearful of God? He will instruct him in the way that he will choose. His own soul will lodge in goodness itself and his own offspring will take possession of the earth." It is also good to express emotions on a short-term basis, whether positively or negatively. This psychologically and physiologically makes for good health. In an experiment on emotions and the immune system by Dr. Margaret Kemeny, a psychologist, Assistant Professor in the Department of Psychiatry and Bio-behavioural Sciences, University of California, Los Angeles, specially method-trained actors, who are trained to use their memories and sensations to elicit very intense emotional expressions realistically when they are on the stage, were used to study whether short-term emotional changes of feeling sad or happy for twenty minutes have an effect on the immune system. The investigator, Dr. Ann Futterman directed the actors to improvise a monologue (a soliloquy) based on standard sad or happy emotions. When the actors were in the desired state, changes in the immune system were observed. To begin with, the actors were asked to have an intense feeling of sadness for having been rejected for playing a part badly. It was observed that in the intense sad state, there was an increase in the number of *natural killer cells* in the bloodstream and that the *killer cells* were functioning more perfectly than they were when the actors were in a neutral state. Then the actors were made to imagine that they played the part well and were successful and happy because they were approved. In this case, it was also observed that the natural killer cells, leukocytes, white blood cells that go about scavenging/hunting and ingesting invading bacteria, increased in number, just as in the sad state. When the actors stopped feeling sad or happy and sat down quietly for half an hour, the immune system returned to its normal condition. The natural killer cells of the immune system are the white blood cells called leukocyte neutrophils that are the first-line defence that confront foreign organisms without prior experience of the organism. They are able to kill cells that are infected with viruses and also tumour cells. They kill by producing toxic substances. In our daily experiences of happiness, sadness, anger, frustration, love, and fear they are there on a short-term basis, producing healthy adaptive enhancement of emotions, psychologically, and physiologically. But if you live with fear day in, day out, and month after month, the mechanisms that pump these killer cells and other chemicals into the bloodstream to increase their activity get depleted over time and hence, lose their adaptive healthy advantage and become psychologically and physiologically detrimental, like in chronic depression, panic attacks, and terror. So beware, constant sadness, as well as depression, can kill easily. You must to be willing to feel the fear.

You have to Be Willing to Feel the Fear

Some people lose money in their stock market dealings. Some mountaineers fall off mountains and die yet there are people training for mountaineering. Many women die during childbirth yet women get pregnant and still give birth. "Oguru negbu nde, **nde afuwo oguru nara**". This is a Nigerian 'Ibo' proverb, meaning that while there are people who are abundantly drunk, there are also people in the same vicinity who are feverishly longing to drink but have nothing to drink. What about driving a car? Every day, people swerve off the road and hit trees and die. All the same, people are still confident going round daily in their cars, and doing their chores without fear of accidents. We are all aware that life is a mixture of some accomplishments and disasters just as it is said: *"Nothing ventured, nothing gained." It is an "all-or-nothing" situation.* Sometimes, when you are in the middle of executing your dream project, someone comes along telling you that you are foolish because he or she sees you heading for an approaching disaster. When Hernando Cortez (Spanish sailor) arrived in Mexico in 1519 AD, he destroyed all the ships in order to prevent the idea of retreating and abandoning his mission in the face of any danger. Most of the time, it is a win-or-lose determination. The wise saying goes, "you don't refuse to go to war because of dying". When I was about to enter the convent, a friend of mine and one of my aunts were bent on convincing me not to go with lots of good reasons. But I ignored them and decided to proceed. Here I am today as a convinced nun. By convinced nun I mean a satisfied, happy, religious nun. One of the reasons given to me then not to enter was based on my level of education. I had only secondary education then, but today, I am a qualified professional graduate. No matter what pressure you face, never give up on your goal; never retreat, just roll on. I advise you at this point to associate with forward-looking people who can move you forward rather than associating with "road-blockers." It is amazingly empowering to have the support of a strong, motivated, and inspirational group of people. You need people with positive minds to facilitate your self-esteem. When you take a loan for a project, you are faced with the terror of taking chances in throwing your money, your credibility and prestige into an unknown, unpredictable mishap. On the other hand, one can positively dare to proceed with the affirmation that all will be well in the end. One can apply what is called the *"Four D's."* That means: **Do it, Delegate it, Delay it, or Dump it.** These four principles help one to assess one's capabilities in confronting a problem. If the matter is urgent and one is capable, then it is proper to attend to the matter at once. But if everything is all right, yet the strength is lacking, then it is wise to find someone who can do it. When strength for doing it will be available in future, one has to delay doing it. When what is expressly prominent in a project is its deficiency with no strength to do it, the appropriate thing is to dump it. However, if you dump it, I recommend you to find an alternative way to reach that objective. Always be mindful of this: when one road closes, another opens. It is only a dead person whose road closes forever in this mortal world. As long as one lives, you have an alternative solution to continue with.

At this juncture, Caroline Myss said,

> *"When one door closes, another opens; but we so often look so long and so regretfully upon the closed door, that we do not see the ones which open for us"*
> -Caroline Myss
> Invisible Acts of Power *by Alexander Graham Bell 2004, (p.182).*

This implies that often, whenever we get disappointed on one plan, then we feel that the world has ended and there is no way out. We lose every hope and patience to look for another means. I am assuring you today that your door does not completely close; just have patience and look for an alternative door to go through. As you move on with your proposal, I would like you to consider this section of the bible; "Our hope will never fail us" (Romans 5:5). Trust in God and believe in the mystery of possibilities because our hope will never fail us. God is the hope of the hopeless and comfort of the fearful in time of despair. The fortification of our fear, as well as the fulfilment of our hope, is not limited to the realization of what we are anticipating, rather in hope itself which is the ability to move on without dropping out.

Two ladies went for an interview for a job in an administrative office and these ladies were both qualified for the job. After the interview, one of them stayed back in the city while the other went home to the village. At home when she was staying idle, her mother inspired her to go back to the city and be near to the job location. Then she immediately sent an e-mail to the administrative office requesting the interviewer to reserve the job for her. Then she went back to the city, and, having dressed herself as a secretary, went boldly and confidently to see the manager. She told the boss that she had come to start working as a secretary in his office. The manager was astounded and embarrassed because he had not yet issued a letter of appointment to anyone. But the lady was insistent, saying that she had been idle at home and that she needed a job to keep herself busy. The administrative officer was highly impressed with her and gave a letter of job engagement to her and asked her to start working immediately. This is an example of a woman of strong capability undaunted by the rigors of protocol or rules of the game of jobs and employment. ***This is the "Do it or never" principle.*** Consequently, it is fear which can make you dump your proposals and your opportunities. Always be positive and aggressive as this lady was when searching for a job. Time waits for no one. Try y to remove fear and forge ahead on your dream goals; don't wait and never quit; you are in and you're in to win. Some people are excited in all senses, feeling heady to stare danger in the face just as when they say that the valiant always wins the laurel. The risk-takers, the thrill-seekers are usually called the T-type personality (T-means tyrosine-amino acid from which dopamine, norepinephrine, and epinephrine are derived, neurotransmitters that prepare the body for high energy expenditure), with high energy minds that crave for stimulation to tackle dangerous problems. They tend to break the rules, ignore tradition, and flout authority. They exert enormous sensations and emotions, and succeed most of the time. They are intensively creative or destructive. They convert their high energy into jobs, hobbies, sports, and adventures. The question is what makes a risk-seeking person? It is a combination of upbringing and genetic makeup.

Section VI: Fear is a Preprogrammed Genetic Aspect of Life

Research studies in Natural Genetics in Richard Epstein's Laboratory in Jerusalem have shown that those with novelty-seeking characters have an unusual version of the D4DR gene (D4 means dopamine gene #4 for DR-Dopamine Receptor) on chromosome 11. It is the recipe for a protein called a dopamine receptor switched on in cells of certain parts of the brain (nucleus acumens, substantial nigra, and ventral tegmentum). Dopamine is a multi-purpose neurotransmitter related chemically to norepinephrine, epinephrine and serotonin essential for controlling complex bodily activities, helping the brain to talk to at least fifty different chemicals at once. Dopamine is the brain's motivational and initiating chemical. With the shortage of dopamine, the brain creates an indecisive and frozen personality, unable to initiate bodily functions. An excess of dopamine in human beings is the cause of schizophrenia, a mental disorder that causes delusion and gross disorganized behaviour. Dopamine in concert with norepinephrine, GABA (gamma-aminobutyric acid) and their close cousin serotonin prepare the body to fight danger or run away from it. Dopamine motivates and initiates a neural impulse; epinephrine generates the high energy chemical, glycogen; norepinephrine stimulates the tissues for an action; GABA modulates the neural impulse and allows the neurons to receive information in an orderly manner; serotonin helps to enhance, and smooth the emotions, so that the risk-seekers are always bursting with energy ready for action. We are created with fear in our system and maintained with fear as a weapon for our success. This is true because the seven gifts of the spirit are (1) wisdom, (2) understanding, (3) counsel, (4) fortitude, (5) knowledge, (6) piety, and (7) fear. We invoke God to infuse fear in us as in prayer to the Holy Spirit.

Fear is factored into all created beings, from microbes to multi-celled organisms, so much so that we are all armed with instructional, warning, and defence genes, genetic functionaries that listen and collect data from the environment and create and use hormones, enzymes and neurotransmitters in response to the situational messages. We all now know that antibiotics, such as penicillin, have been overcome by some bacteria such as Escherichia Coli (E-Coli), Salmonella, shigella, enterobacter etc., because these organisms have developed a resistance for fighting back. Bacterial cells have an outer coat, a cell-wall made up of protein and sugar molecules forming what is called peptidoglycan which runs in a stiff crisscross framework giving the bacteria a structural strength and protection. But there are antibiotics like penicillin, cephalosporins, and vancomycin, which prevent the cross-links of peptidoglycan lattice from being formed during the time bacteria are dividing. The antibiotics replace the protein part of the peptidoglycan so that the connectivity within the peptidoglycan never get formed. In the antibiotic threat, bacteria, like human beings in the fight-or-flight situation, proceed to either deny the penicillin access to the inner chamber of the cell or destroy the penicillin or opt to go into a resting phase until the active level of the penicillin drug falls below the effective threshold. At this point, the bacterium, by studying the penicillin structure, made up of lactam-rings (organic chemical that contains NH-CO), uses its resistance gene to create the deactivating enzyme called lactamase, which shatters the penicillin drugs. Here we learn that a one-celled organism without a brain and a nervous system can perform the emotional fight-or-flight strategy just like us because the bacteria are pre-programed with defensive resistance factor genes by their creator.

Another instance of the natural intelligence incorporated in living beings is an episode of what happened between a ground *Spider and a Wasp*. The wasp built a nest and was ready to lay her eggs. But it had to find prey on which to lay the eggs. Consequently, the wasp found a pit dug by a ground spider. The pit was made up of freely flowing sand so that any trespasser would easily slide to the spider that was waiting at the bottom. The wasp saw this and knew the spider was hidden at the bottom of the pit. Thus, it started to clear the sand to expose the spider. It was not easy but it used its wings to balance itself on the loose sand. Eventually, it reached the spider. As it was ready to sting the spider, the spider sprang out of the pit, formed its body into a ball and quickly rolled away. The wasp was disappointed for it could not locate the spider anymore. This is a fearful threat from the wasp. The spider escaped by an ingeniously inborn intelligent strategy designed by its creator for deceiving its predator.

There is a similar story of a mother-of-pearl caterpillar and a bird. The bird threatened the caterpillar which fell down from the tree where it was, formed itself into the shape of a green wheel and rapidly rolled away. At last, we come to the conclusion that life is programmed with intelligence and a fear factor for all activities which are present for the survival of all living beings. Therefore, fear is unavoidable.

In my naturalized country, the United States of America, I set a goal and I was always fearful of one thing; that is *"failure."* Because of this, I set up a unique strategy to secure myself and my goal, to keep away from anyone that I knew who would be an obstacle or a distracter to my imperative proposal. That is, I hid my phone book inside my box where my hand could not easily reach it to call anyone. And I said to myself *"I'M IN, AND I'M IN TO WIN"* Hillary Clinton, Biography (1996). So, I am in to win. I then disowned anyone who would tell me distractive stories or lead me into things that did not really matter. I maintained contact and associated with only those who directed and uplifted me. Guess what? This worked for me and I succeeded in achieving my crucial dream career and I am happy now. I maintained effective contact with my work, school, and my church. Moreover, I did totally switch off from any distractions and it worked for me. It will work for you too. Always be mindful of fear because it is a two-edged sword. If you do not know this, you mess yourself up. The secret to success is fearlessness and peace of mind. Henceforth, focus on your dream and keep fear behind you. Benchmark Senator Hillary Rodham Clinton's philosophy; *"I'M IN, AND I'M IN TO WIN."* You have to take bold steps and risks in order to succeed. You don't sit down to succeed; you have to be active and become a habitual action-taker. When Hillary was a sophomore in her school time, she was feeling inferior and also struggling with an identity crisis which gave her sleepless nights. This situation enabled her to strive harder to work herself up to the level she is today as a senator and Secretary of State. When I was reading her biography, I said to myself, so even as a white woman felt inferior. I could visualize the picture of myself through her. I was enthralled. Then, I challenged myself and started working hard to get rid of the inferiority complex and I succeeded. I urge you to challenge yourself in order to be what you want to be. You can do it.

Section VII: Fear: Pathological Aspect of a Neurotic Person

The neurotransmitters send their neural impulses in successive waves, one at a time, so much so that as each chemical delivers its impulse, it is immediately either repackaged and released back to its original source vesicles or broken down into its inactive metabolites (by-products). At this point, another chemical, a relative of the dopaminergic family (of family dopamine), the brain enzyme called monoamine oxidase (MAO) comes into play. Its function is to make sure that the on-rush of packets of serotonin, dopamine, norepinephrine, epinephrine and GABA, after they have delivered their impulses to the receptors, are either repackaged and re-absorbed in the vesicles or are broken down into their metabolites, to prevent the successive waves of the neurotransmitters from accumulating and continuing to excite the receptors repeatedly. These neurotransmitter molecules work in a consortium and in a cascade so much so that a failure in one of them has a pathological consequence.

This paragraph itemizes the neurological illnesses that result from individual failures. As a matter of fact, all bodily functions like sleep, emotions, and movements are consecutively operated by multiple regulatory hormones and neurotransmitters. For instance, memory is a function undertaken by acetylcholine (transmitter for memory), epinephrine, norepinephrine, and serotonin. These regulatory chemicals do not act singly but instead, they interact with one another like musical instruments in a symphony orchestra to produce harmonic melodies. In the light of the foregoing statement, because each chemical has a set-point value for a reactive state, there is always a tell-tale episode, should any chemical molecule default in performing correctly. **Neurological fear** is a result of emotion chemicals not functioning correctly. The depletion of dopamine causes persistent tremors of Parkinson's disease, shaking of hands and legs, tightness, and stiffness of the muscles. Because its presence causes alertness, its low level results in narcoleptic apnea (frequent irresistible sleep during the day). In the excess of dopamine, an intense schizophrenic agitation and manic unreality abound. Another kind of schizophrenic person is one who is passive and immobilized and withdrawn into a shadow world of internal terror and fear. These conditions create in a patient neurological episodes of delusional hearing of voices, seeing objects that do not exist and fearing that those trying to help her are attempting to kill her. A patient of these ailments is in an **apathetic fear**. With the dysfunction of GABA, severe forms of stress, terrifying panic attacks, and sudden acute anxiety manifest. About 2 to 5 percent of the American population is affected. Other affectations of the stressful disease are sweating palms, unstable knees, palpitating heart, gasping breath, and a bizarre sense of unreality.

Normally, GABA, by an inhibiting action on a neural activity, helps neurons to receive pulsating impulse information in an orderly way. In some cases, what is called post-traumatic stress disorder arises from the internal unconscious memory of past forgotten emotionally devastating episodes such as soldiers involved in wars, rape, and physical assault. The individual is in constant fear. For instance, in some nursing homes, most clients who were ex-soldiers are always ready to fight, kick, and hit anyone who comes in to attend to them, presuming that the person is an enemy. They are always exhibiting transfer aggression; taking everybody as an attacker. A discharge of norepinephrine, serotonin and epinephrine in a human body in normal circumstances helps the body to exhibit normal behavioural alertness, pleasure, and excitement necessary for performing functions for its survival. But, in a neurological disorder, too much norepinephrine, epinephrine, and serotonin causes agitation and too little creates mental depression (loss of interest in all pleasurable outlets such as food, sex, work, friends, hobbies or entertainment).

Section VIII: Fear: Biological Function of Emotions of a Person

The capacity for imaginatively creating and responding to dangers that never materialize is unique to our species. The anticipation of a loss of face in front of others, of one's job or a financial status being at risk of making a bad impression and of a whole variety of problems, all *provoke anxiety and fear* in some people. Teachers, administrators, and supervisors often say to workers: *"People have to be kept on their toes. Let them relax too much and they become unproductive. A little anxiety is good because it keeps everyone motivated."* But when anxiety continues for a while, the benefits decline and people work less efficiently and less productively.

Sigmund Freud defined fear and neurotic anxiety as,

"An apprehension of an actual danger from an external object, a person, or a situation but the neurotic anxiety has its source from an unknown danger of a vague nature, lacking precisely definable substance. Someone asked, "When does fear escalate to terror or neurotic anxiety? The answer is when the element of unpredictability of the source is involved. Psychologist Raymon Cattel and his fellow teammates in the 1960s conducted questionnaires, interviews and extensive psychological, physiological, and behavioural tests

to answer the question of how we are to draw a line between "normal" anxiety and anxiety that is pathological. From these exercises, symptoms of the anxious person were derived. He or she lacked confidence, regularly experienced guilt or worthlessness, feared new ventures, fatigued easily, and often expressed irritability, discouragement, and uncertainty along with a degree of suspicion, and distrust of the motives of other people," said the team Receptors 2004, (pp. 155-156).

Anxiety is a persistent emotional disorder that generally generates phobias as a means of avoiding an anxiety-provoking situation. About 19.9 million people are affected by these two disorders. But there are anxiety-stricken situations that have become entrained in the biological setup of some people's brains. Take, for instance, the soldiers who have to fight in a war or those who watch war movies or television shows. We have come to live with terror-causing fearful natural disasters like mad cow disease (1986-88), floods and storms, (tsunami 2004, Katrina 2005) and the present-day epidemics of HIV and AIDS (human immune-deficiency virus and acquired immune deficiency syndrome), Ebola virus as well as coronavirus - COVID -19. It is said that images of fear, horror, danger, and violence affect the right hemisphere of our brain more than the left hemisphere and so those of us prevalent in the **right hemisphere** are more seriously stricken than the **left hemisphere** people in such a way that they cannot be easily calmed down. An important part of terror, which we sustain in us is from the biological fear which we acquired when in the ancient times, was that we were trained to look out for unexpected terror scenarios hiding in the grass. For over a billion years, our body genes have been re-writing themselves by adding, deleting, and amending portions of themselves in response to the environmental threats of fear. Now we have, in our biological makeup, recipes for instructions about fear and how to defend ourselves when confronted by fear-inducing situations.

Section IX: Instances of Fear

It is said that when stress, in its pathological and psychological forms, gives rise to fear, anxiety, and neurotic crisis, then it becomes a neurological disorder creating all different types of phobias. Hyperadrenalism (caused by increased secretion of adrenaline from the adrenal gland) and hyperthyroidism (a condition caused by an excessive secretion of the thyroid gland which increases the basal metabolic rate and increased demand for food thereby causing nervousness, excessive sweating, and increased heart rate) are source causes of fear which generate phobias because they rev up one's metabolism with insatiable hunger, so much so that one's energy is drained, giving way to apathy, loss of enthusiasm, role conflict and mood swings. The following phobias are adapted from Campbell, R.J. Psychiatric dictionary, ed. 5 Oxford University Press, 1981, from Taber's Cyclopaedic Medical Dictionary, ed. 15, 1985 edited by Clayton L. Thomas, M.D., M.P.H. (Master of Public Health).

Common Fears

1. Fear of Aloneness (monophobia)
2. Fear of Animals (zoophobia)
3. Fear of Bees (apiphobia)
4. Fear of Blood (haematophobia)
5. Fear of water (hydrophobia)
6. Fear of Mirrors (eisoptrophobia)
7. Fear of Colours (chromophobia
8. Fear of Contamination (mysophobia)
9. Fear of Crowds (demophobia)
10. Fear of Darkness (Scotophobia/nyctophobia)
11. Fear of Demons (demonomania)
12. Fear of Death (thanatophobia)
13. Fear of Devil (satanophobia)
14. Fear of Flying (aerophobia)
15. Fear of Dog (Cynophobia)
16. Fear of eating (phagophobia)
17. Fear of Failure (kakorrhaphiophobia)
18. Fear of Fearing (phobophobia)
19. Fear of Filth (mysophobia)
20. Fear of Filth or odour, personal (automysophobia)
21. Fear of Food (cibophobia/sitophobia)
22. Fear of Glass (Crystallophobia)
23. Fear of God (theophobia)
24. Fear of Height (acrophobia)
25. Fear of High objects or being on tall buildings (batophobia)
26. Fear of Insane, becoming (maniaphobia)
27. Fear of Insects (entomophobia)

28. Jealousy (zelophobia)
29. Fear of Justice (dikephobia)
30. Fear of Marriage (gamophobia)
31. Fear of Medicine (pharmacophobia)
32. Fear of Needles (belonephobia)
33. Fear of Night (noctiphobia)
34. Fear of People (anthropophobia)
35. Fear of Poison (toxicophobia)
36. Fear of Poverty (peniaphobia)
37. Fear of Punishment (poinephobia)
38. Fear of Rain or rainstorm (ombrophobia)
39. Fear of Red (erythrophobia)
40. Fear of Responsibility (hypengyophobia)
41. Fear of River (potamophobia)
42. Fear of Sea (thalassophobia)
43. Fear of Sinning (peccatiphobia)
44. Fear of Snake (ophidophobia)
45. Fear of Snow (chionophobia)
46. Fear of Solitude or being alone (eremophobia)
47. Fear of Sound (acousticophobia)
48. Fear of Speaking (laliophobia)
49. Fear of Spider (arachnophobia)
50. Fear of Strangers (zenophobia)
51. Fear of Thunder (brontophobia)
52. Fear of Vaccination (vaccinophobia)
53. Fear of Open space (Agoraphobia)

There is a story about a family called the Eke family, suffering from a pervasive hatred for anything or any person **filthy** in behaviour. This form of phobia is called **mysophobia (fear of**

contamination). The members of the family would not eat your food if they saw you handling food in a messy fashion or if you did not wash the cooking utensils immediately after cooking. So, one of them got married to a woman who did not wash her cooking utensils, pot, mortar, and pestle but instead left them unwashed till the following morning. When Eke saw this, he felt nauseous and filled with anger. He told the wife because of this attitude of leaving the cooking utensils in a messy condition, that he was divorcing her. He asked her to pack and go back to her parents. The woman collected her things and went home to her parents. She told the parents what happened. Her parents then told the story to their community.

The news of this episode spread to other places. Consequently, Eke decided to remarry but no parents would give their daughter and no woman would agree to marry him because they said he was too **fussy** for any woman. Everywhere, he went for a woman, he was asked to tell the story of the first wife. Eke got disgusted and lived as a bachelor and died a bachelor, childless, and wifeless. Consequently, this attitude became known as the "Eke Isoyi" legend. Today, the present members of the family are cautious when dealing with the public and are conscious of their brother, Eke, who, owing to his extreme phobia for filth, lost his wife, died a bachelor and without a child. Theophobia is the spiritual act, forbidden by God because of the fear of Divine or Spiritual retribution capable of affecting both the clan and the individual offender. According, to the original ancient Orusa worship in Igboland, taboo, which is Theophobia, has been practised with respect to god "Ali" (divine entity in charge of the land and the people). Taboo has many forms. For example:

(i) Causing a lamb to die or break a leg.
(ii) Impregnating a girl before her official spiritual "ikwezi" (native cultural marriage celebration and ceremonial offering of a sacrifice to the god, and "Ali the goddess."
(iii) Stealing of yams (yams are sacred to the god "Ali" who gave yams to mankind,).
(iv) A woman in her menses is forbidden to go to the family shrine to eat the food offered to the god at the shrine. This taboo can be traced to ancient Egypt and to Leviticus in the Bible. As early as 1850 BC from the Papyrus Kahum during the middle kingdom period in Ancient Egypt, there was an inscription at the temple of Hathor (Hathor-Egyptian goddess of a number of the pleasurable aspects of life such as dance, music, sexuality, alcohol, and love), in Edfu, Ancient Egypt, that contains a list of gods with specific dislikes for menstruating women. In Leviticus 15:19-20, we read, in case a woman having a running discharge and her running discharge in flesh proves to be blood, she should continue seven days in her menstrual impurity and anyone touching her will be unclean until the evening. And anything upon which she may lie down in her menstrual impurity will be unclean and everything upon which she may sit will be unclean.

(v) A hen hatching only one egg or a dog giving birth to one young one is defiled.

(vi) A cock crowing too early at midnight before dawn is defiled.

(vii) Anyone murdering a person deliberately or accidentally must leave the land and stay outside for a year and after that, must pay atonement to the family of the dead and to the god "Ali" of the land if the murder was by mistake. Hence, if one deliberately commits murder, he or she must be banished forever from his clan.

Scotophobia (Fear of Darkness)

There was a young girl called Nnenna who would not enter a dark room in the night because she said her dead mother was hiding there. Immediately it was dark, her ordeal would begin wherever she was in the dark. To overcome her problem, she had to have an escort to assure her that everything was alright. For cibophobia or sitophobia, there was one girl named Ada Obi who was afraid of eating the staple food, cassava "fufu." When under pressure from older adults, she would swallow food until she would suddenly vomit all she had swallowed. No one could convince her to eat the staple food. One day, a group of adults determined to force her to eat "fufu." They succeeded and forced the food into her stomach with water. After this, she was cured and she started eating by herself. There was one Igweke family of nine boys. The boys were very boisterous (full of energy) and menacing to people. The villagers were very afraid of them because the boys were suffering from extreme **jealousy, (Zelophobia)**. One day, they invaded a farm and stole yams. The news of the incident spread in the village. The village head and the high priest of the god "Ali," to whom yams were consecrated, summoned everybody to find out who had committed the offence. All but members of this family came out. They all swore before the god "Ali" that they did not steal the yams. There and then, the priests of the god "Ali" invoked "Ali" to expose the offenders. It was not long before the epidemic of "Otiwu," (black-death) began. The nine boys, in one night, died of the "Otiwu." They died because they were afraid of owning up to what they had done. They died out of fear.

Section X: All Power to Your Elbow Hang Tough

Fear can lead you into the avoidance of responsibility. Rose and Rita were friends and classmates. The two of them were not good at mathematics, so, Rose became very apprehensive and left school and became a dropout because she lacked confidence in herself. For Rita, she became courageous and eager to learn and was able to make it to graduate level. Rose easily lost confidence and was discouraged by fear. The sooner you are aware of what you fear, the better for you. You have the power to turn everything around; that is, conquer your fear; never allow fear to defeat you. According to Albert Einstein,

"Life is like riding a bicycle; in order to keep your balance, you must keep moving."

Simple Ways to Gain Confidence

- Maintain a positive frame of mind and stop blaming yourself or others.
- Stop blaming others for your fault.
- Appraise yourself and do not cast any negative image on yourself.
- Be sure you know when you are wrong and then know the fact and accept the fact in order to remedy the situation.
- Know yourself and do not be misled by distractions.
- Determine your goal, stick to it, and devote your energy to what you plan to accomplish.
- Finally, rely on your option and develop strategies to achieve it.

In his autobiography, Martin Luther King Jr. said,

> *"I have always felt that ultimately along the way of life, an individual must stand up and be counted and be willing to face the consequences whatever they are. And if he is filled with fear, he cannot do it. My great prayer is always for God to save me from the paralysis of crippling fear, because I think when a person lives with the fears of the consequences for his personal life, he can never do anything in terms of lifting the whole of humanity and solving many of the social problems which we confront in every age and every generation."*
> bz*https://kinginstitute.stanford.edu/king-papers/documents/interview-joe-azbel*

More so,

> *"Just do what confident people do" "You should move your body like a confident person, give yourself positive self-talk, use a confident tone and just do what confident people do. The more you act as if you are confident, the more you will become confident".*
> Steve Miller
> 7 Secrets of Confidence 2010, (p. 74).

Reminding yourself always that you are confident and you can do it helps a lot. Remember, once you say to yourself, I am unable, I am an idiot, I am stupid, your unconscious mind takes it and stores it for you. Whenever you are about to take responsibility, your unconscious mind retrieves it and begins to say to you, "You cannot do it... and you must not." It will be reminding you whenever you want to take responsibility. Here is another vision from 7 Secrets of Confidence:

> *"What you put in mind is what you are; so, in order to be mentally efficient, you to have to keep the positive part of life. When you remain in the positive side of life, your thoughts will be well refined. According to Steve Miller, "The commands and information you have been sending to your brain have done little or nothing to spark the confidence that you desperately want. And do remember that the unconscious mind cannot distinguish between what's good and bad for you; if you tell it you are useless, it will accept you are useless..."*

How Fear Leads to Failure

Fear leads to failure because once your mind perceives that you cannot do it, it will always flash it to you each time you want to perform. Once you tell your inner consciousness you cannot, it registers and no matter how much effort you put therein after all, it becomes fruitless. Brave people never give up. Once they fail, they look for an alternative. This is how they succeed and become famous. They took risks and challenges before they reached where they are now. Their self-confidence was not built in a day. What I am trying to say to you here is that you should never think of failure as a justification for giving up. Failure means setback. Many students fail their exams not because they do not know what to write but because they fail to express their points the way the teacher expects them. Then their challenge is to sit back and examine the cause of their failure to fix it. All the confident men do likewise when they fail. Only the losers give up. Be mindful that failure never lasts forever. It is a temporary occurrence but cowards make it permanent. You need to face challenges before you reach a goal. Nevertheless, face the challenge of failure and keep running till you overcome it. How do you overcome failure? To overcome your failure, you must learn a new approach to get to the solution. This new approach is applicable to all aspects of life including the company one keeps. If the company you keep brings failure in your life, step back and seek the one that would help you to move forward. Success is meant for everybody, especially those who work hard. Never allow fear to overtake you and stop you from reaching your desired target.

> *"Being defeated is often a temporary condition. Giving up is what makes it permanent."*
> *- Marilyn Vos Savant.*

Remind yourself that you will not even experience any failure; your ambition is success. There was a time when I set a goal on win, win and it happened that way and has continued. The quote below, from one of the famous writers, may also assist you to strive higher in your career. Here it is:

> *"Promise me you'll always remember: You're braver than you believe, and stronger than you seem, and smarter than you think."*
> *Christopher Robin to Pooh, A.A. Milne.*

In fact, this quote is for me. Someone said that I am smart, not intelligent; since I learnt it, I translated my smartness to intelligence. Many a time, when people say something against us, we take offence, but in actual fact, we learn from it. As a result of that comment, I have become smarter, braver and stronger in all my endeavours. Keep pressing forward and never place your dreams on hold. Whenever you experience a setback in your confidence-building, don't be disheartened. Here is a short story according to Joel Osteen:

> *"That almost happened to my father. My dad was married at an early age, but unfortunately, the relationship didn't work out. My father was devasted. He felt certain that his days of ministry were over and that he'd never have a family again.*

He felt sure that he had ruined his life and destroyed any future impact for good that he might hope to have. He spent long hours just sitting around depressed, defeated, and dejected. Then one day, he did what I'm asking you to do. Instead of settling for good enough, instead of focusing on all his mistakes and dwelling on his failures, he decided to let it go. Years later, he told me the hardest thing for him to do was to receive God's mercy. But the Bible says that when we confess our sins, God not only forgives us, He chooses not to remember them anymore. If somebody keeps bringing up your past, you need to know it is not God. If God has let go it, why don't you let go of it too?

That's what my father did. One day, he got up, dusted himself off, and said, "Yes, I've made some mistakes; I've made some poor choices. But I know God has another seed. I know He has another plan." Shortly after that, he met my mother. Eventually, they got married and over the years, God blessed them with five children!

Many people who, like my father, have experienced hurt and pain, are sitting around wallowing in their mistakes, feeling guilty, condemned, and frustrated. Feeling like they're washed up in life, they allow their gifts and talents to waste away; they place their dreams on hold. Please, don't let that be you. If you've made mistakes, know this: God is the God of a second chance, a third chance, a fourth, and more." I am not saying to take the easy path and bail out of a marriage. No, if at all possible, stick with that marriage and make it work. However, if you're already past that point, don't sit around thinking that life is over and that you're never going to be happy. No, God has another seed. He wants to give you a new beginning. Let the door open completely and step forward into the future God has for you. Quit looking back. Instead, receive God's mercy and start pressing forward in life.

The car you drive has a large windshield, but only a relatively small rear-view mirror. The importance is what is in your future. Where you are going is much more important than where you've been. If you stay focused on the past, you're liable to miss numerous excellent opportunities ahead."

-Joel Osteen
7Keys to Improving Your Life Every Day
Become A Better You 2007, (p. 23-25).

I have the audacity to ask you to never despair when you fail to get it right. "Disappointment produces despair and despair produces bitterness". Martin Luther King. Jr. (p. 316) The Autobiography

Chapter Two

Section I: How to Treat Fear in Case of Pathological Situations

But when fear, a mild apprehension necessary for normal existence, grows in a continuum, neurotic anxiety ensues.

In a biological framework, the mood-regulating bio-chemicals flow from the limbic, hypothalamus, pituitary, and adrenal glands (LHPA) axis (bio-chemicals- serotonin, dopamine, epinephrine, norepinephrine, gamma-amino-butyric acid (GABA) and mono-amine oxidase (MAO). When you are angry or fearful in unmanaged stress, the hormonal overload does not have enough mood-regulating bio-chemical connections to handle it and so the imbalance upsets the LHPA axis. Remedies in each case and how to restore normalcy to the system by creating hormone-balancing techniques shall be discussed. To start with, if you have panic, phobia, and fear-inspiring anxiety, you have to ask your doctor, therapist or counsellor to examine your inner psychological conflicts. Then follow up with personal care as follows.

> *"Treating the whole person with psychology and nutrition is better than psychology and medicine and by using herbs, food, vitamins, and minerals instead of drugs. When behaviour therapy is called for, it is usually in conjunction with proper diet and nutritional supplements to achieve a reasonable result. By listening to the body for subjective symptoms like mental fogginess, agitation, anger, dizziness, and panic, which are the products of how you think and feel emotionally, your lifestyle choices, medical, nutritional, and exercise records, you will be in a position to locate the cause of your problem."*
>
> By Arthur Hochberg Ph.D.
> A herbalist-psychologist

Follow up with personal care as follows:
A. Put limits on alcohol, coffee, and smoking

Research studies have shown that substances such as cigarettes, alcohol and caffeine have the power to ruin our hormones, thus creating a hormonal imbalance. They say that smoking drains women's bodily stores of hormones, especially oestrogen, both the natural and the supplemental oestrogens. Even when we take therapeutic glandular supplements for helping the endocrine glands like thyroid, adrenals, ovaries, and testicles, and smoke, we run the risk of consuming toxic chemicals like pesticides, fertilizers, and antibiotics which are contained in them and which build up in the brain and cause dementia, and other neurological disorders. Consult your physician whenever you suspect that the above harmful substances have created some imbalance in your system.

B. Reduce your caffeine intake

Tea is recommended as a relaxing beverage and, in fact, a hot cup of tea is psychologically calming. Truly low doses of caffeine make us joyful, energetic, and self-confident but high doses drain the B vitamins and so render us anxious, irritable, and sleepless. If you find it difficult to quit, go for counselling.

C. Drink Lightly or Quit

"Alcohol provokes the desire but takes away the performance."

- William Shakespeare
https://www.bing.com/images/
search?q=shakespeare

Alcohol causes the loss of water-soluble nutrients, especially B vitamins, potassium, and vitamin C, thereby causing deficiencies. B-vitamin deficiencies cause nervousness and irritability, fatigue, aches, and pains, loss of appetite, itching, burning eyes, mental depression, and impaired thinking. But moderate drinking is defined as a drink per day, a drink meaning 12 ounces of beer or a 5-ounce glass of wine or a mixed drink of 1.5 ounces of whisky.

When your fear is out of control, it results in mood disturbances

Symptoms of Mood Disturbances

- Loss of interest in hobbies, food, sex, and other pleasurable pastimes.
- Persistent anxiety, sadness, and emptiness.
- Feelings of hopelessness, helplessness, guilt, and worthlessness.
- Unexplainable fatigue, changes in appetite, and weight.
- Constant headaches and pains.
- Inability to sleep well or too much sleep.
- Difficulty in concentrating, remembering, or making decisions.
- Preoccupation with death, and withdrawal from friends, and family.

If you are always moody with **chronic depression or photophobia (fear of fearing)**, dragging yourself along to places but without the energy, enthusiasm, and enjoyment that quality of life brings, you should book an appointment with your doctor or psychiatrist to evaluate your condition by undertaking physical tests to underpin the underlying causes.

Meditation

Meditate on anything good that refreshes your mind. Recite some ejaculatory prayers and as you say them, breathe in and out and pause and reflect for a while. Visualize the beauty of creation and think as much as possible about the wonders of God's creation and wisdom endowed on man. Reflect on the things God has done for you. Think about your good friends and well-wishers. Think about your good health, your parents, families, the natural wisdom given to you. Thank God for all these. God never created you and left you with nothing. He gave you and me something to live with. It is our duty to discover those talents in order to develop them and make use of them. Never say you have nothing; you have to find them out and make use of them. Ask for God's guidance and stay with the struggle to the end.

For Your Meditation

1. Retire to a cool place.
2. Relax your system by remaining quiet for a while and then take a deep breath.
3. Thank God for creating you.
4. Ask yourself, as God created me, has he any goal for me?
5. What is that goal all about and how would I go about it?
6. If you are afraid to carry on with your career, invoke God to empower and enlighten you and ask him for strength and integrity.
7. Ask him for perseverance and invoke him to inspire you with more wisdom.
8. Ask God to give you a good career and understanding.
9. Pray for longevity and eternal life.

10. Pray to God to give you good relatives, friends, and well-wishers.
11. Entrust all your being to him to lead and guide you in all your endeavours.

Once you trust, believe, and work harder, the sky is your limit. Never fold your hands, waiting for miracles. If you fall in a pit, raise your hand for someone to lift you up. But if you hold your hand down, no one will help to lift you up. Thus, faith without good work is dead; hope, believe, trust, and act.

Overview Sources of Fear

Before I list them, I would love you to have in mind how Paul McKenna defined fear. He said,

> *"It's really just a warning, that something bad could happen, so you'd better be prepared. If you feel that you are fully prepared, or if you are experiencing fear in a situation where you normally feel comfortable, it could be a genuine warning of physical danger."*
>
> -Paul Mckenna, 2006.

A lot of things could cause us to fear and such things are:
- Preoccupation with negative thinking.
- Overprotection from parents which inhibits self-confidence.

- Lack of self-trust.
- Lack of self-belief.
- Making a public speech.
- Height.
- Snakes.
- Filth.
- Loss of money.
- Loss of a loved one.
- Being alone.
- Having intimate relationships.
- Loss of one's image.
- Being cheated (conned).
- Being rejected.
- Unknown circumstances.
- Change in technology.
- Changing one's career.
- Unable to raise one's children.
- Making mistakes.
- Fear of maltreatment.
- Failure.
- Success.
- Crowds.
- Changing job.
- Unable to make decisions.
- Rape.
- Accident.
- Ageing/retirement.
- Illness.
- War and fear of dying and so on.

If you know the one bordering you, work on it. Susan Jeffers said, "Feel the Fear and Do It Anyway." So, your fear is always there with you, you must muster enough courage to handle it, touch it, feel it, and work with it. To combat fear, you need to be determined and maintain strong mental strength.

Section II: Fear Breeds Stress

How do I Gain Confidence to get Rid of Fear?

The question is, how do I obtain self-confidence and get rid of fear? Where do I get it? You are not making a long trip to obtain it; it is just right there where you are now. It is in front of you, behind you, on your right side, on your left side, even above, and underneath you. Are you ready to get it? The ball is on your court. Catch it, roll it and score it. You must be ready to score well to merit it. Therefore, pay attention to the point I stated earlier in this book on how to upgrade self-confidence. With the application of those factors above, you become master of yourself. Keep track of all your efforts and make progress reports on your achievements. What I am doing now by putting these thoughts together is also a way of enhancing my own self-confidence and conquering the fear.

> *"The secret and ultimate way of earning self-confidence is through self-reliance, self-affirmation, self-esteem, self-affection, and self-belief." "But without it, God help those who have to live with you; because without these attributes, a*

person either becomes a withering worm or a rank, obnoxious egotist."
- *Robert H. Schuller*
Discover Your Possibilities
Positive, Inspirational guidelines that will enrich your life as you reach for your highest potential!
(1978)

Robert H. Schuller also advocates to self-confidence-builders thus,

"Finding and following God's plan for your life is the soundest, surest way to self-confidence. It is also the best way to keep the feeling of self-confidence growing within you now!"
- Robert H. Schuller
Discover Your Possibilities 1978, (p. v. 8).

William Shakespeare said a long time ago to the ghost of a murdered king flashing its eyes; **"There is no speculation in those eyes: "It is the eye of childhood that fears a painted devil."** Thus, life without confidence is an empty one. Therefore, never be afraid to discover your possibilities and if you do not know how, ask questions so that you will be directed. Never anticipate failure first; rather, be optimistic. Just claim it first that you already have it.

In one village, a young man was in search of self-confidence. He attended daily masses and Sunday masses in his local church and the pastor was a brilliant and eloquent preacher. This young man always admired this well-expressed priest. One day he said, "I would be like this pastor." He maintained and nourished this thought in his heart. This young man was twelve years old then and was an orphan too. He started doing menial jobs to raise money to go to college to be qualified to enrol in a junior seminary institution. He had every hope of achieving his ambition. Fortunately, he was a clever student too and one rich charitable man spotted him as being responsible, hardworking, and determined and took the responsibility to train him to any level he wanted. He did his best in the school and was admitted to a seminary. Today; that orphan boy is a fulfilled priest and an eloquent preacher like his role model. The young man obtained his self-confidence through listening and ardent effort. Truly, the responsibility for your success lies more squarely on your own shoulders than on anyone's.

Self-confidence is also defined as your belief in yourself armed with self-esteem and self-assurance. It is a deep-seated belief that you have what it takes, namely, abilities, inner resources, talents, and skills to achieve the desired results.

To achieve your desired results, you must avoid anything that would put you in fear and take away your strength.

Sarah Litvinoff called it "**energy vampires**." These are always pessimistic and have negative ideas that could drag you down; "They are often people who complain a great deal, who use you and don't give anything positive back, or who make themselves feel good at your expense. These people are usually more demanding of your time than your truly good friends, whose company, in contrast, recharges you and makes you feel good about yourself and about life."

Your success depends solely on the company you keep. Follow positive people so that you will succeed like them.' Avoid "energy vampires" because they will drive you crazy.

Who are Confident and Who are not Confident?

Confident people are those who have the extra-ordinary energy to accomplish their desired goals. They know how to set their targets, tackle problems and always anticipate ups and downs and know how to fix them and move on. They always apply effective strategies to carry out their desire goals. The confident individuals focus on those things they are good at, enabling them to develop more effective confidence. They always give out positive thoughts that uplift their strength. They apply checks and balances to keep track of their aims. They are assertive and aggressive. Confident persons walk with their head up and always look directly into people's eyes when talking. They are self-contented. Confident fellows have faith in themselves even if they fail many times; they keep striving without fear and despair, like the former USA President-Abraham Lincoln who never gave up till he achieved his desired goal.

Non-confident persons are the opposite of confident people. They easily slip off once there is a lack of confidence or an obstacle. They have reasons not to perform and often live to remain in their comfort zone. They lack courage and will-power. Those with low self-esteem always feel hopeless and hardly believe in themselves and discourage themselves, saying, "We cannot do it." They always feel inadequate. Most of these groups who are students drop out of school because they never believe in themselves and easily give up. There was a woman who lacked confidence in herself. She never liked to see herself in the mirror. Though she was fat, her body shape was very attractive, and others admired her, but she disliked herself completely. She lacked self-confidence.

What are Those Things Undermining Your Self-Confidence?

Avoid those things that lower your self-confidence. They ruin your self-esteem

> "Confidence is not a steady state - you have more of it at *some times than at others*. *The more you concentrate on building up your confidence- in any area – the more easily you will be able to access it when you are challenged. Whatever you focus your attention on, grows and develops. If you focus on your weakness or failings, you will entrench your sense of hopelessness and lack of confidence. When you focus instead on what you are good at, what is valuable about yourself and where you have succeeded, you will generate good feelings, and these will expand. Most people with confidence issues find focusing on their good points extraordinarily hard. They have usually got into the habit of fixing on the negative aspects of themselves and their abilities. To build your confidence, you will have to do the opposite."*
>
> *- Sarah Litvinoff*
> *The Confidence Plan (P. 64).*

Never Pile up Negative Thoughts; it Punctures your Ability to Perform.

Build Your Confidence, Maintain a Positive Approach, Change Negative Attitudes, and Embrace the New You

A typical example of the positive approach to life is that of a young British teenager, Marc Woods, a former British swimmer, who competed at five Paralympic Games and won twelve medals. He was diagnosed with cancer as a teenager. He had his leg amputated yet he infused meaning into his life. He became a world legendary swimmer and won four Paralympic gold medals. He was physically challenged but that never deterred him from injecting meaning into his life. His amputated leg did not deter him from attaining his career objective. He had absolute confidence in himself. This young man would have given up every hope and termed himself a 'good for nothing' and cursing God. He could have decided to take to the streets to beg for food and money. Yet he stood up courageously and devoted his time learning the skills of swimming till he became an expert. Marc Woods did a wonderful job in fostering his self-confidence. He is a typical role model to many. This young Britton believed in himself and trusted the other parts of his body. His amputated leg did not limit him from achieving his desired career. One can see in our world today a lot of people with amputated arms and legs who are on the streets begging. Many decide to steal to survive. They do this because they lack confidence and self-esteem.

In the USA, one of my tutors was a blind lady. I wondered how this blind lady had gone to school, learnt and was able to teach? But some students with normal eyes were finding it difficult to understand the subject she was teaching. I always took her as a point of reflection. I was always reinforcing myself then that, if this blind person could do it, I could do it too. And that was how I overcame my difficulty in that subject. Remember, if you consent, God affirms you. At that time, I never knew how to operate a computer and research for information. But then, I knew how to learn. During Bill Clinton's Presidential Trial in 1998 - 1999, one of his lawyers was in a wheelchair arguing smartly. I admired his intelligence and self-confidence then. Many people in wheelchairs are out there drinking, smoking cigarettes, and begging because they think they are incapable. If these three people could do it, you can do it also. Ignite your confidence and shine. Remember, heaven helps those who help themselves. Discover your possibilities now and assume them just like the British amputee did and became a world-famous medallist. Stop blaming yourself and others; you can do it - be in to win and never quit.

> *It's lack of faith that makes people afraid of meeting challenges, and I believe in myself."*
> *Muhammad Ali*

Believe in yourself in order to exceed. Moreover,

> *"Without a humble but reasonable confidence in your own powers, you cannot be successful or*

happy. No matter what has happened to you in the past or what is going on in your life right now, it has no power to keep you from having an amazing good future if you will walk by faith in God."
— *Muhammad Ali*

"The way you think about yourself in relationship to the challenges you are currently facing in your life will have a profound impact on your ability to succeed."
— *Albert Bandura, a psychologist.*

Maintain Your Bill of Rights; What are Your Bills of Rights?

Right to Believe in Self: Believe that you are confident.

Right to Love Yourself: Love yourself. If you don't love yourself, **you** will always feel like an empty bag that is unable to stand.

Right to Trust Yourself: You have absolute right to trust yourself; to say to yourself I am in charge, I am in control, I am the boss and I can do it.

Right to Self-Confidence: Self-confidence is equal to self-trust. When you have a firm conviction of your ability, you can achieve a lot. Whenever you have some doubts, condemn them, and say, 'quit now, and be calm!'

Right to Positive Self-Talk and Affirmation: Positive self-talk is necessary for self-enhancement. Always think well of yourself, thoughts that would uplift and motivate you positively.

Right to Projecting Your Authentic Self: Authentic self-fills you with "dynamic energy to go for what you want." Be bold and proud of what you are and what you can do. Be content with your talent and proudly develop it.

Right to Call Yourself to Your Senses: Whenever you are preoccupied with negative self-talk, stop yourself, tell yourself to stop immediately and occupy yourself with past success and the many other good things you have achieved.

Right to Self-Determination: You have the right to determine what you would be. Never depend on anybody to decide for you; you must make your own decisions but could consult anyone for a certain opinion because no one knows it all. You are the boss of yourself and the captain of your ability. You must play 'confidence captain to yourself.' You have a right to set a goal and decide your plan of action. Always have Mahatma Gandhi as your role model as action-doer. Be a self-dynamic leader who motivates self to effect results. I, the author of this book, motivated myself to become an author. I have no authors in my family or in my ancestry. You can do it. So, play confident now.

The Right to Choose a Good Role Model: Marc Woods said,

> *"We need guidance from somewhere. This is where role models come in. But not just any role model, not the conventional pop, movie, and sports stars.*

Role models are all around us, we just need to find the right ones. Well-chosen role models and mentors help us help ourselves to get better."
Marc Woods
Personal Best by Marc Woods
How to Achieve Your Full Potential 2011, (p. 25).

"Setting an example is not the main means of influencing another, it is the only means."
Albert Einstein

The Right to Self-Awareness and Self-Acceptance: An individual exists in the context of a community, family, workplace, religion, and society. He must understand that he has abilities and talents which he never knew he had and that he has people around him he never knew he had. People learn to love themselves and accept themselves for what they are. They understand that they can adapt and can carry out their daily routines despite discomforts in stressful conditions.

Rachel Naomi Remen M.D., founder and director of the Institute for the Study of Health and Illness at Commonweal Bolinas, California, said about **self-acceptance:**

"You know, some of the most important times of my life have been those in which I have had a much deeper sense of the integrity in myself even though I wasn't feeling very well physically. That I am what I am. And that there's no need for me to find your

approval or to seek it. And there is an essence and uniqueness and a beauty like other people have too."
Rachel Naomi Remen M.D.
California

The Right to Self-Organisation: On the micro-level, let us look at self - little beings, socializing among themselves, unite to form a machine for doing their functions. All living systems own self-organising capacity in forming themselves into social groups of enzymes, lymphocytes, and hormones etc., capable of assimilating and manipulating environmental data to perform their functions. They know what they must do, and they do that perfectly.

The Right to Belong: You need to feel and have a sense of belonging whenever you think about self-confidence. Endeavour to have a good rapport with God and those around you.

The Right to Change the Negative Picture of Self: How do you project yourself? What picture do you have of yourself? If you hold the kind of picture I held of myself in the past such as, "I cannot do it, they will laugh at me", please do not hesitate to drop these kinds of thoughts. They are very destructive, so avoid them.

The Right to Assert Yourself: To assert yourself, you must be calm and respectful. Most often, asserting yourself confidently might not be right for you or for the situation. But sometimes one must behave like a lion rather than a lamb. Communicate fluently, never shake, and do not stumble over your words; maintain a strong and firm voice; it should make you feel more confident. You could practice taping your voice, listen to yourself and your voice over and over. Make amendments till you become more confident. Monitor the pitch of your tone; a low voice increases your confidence. Never use 'uhh' too often as it is a nasty rhythm because it is distractive. Maintain a good volume of your voice when speaking. Try to make your speech clear and concise and be in control. Be constant and coherent as you communicate because it is an essential signal to the listeners. Assertive people have the right to express their opinion assertively but not aggressively: Do not be afraid to say what you feel is right to say. Express your opinion in a respectful manner. Assertive people put their thoughts articulately, but aggressive people lose their points.

The Right to Say 'Yes' or 'No': Say yes when you are supposed to yes, and no when you're supposed to say no. Never please anyone to hurt yourself. This insight here will help you a lot.

> *"Remember that saying yes to something you don't want to do damages your confidence, but saying yes to something you do want to do is an opportunity to do it joyfully and confidently".*
> *Jan Ferguson (p. 83).*

The Right to be Firm but Polite: Most often, we lose confidence when we fail to be firm and polite. Always present your points in a polite manner. Many unconfident people lose their court cases for being impolite and nervous. Anxiety could lead you to lose your stand. Be strong and be firm.

The Right to Communicate Clearly: You need to acquire communication skills to obtain self-confidence. Visualize what you want to talk about and gather your points and plan to execute them.

The Right to Make a Decision: Make a good decision that could enhance your career. Set a goal and stay with it. Evaluate it, then give yourself feedback. Move on to achieve it. Be focused and determined. Break your goal into achievable sections to make it easy for yourself. Determination and willpower lead to success. Always look ahead of what you want to achieve, and remember to mount your signpost further ahead to enable you to strive harder to reach it.

The Right to Self-Motivation: Motivation is confidence in action - and confidence in action is what will carry you all the way to a life of BIG goals and dreams!

The Right to Change Your Mind: You have the right to amend your decision and make a better one. "The secret of success is to set the right goals and priorities and never take your eye off of them." Jesus said,

> *"No man, having put his hand to the plough, and looking back, is fit for the kingdom of God." (Luke (9:62). Set a goal and keep your eye on it."*
> -Robert H. Schuller.
> *Discover Your Possibilities*
> *Positive Inspirational Guideline that will Enrich*
> *Your Life as*
> *You Reach for Your Highest potential 1978,*
> *(pp. 112-113).*

The Right to Powerful Visualization: As you build your self-confidence, visualizing your future success is necessary.

> *"As you become more practised at visualizing yourself succeeding rather than failing, your feelings of confidence and motivation will increase. As a result, your behaviour will begin to change. Soon, you will have reprogrammed yourself to go for what you want with ease and comfort - a natural sense of confidence." (2006).*
>
> *- Paul McKenna*

When I was a student, I used to visualize my grade in each course. I always drew a line from 'A to B+' grades. Each time I worked harder to be within that range, most often I landed with 'A and B.' This worked for me and I found myself on the honour roll. With determined effort, I programmed myself on this powerful visualization and automatically, I moved away from being an average student to an excellent student. I call this action 'willpower.' Develop your willpower; it is necessary for your success. Willpower is a rightful ultimate means of upholding your self-confidence.

Finally, based on the bill of rights, whatever you intend to do, choose a role model to assist you to build, a good role model now who will influence your life in a positive manner. A good role model is a treasure. Role models offer you something great; they inspire you and they always enthuse about the success of your career. They help you to achieve and they also celebrate with you. I, the author of this book, made a good choice of role models. Who are my role models?

My parents and siblings were the first role models I had, then the Marist Brothers of the Schools in Nigeria, a good friend of mine and one of my classmates. I will never tell my history without mentioning them. I always benchmark and copycat them in everything I do because they're good role models and good mentors. Even though they are now far from me, I do still visualize them, what they do and how they do things. Who is your role model? Whom are you benchmarking? Or copycatting? Be sure you have a good guy to influence your self-confidence. You have a great deal to learn from good role models. Successful confident individuals learnt from good role models. Benchmark them but never compare yourself with them because it is detrimental to compare yourself with another person. No matter what, you cannot be like him/her because every individual is a unique person. Always be of yourself but keen to learn. As you choose your role models, just look out for role model as described below:

> *"Role models are people who possess qualities and abilities that we admire and would like to have. They show us what is possible and motivate us to achieve greater things."*
>
> - Marc Woods
> *Personal Best*
> How to Achieve Your Full Potential 2011, (p. 188).

In conclusion, we see that people low in self-esteem do not possess the above-stated principles and are more likely to have feelings of resentment, alienation and unhappiness. They are also more likely to experience insomnia/restlessness and psychosomatic symptoms (abnormal circumstances experienced by an individual in mind and body).

Effective Communication Skill

Ability to communicate and express our thoughts uplifts our confidence. If one is unable to communicate and put her opinion across, frustrations and lack of confidence set in. To create one's confidence, effective communication skills are vital. Whenever you intend to speak, stand up boldly, look into the faces of your audience, make eye contact as you speak, speak audibly, directly, and clearly. Maintain a sense of humour as you speak. Be sincere and be yourself. Always consider your audience. Be conscious of time to avoid boredom. Avoid nagging when you are talking. Gather positive points that can be easily remembered. Your approach of communication could influence, attract, and persuade your audience to be moved to action. Being articulate boosts your self-assurance. If you fail to communicate well, automatically, low self-esteem would set in. Always listen to people when they are speaking. Do a thorough rehearsal before your speech. Whenever you are about to make a speech, always have these in mind:

- Maintain eye contact.
- Be brief and go directly to the point.
- Never panic, rather remain calm and be in control.
- A good speaker listens to his audience.
- Take responsibility, and
- Learn from your mistakes.

Taking Responsibility

Taking responsibility involves acting. Once you have a goal to attain, automatically you have something to think about every moment. Your objective is how to go about it and how to succeed. You must think about the resources to carry on etc. Once you act in this way, you are performing an action. According to Aristotle:

> *"Man is a goal-seeking animal. His life only has meaning if he is reaching out and striving for his goals."*

I strongly agree with Aristotle because since my university education and with continuous researching and working, I find meaning in my being. I also feel fulfilled. Self-confidence and belief in yourself, armed with self-esteem and self-assurance are parts of a deep-seated belief that you have what it takes, namely, abilities, inner resources, talents, and skills to create your desired results.

Make-Ups- Self-Confidence is Built on the Following Factors:

- Faith in God and yourself.
- Experience in the real world.
- Core values.
- Strengths and weaknesses.
- Expectations and resiliencies after failures.
- What you do to reach your peak performances.
- Celebrations of success.

1. **Faith**: You must have faith in yourself and in your God, as in the following statement. *"No matter how tough it is and how tough it gets, I am going to make it."* The best answer to this is, I am making it already. So, say it, do it, claim it, and have it. You must listen to your inner self which has been fed with positive thoughts, words, actions, and result in a plea to God. You will hear or see something suggesting the direction and the result of your vision.

To send signals of confidence in the face of an intimidating audience, one needs to take micro-actions such as these:

1. Make an effective entrance by first impressions of a warm handshake and a warm greeting.
2. Stand upright and walk tall proudly.
3. Be a strong presence - that is, making positive eye contact and giving a warm smile to put others at ease.
4. You must stay connected by networking with a group of people in related businesses and social groups that have common interests.
5. You must do a preparatory rehearsal of your presentation by using the Boy Scout Motto: *"Be prepared for an emergency may be looming."*

Rehabilitation for Vulnerable Single Mothers

To give hope and empowerment to those who are most vulnerable in living on the fringe of life where the availability of materials of life is scarce, mostly jobless single mothers, a workable plan must be set up. When a woman is not with a man on whom she can depend for her maintenance, and is not working, she will fall prey to vagrant lovers who may make her pregnant.

In this case, her condition becomes unsafe and wanting. The way to go about remedying the situation is to provide her with a means of living. If she is skilled in doing something, those in charge of her can help in procuring a job in her field of expertise. If she is unskilled, a satisfactory job in any additional facilities like dis-washing, housekeeping, social welfare work, etc. can be arranged. If she can be trained, consider Technical Learning Centres where she can train for medical programs and computer programs. After training in these centres, job placement, career counselling and financial aid are available. We are talking about empowering her to take care of herself and her child.

Life is precious. It cannot be taken for granted or be treated with casual attention or be managed with halfway measures for solving problems. It must be lived with full involvement and full results. It cannot be handled clumsily. It is said a woman should be educated so that she can work and provide for herself and others. But love is a life requirement and must be handled with a plan that is responsible and healthy. If a mistake has been made in having a love affair which resulted in having a child, the situation can be revamped with a training scheme that produces the capability for earning a wage for the maintenance of self and any dependents. It is also worth exploring the job market in order to locate areas of availability of jobs. Life needs preparation and careful attention because it is full of risks and uncertainties. Therefore, to cater for the hopeless, it is necessary to organize a training scheme as well to engage them.

2. *Experience in the Real World:* What you are made up of are the truths coming from your triumphs over all life's struggles. When you eat a cabbage salad and get sick, you know cabbage salad is not good for you. That impression is stored in your memory. If you see cabbage salad again, your mind remembers your past experience with fear, and you shrug your shoulders and say not for me again. Once bitten, twice shy and so an experience and its revolting reminder apply to all events. But now you know all the truth about this matter so that you can proceed with caution and have your way. Here is a piece of advice by author, Susan Jeffers; *"Experience your fear and take action anyway."* Do not let fear stop you from taking the necessary steps to achieve your career goals.

Many things can trigger chain reactions of surprise, novelty, sudden change, conflict, uncertainty, increased complexity or simplicity and fear of the unknown. Novelty, for example, excites by pushing us off balance and weakening our stranglehold on habit, pushing for an urgent need to improve new skills, learn new rules and habits. Our curiosity and passion for mystery, exploration, and adventure arouse tension, fear, and suspense at times but we use confident feelings of safety and serenity to prevail.

3. Core Values Your inner resourcefulness tied to your mission in life, gives rise to values which propel you to plan, do and achieve good results. These values must be tried in good times and bad times and the results acquired, fed into your mind as bases for accurate judgement which results in self-confidence. Confidence drives fear away because fear is based on the lack of accurate knowledge.

To have self-confidence in a balanced and successful life, your vision needs your core values in seven areas:

- Work and career (mission).
- Finances (resources you need to procure fine work).
- Recreation and free time.
- Health and fitness.
- Relationships.
- Personal goals (achievements).
- Contribution to the welfare of others in the community.

4. Strengths and Weaknesses: Everyone has core strengths based on doing what one loves best and weaknesses which originate from one's pet aversions. Everyone has dislikes but such feelings should not be a cause for alarm. They should be smoothed over with positive strengths. You can overcome your weakness and empower your self-confidence by expanding your strength, improving professional skill sets, listening, researching, and learning new practices. With these, fear is subdued and your strength waxes brilliantly.

5. Expectations and Resilience after Failures: Most people have high expectations when they make plans, but often, result from the execution shortfall of their expectations. You must check your feeling of despondency being more resilient. Sometimes, the expected event occurs with surprise and fear, but a person of strong character and practicality knows the way out. Here, you must emulate the very patient and long-enduring former President of America, Abraham Lincoln, who failed eleven times and at the twelfth attempt became the President of USA. He is worth being emulated.

1. When he was 22 years old, he failed in business.
2. When he was 23 years old, he ran for state legislature and did not make it successfully.
3. Then, at the age of 24, he went back to business and could not make it.
4. The worst happened to him at the age of 26 when his sweetheart died.
5. He continued striving at age 27 but his nervous system broke down.
6. He never gave up but regained his health, then he ran for Congress at age 34 but did not win.
7. He paused for a few years and began again to run for Congress at the age of 39 and failed again.
8. He picked himself up, dusted himself off and kept running; accordingly, at the age of 46, he ran for the Senate and lost again.
9. But he never lost hope, and at the age of 47, he ran for Vice-President and lost again.
10. Lincoln put all these failures behind him and continued the struggle, even at the age of 49.
11. Finally, he won the fight and was elected President of the United States of America at the age of 51.

What great self-confidence! President Lincoln exhibited absolute confidence and positive self-reinforcement to win and he won. He remains a role model for confidence-builders. The downfall of a man is never his end. If he fails and remains there without making alternative efforts, then comes real downfall. He made efforts and succeeded. As you fail you get up... Never allow your initial failure to influence your success. Try to change your method of approach to things in order to transform your situation and boost your confidence. Never say yes to failure; rather keep striving. The action, goal and aim of President Lincoln tallied with the wisdom of C.S. Lewis,

> *"You are never too old to set another goal or to dream a new dream. Many people feed their mental strength with negative of old age. I am getting old so I cannot set any goal now; it is for the youth. No, it is for you too."*
> **(www.goodreads.com/author/ quotes/1069006.C.S.Lewis).**

Remember, what you tell your brain is what it works with so be positive.

6. What You Do to Reach Your Peak Performance and Boost Self-Confidence: The game of life is like the game of football. If a team catches the ball at one end of the field and through many rigorous means gets to the 99th yard of the other end of the field and cannot get into the end zone because it cannot cross the last one-yard line to win, it is really very disappointing. Likewise, in business or in life, some people can move a project to 98 percent of completion but fall short of success because they cannot finish the last 2 percent. In life, as in football, winning is paramount. Sometimes, people through lack of confidence, commitment, strategy, and action, create their own one-yard barriers that prevent them from fully reaching their aspirations. You must not shun ideas and actions which facilitate us to destroy the self-defeating barriers of inaction, indecision, insecurity, and unpreparedness. The tools and techniques needed to put you across the one-yard line are as follows:

1. Refocusing on Your Purpose and Vision
By readjusting your choices, priorities, and dreams, you direct your actions towards achieving your goals and fulfilling your purpose. Never allow any unfulfilled dream in your life.

2. Assessing Your Room for Growth
If you are falling short of attaining your full potential, you might expand your vision to encompass a bigger horizon of mission and more far-reaching goals, creating a written action plan and improving your organizational skills.

3. Living Your Mission
You must write your mission statement, for example, "My mission is to educate, motivate, encourage others, and cater for them." You need to ask yourself questions like these: What hopes, dreams, actions make your heart pound and your palms sweat? What do you love most? What drives you? What makes you willing to push through tough times?

4. Setting Aggressive One-Yard-Line Goals such as Re-Emphasizing Essentials
Improving systems, gaining competence, and tracking daily progress, you can attempt to contact 25 people per day. You

can, as your one-yard-line goal, host at least five face-to-face client appointments every week. You can read one book a week, thus improving your understanding of your job, your life, and the world around you. Successes do not evolve; they are created. You must identify and move beyond the artificial barriers between you and peak performance. Anyone who has skills and experiences that you do not have can serve as your mentor.

5. Building and Using One-Yard-Line Resources

You must willingly channel your time and energy into the things that matter to you. Take time to give yourself permission to break stagnant non-productive routines of mistakes and move actively towards your goal.

6. Embrace the Power of Perseverance

Many people grow complacent and weary before they reach the end zone; they quit striving just before they hit their goals. These ideas help you as a springboard to explore the resources unique to your own objectives. They are seeds of change that can take you towards the fulfilment of your personal and professional destinies.

7. Celebrations of Success

Anything worth doing is worth doing well, the success of which is the cause for rejoicing. Your personal achievement should be celebrated with thanks to the Great Creator who infuses your system with great ideas through his spirit which brightens you, directs you, and helps your life target. Celebrations help you to feel that fear does exist but does not stop you from success. When you celebrate, it means you are trimming off your fear and embracing victory. Thus, get rid of your fear and celebrate! Victory is that confidence we have been discussing throughout this book. Academic success is not the only victory to celebrate. Things to celebrate are; you being able to take responsibility, surmounting obstacles, making daily decisions, motivating someone to succeed in life, ability to train your children, ability to make a right judgement, ability to trim down excess weight, and a lot of others. Always acknowledge your little accomplishments and once you do this, you are there to acknowledge enormous successes.

Fear always occurs as a result of a lack of confidence. One must bear in mind that fear is inevitable, thus, as long as one advances in life, fear will never leave one. Once you have a task to embark on, the fear is there. The only way you can get rid of the fear is to persist and do it. If you want to feel better and fulfil your objective, just go out and do it because practice makes perfect. Nobody is above fear. Everybody experiences it. What matters a lot is to overcome fear by doing those things you fear.

> ***"Pushing through fear is less frightening than living with the underlying fear that comes from a feeling of helplessness."***
> *- Susan Jeffers*
> *Feel The Fear And Do It Any Way*
> *How to Turn Your Fear and*
> *Indecision into Confidence and Action 1987,*
> *(p. 28).*

> *Bernard Shaw said, "A man learns to skate by staggering about making a fool of himself." "Many fail to achieve efficiency at school as well as at work because they are terrified by the possibility of failure or ridicule and so they deprive themselves of pleasures, adventure or just plain fun by being too concerned with what people will think. Mistakes are not only an acceptable part of life; they are essential to a full life."*
>
> *- J. Maurus*
> *How to win Personal Efficiency*
> *A Valuable Help to Win Personal Efficiency in*
> *All Walks of Life 1988, (p. 19).*

Creating Confidence (addendum)

From the Psychologist's Book of Self-Test-Intelligence, Career and Personality

Test by Louis Janda, these questions are drawn to reveal the real you:

1. How comfortable are you with yourself? - Your self-esteem.
2. Do you rely on yourself or someone or something else outside you?
3. How comfortable are you with success? Do you falter when asked to lead?
4. How much experience do you have?
5. How successful is your life? Do you sometimes have despair, alienation and emptiness or a

measure of self-fulfilment? Moderation is key to self-sufficiency.
6. How are you affected by the unexpected?
7. How comfortable are you in social situations? Giving your best to others and being nice and tactful is the key.
8. How much faith do you have? Your core beliefs and core values matter here.

True Projections of Confidence

1. Examine yourself; are you generally happy within yourself?
2. Are you always in control instead?
3. Do you encourage and motivate others?
4. Do you imitate others' achievement?
5. Do you accept praise graciously and criticism constructively?
6. Are you ready for difficult situations?
7. Do people feel relaxed and comfortable associating with you?
8. Are you flexible in analysing things? (They don't tend to analyse everything.)
9. Do you know your limitations?
10. Do you communicate assertively?
11. Do you treat people well?
12. Do you accept your mistakes?
13. Do you regard yourself equal to others regardless of your skills, background, and status?
14. Do you maintain eye contact, cheerful mood, and smiling face when dealing with people at gatherings?

15. Do you have open arms, open body language?
16. Do you cut your coat according to your size?

If you can answer "yes" to all these questions, you have obtained self-confidence. People with self-confidence exhibit these characteristics. Do you? I would love your answer to be "yes I do"; if not, begin now to strive to acquire these virtues.

Cultivate Confident Posture
Sending Signals of Confidence

To be a leader, you must present yourself as a leader. You must walk like a leader, dress like a leader, feel like a leader, and talk like a leader. Some people are born with these qualities and others must learn to strengthen these high-quality skills. Here is a series of favourite actions to give you a score of 55 percent of the world's opinions.

1. **Make an Effective Entrance:** Make a firm impression by saying you are glad to meet them. Step out towards them quickly with a smile and a warm handshake to show you are excited.
2. Stand up straight and walk proudly. Regardless of your height, just stand tall and walk tall.
3. **Have a Presence:** Always maintain good eye contact. Be sure the principal players in the meeting room have direct contact with you. Place your table midway so that those at the end have visual contact with you.

4. **Relax and Communicate Effectively to Deliver Your Message with Excitement:** When you are relaxed, engaged, and energetic, people feel you are listening to them and ready to help them.
5. **Listen Attentively:** Lean forward, watch the person speaking to you and repeat the message to them so that they know you understand.
6. **Dress with Respect for Others:** In business, casual dress is not appropriate. To be successful, wear a business suit. Clothes determine how others feel about you and how you feel about yourself.
7. **Stay Connected Through Networking:** Networking means maintaining contact with a "network" of people in your business, related business, and other organizations of shared interests.
8. **Describe Your Business:** Do you really know what you do? You need to be able to describe yourself, your products, and services in a way that clearly differentiates you from your competitors.

Select a Confident Role Model Persona

Write down the names of those whom you imitate.

What do you admire about them?

Act as if you are your role model.

Become your own role model.

Ask yourself, "how I do to become my own role model?

Find it out and start acting on it and succeed.

Assertiveness- an Effective Way of Building Self-Confidence

What is assertiveness? It is being able to communicate a point clearly, precisely and without being too pushy and aggressive. It is a way of being more at peace with oneself. Humour - essential tool for assertiveness – a bit of humour, a laugh, a smile... Avoid tension. Being assertive does not mean being arrogant, naughty, bossy, being naïve, unfriendly, intruding, etcetera. One of my friends said that people hate her because she is assertive. I told her that they do not really hate her but the character she exhibits, and I told her that most often people do not like the truth.

Restore Self-Esteem

People with high esteem feel good about themselves and tend to like others while accepting their failures. Because of their genuinely positive feelings towards the acceptance of others, these people tend to elicit the best in those around them. There is truth in saying that a person who feels good about herself makes other people feel good about themselves too. This attitude makes these people very attractive to others who cling to them in both social and professional gatherings.

The Psychologist's Book of Self-Tests (pp. 73-75).

According to Psychologist Don Hamachek, people with low self-esteem have an inferiority complex and in his book about self-esteem, he outlined seven signs of this inferiority complex as follows:

1. **Sensitivity to Criticism:** People who feel inferior know their shortcomings and do not like other people to point these out.
2. **Inappropriate Response to Flattery:** Some people are desperate to hear anything good about themselves and will be constantly fishing for compliments; others may refuse to listen to anything positive about themselves because it is not how they feel.
3. **Hypercritical Attitude:** People who do not feel good about themselves have trouble feeling good about anyone. They look hard for flaws and shortcomings of others to try to convince themselves that they really are not so bad after all. These people cannot feel intelligent, attractive, and competent unless they excel in everything.
4. **Tendency Towards Blaming:** Some people project their perceived weaknesses onto others in order to lessen the pain of feeling inferior or their failures.
5. **Feelings of Persecution:** Carried to its extreme degree, blaming others can extend to believing that others are actively seeking to ruin you.
6. **Negative Feelings about Competition:** People who feel inferior like to win games and contests as much as anyone else, but they believe they cannot win.
7. **Tendency Towards being Seclusive**: Because people with an inferiority complex believe that

they are not as interesting or intelligent as others. They appear to avoid social situations and avoid speaking up because doing so will betray their dullness and stupidity. Do you depend on a plan or fate for your actions? These people seem to exhibit self-confidence to the point of arrogance, but they also show many signs of low self-esteem. It is generally accepted that people with moderately high self-esteem are the well-adjusted ones.

Part of building self-esteem is recalling your good image and your pleasant times. Now that we are in the realm of ascertaining self-confidence, I would love you to provide yourself with a personal journal and begin to jot down all the good things, positive thoughts, positive actions, positive experiences, positive deeds performed in your life, admirations you received from people, praise and recommendation you received and are receiving from your various bosses, teachers, pastors, mates, parents, etcetera and the ones you exchanged with others and with yourself. Write them down each day as much as you can and never stop writing till the end of your lifetime. Every day brings its goodness. In addition, make it your daily habit by jotting down each positive experience. By the time you finish this exercise, you will observe a tremendous change in your life. Your whole self will be full of positivity and be uplifting. Keep on writing and never give up. Mind you, as you strive, always base your effort on the hope that God will bestow on you the wisdom to gain your confidence.

Section III: Factors Affecting Confidence

An unexpected event without warning shocks you and makes you lose confidence but a person with high self-esteem reacts as if nothing happened. With her experience, she will bounce back and challenge the situation.

When you react to criticism, you have low self-esteem. People such as this always withdraw from society; also, they find fault in everybody. More so, they blame others in most situations.

- **Self-Identity Crisis:** Causes of identity crisis- having lack of trust for oneself, not believing in ones' capability, looking down on yourself, feeling inferior and being ashamed of one's self, being unable to handle responsibility. The key to success in this challenge is one's strong belief in self.
- **Fear:** Never consent to fear; find a way to combat fear, and invent a solution to prevent fear from getting out of hand in your life. Learn from your past mistakes and difficulties.
- **Feeling Defeated:** Never feel defeated because it brings about a lack of self-esteem, depression, and hopelessness, an inability to cope, and an inability to perform to achieve your ultimate career goal. As long as you are alive, you are not defeated. Just avoid feeling overwhelmed because it results in a huge amount of psychological damage. Keep on thinking positively till you acquire confidence.

- **Low-Self-Image:** Undermining self. Self-deflation (degradation); for instance, I am nothing, everybody hates me, I don't count, I am not worthy, no one knows me, etcetera. Avoid self- deflation because it leads to chronic depression and self-condemnation. Once you lose confidence, you equally lose courage which escorts to lack of motivation to achieve and to succeed. When you say you are nothing and you are unable to perform, it means you are nobody. You are somebody as no one is born insignificant. You are created for a purpose and you are a unique individual.
- **Self-Flagellation:** This means intense remorse or regret. Avoid too many regrets in your life because it undermines your self-confidence.
- **Self-Negation:** Self-negative thought is a cancer that destroys your entire system. It is a parasite inside you. In order to cure this, you should stop projecting a negative image of yourself.
- **Obstacles:** Try to turn your obstacles into opportunities. Turning your obstacles into opportunities is like this example of an ex-slave girl: This girl was sold as a slave and her mistress used her for every bit of her domestic work. Do you know what happened to her? The young girl exercised patience and did every bit of the chores. As a result, she became skilful in all aspects of household chores and beyond. In fact, she was able to build up her self-confidence in serving as a slave. During the abolition of the slave trade, she immediately re-established herself

and became a wealthy woman as a reward of being industrious as a slave girl. The story of this former slave girl is similar to that of King Jaja of Opobo. He was about 1821 at Umuduruoha, Amaigbo village in the Orlu district, now Imo State of Eastern Nigeria. Jaja was sold as a slave boy at Opobo. He became the King of Opobo as a result of being industrious and was able to pay off his master's debts. From grass to grace. I refer you to google to search and read more about King Jaja of Opobo. Very interesting. He was from my original district Orlu in Igboland before he became a slave.

- **Self-Pity:** This is not allowed as you are making your journey towards self-actualization. If you dwell in self-pity, you are depriving yourself of your power. Avoid negative thoughts about yourself because that takes away your power and willingness to perform. If you fail to learn from your mistakes, you are doomed. You are not heading anywhere. However, accept your failures, fix them up and have a new self. We learn through trial and error.

How to Build Your Confidence and Strategies to Overcome the Fear that Invades Self-Confidence

Taking Action - Motivate Self: Make a daily roster of what to do, map out time for it, be focused and get it done. How do you do this? For instance, as a student, remind yourself; I have examinations to take next week, therefore, I must plan well to cover all my textbooks. Then motivate yourself positively on the things that could help you work harder towards success. Assuming you have ten textbooks to cover before the examination, you must divide your time for each book to enable you to read all of them. First thing in the morning you should read psychology and English textbooks with no distractions. After this, you have a bath, have breakfast, do your chores, and have some relaxation before you then read biology and chemistry. Later, you go and do a little shopping and prepare lunch, take a nap, and read your books again. Afterwards, have a break and some refreshment before you start reading. What you are doing now is mastery of your self-confidence, taking action, and taking responsibility. You must decide what to do and how to carry out your plan. Schedule your plan to make it easy for yourself. Plan your schedule bit by bit in such a way that you can cope with it. Although I just cited a student here, this is for all walks of life. A farmer, a carpenter, a trader, a housekeeper, etcetera; you must plan your daily activities properly. When I was a student, I used to take a yearly schedule booklet with me and map out the courses I would take each semester and began early to plan on how to go about them. After that academic year, I cross checked my performance and ticked the subjects off. Then I was ready for the next session. One significant thing was that, all the time I was doing this, I never knew I was developing my self-confidence. It was when I started writing this book and reading so many books on how to build confidence that I came to the realization of what I had been doing then. No one is born insignificant. You are created for a purpose.

Affirm yourself; do not wait. Affirmation of self is the key factor in building one's confidence. What is self-affirmation?

(a) It is self-rating talk.
(b) It is an effective instrument that helps you build your self-confidence.
(c) It is giving you a good mark for your performance.
(d) An affirmation is a positive thought or a positive statement about oneself. For example, I am doing well at my work. Before, I couldn't read fluently but now, I can read well. I used to be shy but at present, I have a good relationship with people. I am no longer afraid; I can now stand up in public to air my view. I am in control of my fear, so I am becoming more confident daily. Finally, I am no longer depressed; I am doing well. I am a master of daily responsibilities; I am strong and hardworking.

Now that you have the idea about self-affirmation, try as much as you can to make it more effective and put it into practice continually. Make more positive affirmative statements to enhance your self-confidence. Have a sense of belonging. A sense of belonging is very crucial in the development of self-confidence because:

"The seed of self-confidence comes through a sense of belonging and through an awareness of being God's child. And it comes through a consciousness of the expectations that people have from you.

When people expect you to be something and you know they expect it, that brings the best out of you."
- Robert H. Schuller
Discover Your Possibilities
Positive, Inspirational Guidelines that will enrich your life as you reach for your highest potential!
1978, (p. 18).

Through Self-Approval or Approval from Others: Take an example from one of the charity homes in Central London where I helped vulnerable young mothers; I always tried to encourage them and praise any little efforts they made to uplift their self-confidence. Self-awareness - being aware of your strengths and limitations will enable you to build your self-confidence and self-esteem. Working harder on your limitations will help greatly to gain self-confidence.

i) Listening and paying close attention to what people do and say will widen your knowledge and self-confidence.

ii) Joining assertive clubs, debating clubs, church meetings and activities, drama clubs etc. will assist you so much in upgrading self-confidence. Having a good support system means obtaining motivation from your friends and well-wishers. For instance, you intend to learn computer skills and you tell one of your friends and she says 'O yes! that is great, go ahead, it is a good idea. I wish you good luck'. This support system and motivation from your friends uplift your spirit and energize you to move on. Your self-confidence increases when you have people to encourage you instead of discouraging you.

Their language is always negative; "Hello, man, forget it, and it is a waste of time. Aren't you taking a big risk?" A girl wanted to enrol in a graduate course and was confused about what subject to study. She approached her friend to help her make a choice. Her friend suggested to her to enrol in a psychology course and she did. After her graduation, she felt so happy and kept on thanking her friend for advising her to choose psychology. She said, "Psychology enabled me to learn more about myself and human behaviour." Remember, a blind man cannot lead a blind man, therefore, when you make friends or add team builders, choose those who are farther along the journey than you are as the moment. For this reason, attempt to surround yourself with good people. Marilyn Ferguson, in her famous book "The Aquarian Conspiracy", wrote:

Fr. Benedict

"If we are to find our way across troubled waters, we are better served by the company of those who have built bridges, who have moved beyond despair and inertia."
- Marilyn Ferguson
"The Aquarian Conspiracy" 2009, (pp. 91-92).

One has to associate with people who could edify one instead.

iii) Using affirmations and inspirational tapes: Affirmations help your self-confidence.

- **Forming Self-Confidence:** Work towards creating confident relationships; one must maintain positive relationships with potential friends and well-wishers who would influence ones' life effectively. It is advisable to be around positive people with positive thinking because they will influence you positively. They are worth being around. Avoid negative individuals because they will influence you negatively and will make you feel negatively like them. Try to avoid negative thinkers because they mellow you down and strip you of your self-confidence. I always keep away from such people. If you really desire to build your self-confidence and get rid of your fear, always be around positive /individuals. Positive ones will encourage, support, direct, enlighten you and compliment you.

Whatever you do, try to maintain a positive mind because it enhances personal growth and self-improvement while a negative mind prevents you from functioning well.

Belief, Faith, and Trust: Believing in oneself, having faith in oneself and trusting oneself are the powerhouses of self-confidence. Believe in yourself by accepting and trusting yourself. Feel positive about yourself. Don't worry about your performance but have trust in yourself. Accept yourself and accept people around you and believe they will also accept you.

Self-Affirmation

What is self-affirmation? It is positive image projection. That is, seeing and regarding oneself as being capable of doing it right. For instance, claim that you are already doing well, performing well, and you are getting along well. See things happening in a positive frame of mind about yourself. Whenever obstacles arise, try to see them in a positive manner that can allow you to handle the situation easily. Don't panic, but rather see things in a positive way. Good personal principles tremendously differentiate your personality from the others. Be able to live assertively; that is, saying "yes" when you need to say yes, and saying "no" when you ought to say no. This also enhances your self-confidence. Do not be a "doormat." Do not be afraid to voice your opinion. Affirmation is a positive statement about oneself which enables you to fasten and affix your mind towards a more positive frame of mind.

Nine Guidelines for Creating Effective Affirmations

1. **Start with the Words "I Am"**: The 17th-Century French Mathematician and Philosopher, René Descartes once said, "Cogito ergo sum" (I think, therefore I exist). It is a command to your mind to make it happen.
2. **Use the Present Tense**: Live the life of what you want as though you already have it; as though it is already consummated.

3. **State it in the Positive**: Affirm what you want, not what you do not want. This means that you do not use negative words to describe your project. Your mind dwells on pictures and words. Positive words and images generate good mind signals which evoke harmony and order leading to a clear vision, thinking, and the right action.
4. **Keep it Brief**: Be brief and use keywords to command yourself into action. That is what the mind remembers easily.
5. **Make it Specific**: Vague information makes for vague results. Earmark what you want.
6. **Include an Action word Ending with- "ing:"** The active verb gives power to the effectiveness of the image doing it right now. For example, 'I am confidently organizing and doing it myself.'
7. **Include at Least One Dynamic Emotional or Feeling Word**: Use the good emotional state you will be feeling when you have achieved the goal. For example, enjoying, joyfully, happily, proudly, peacefully, delighted, and triumphant.
8. **Make Affirmations for Yourself not Others**: Relate the way you construct your words to your behaviour, not that of others.
9. **Add Words or Something Better:** When you are affirming getting a specific situation (job opportunity, vacation), material object (house, car, television) or relationship (husband, wife, and child), use the words 'something or someone better' in your wish, for that will uplift your mind. The

wise man says, "what you accept, your spirit also accepts". Also, as James Allen, the author of 'As A Man Thinketh', said: *"A man is literally what he thinks."* So, what your mind believes is what would reflect in your life.

Experience exposes you to actualizing your confidence and that leads you to overcome your fear. But I can tell you, all the disappointments one encounters in life enable one to build one's self-confidence. Thus, one's life experience is always an eye-opener and enhancer of confidence. If you are the kind who feels inferior, start now to work on it. How do you do it? Start by attending social gatherings, contribute your opinions, and give talks as much as you can. Sometimes, accept a leadership role, read interesting books, listen to the elders' deliberations etc. From these, you will gain self-confidence. Never pity yourself; rather be active and work tirelessly to upgrade your self-confidence. There should be no postponement of any action you want to take. Your core values are worth a lot. Always resist negative thoughts as you journey towards self-esteem. Never give up hope if you are not approaching your target. Rebound and keep on till you get there. Never forget to project positive thinking of self and others. It is very important. Benchmark what others did to succeed. What is "benchmarking?" It is learning what the others did to make it happen and copying from their ideas. Steve Miller called it "copycat." As you move on, pay attention to famous inspirational quotes and sayings like those of Shakespeare, Martin Luther King Jr., Mahatma Gandhi, Nelson Mandela, and Abraham Lincoln, Mazi

Nnamdi Kanu and a host of the others. These will aid you in building your assertiveness and confidence.

As you strive for this, never allow anybody to negatively influence you. Always be yourself and never mind what they say or think about you. The way you present yourself is the way they will regard you. Somebody said to someone, "You are not intelligent; rather, you are smart." Then the person responded, "Your view depends on what you mean by being smart." The latter said that she considered smartness as being intelligent. Then she narrated how she used her smartness to achieve her goals as an intelligent person could do. So, smartness and intelligence complement each other. If you are smart, you are equally intelligent. She is smart and that is the reason why she was able to succeed. She proved her self-affirmation and self-assertiveness. Start now to prove your worth. Change your inferiority complex to self-contentment. Begin today to be a role model and star you would love to be. Turn your inferiority complex into being a superstar. Those who are superstars were born as you were. Remember, confidence is the dynamic power behind every success. Try to discover that dynamic power to overcome fear. Fear is a disease which has a cure; that is, once you think positively and constantly do those things you fear most, you are sure of self-confidence. Always be a positive thinker so that you will regain your lost confidence. Positive thinking hastens your confidence and self-image. Want a word to turn your disappointment into a huge success? Avoid blaming others, but rather take responsibility for your action; claim your success and your failure. The fundamental aspect of life is, no matter your family background, work harder to make it better. You can make it and you can celebrate your success.

Live a life that encourages growth and enhances progress. Now the ball is in your court, plan well to score; that is the game of life. It is up to you to make a wise decision that yields you a positive result. Bloom and actualize your aspiration. You need to make wise choices and decisions yourself. I made an effective decision that led me to secondary school, to convent, across the Atlantic Ocean to America, to Universities, and to the United Kingdom. That effective decision earned me degrees and self-confidence. The same effective decision empowered me to write this book. Is your decision going to earn you confidence, success and happiness? If not, retreat! If you want to build your confidence, make a good choice and good decisions. William Shakespeare said, *"If you want to live long, live slowly."* For this reason, if you are to succeed, make a right decision. If you are to succeed, strive harder. Be in the circle of positive people that can uplift you. Make a choice and decision that could bring a magnificent change and assist you to realise your ultimate dream ambition.

> *"We faced hard days and our share of failure, but I learned then that no matter how great the challenge or how difficult the circumstance, change is always possible if you're willing to work for it, and fight for it, and, above all, believe in it."*
> *-President Barack Obama*
> *Foreword (2001).*

Wake up and make your choice and change. Our world is the world of ups and downs; if you want ups, it is up to you. If you want downs, it is up to you. We are in an era of great challenges along with great opportunities. Those who make wise choices surpass. You have the strength to turn your adversity into opportunity. You have the wisdom to see a little further down the road to make a great change in your life. You need to muster the courage to face the challenges that pave your way. You need innovation. This means enriching your life with an increase in knowledge and being open to new skills and technology. Try to invest your time in anything that leads to you being uplifted. Embark on dos and drop the don'ts that set you back. Just move on to establish your self-esteem. Self-esteem is both a cause and an effect of confidence. We could have such a good time learning to work on our weaknesses and celebrate our strengths if only we would let ourselves. At this point, you could write out your strengths. For example, I am a good teacher, I am a good reader, I am a writer, I am a good dancer, I am a good worker, etcetera.

Key Factors Leading to Lack of Confidence and Low Self-Esteem

1. Feelings of an inferiority complex.
2. Not liking people to point out their weakness (remedy- you have to be open to receive and offer criticism in a constructive, assertive manner).
3. Constantly fishing for compliments from others.
4. Always blaming others.
5. Always having negative feelings about winning.
6. Always dodging social activities.
7. Not liking to speak up to avoid making mistakes.
8. Lack of adequate information.

Low Self-Esteem Leads to Mood Disturbances

- Loss of interest in hobbies, food, sex, and other pleasurable pastimes.
- Persistent anxiety, sadness, and emptiness.
- Feelings of hopelessness, helplessness, guilt, and worthlessness.
- Unexplainable fatigue, changes in appetite, and weight.
- Constant headaches and pains.
- Inability to sleep well or too much sleep.
- Difficulty in concentrating, remembering, or making decisions.
- Preoccupation with death, and withdrawal from friends and family.

How to Treat Low Self-Ssteem in a Psychological Point of View

Always be positive in all your dealings and try to change your old self. Get rid of the old way and embrace the new way. Focus on the present and the future. Look forward to the future and what it brings. According to L.P. Hartley the author of "The Go-Between",

> *"The past is a foreign country; they do things differently there"* but *"the future, too, can be a different country."*
> https://www.goodreads.com/
> quotes/66426-the-past-is-a-foreign-country...

Hence, I may have something great to offer you. Try as much as you can to avoid focusing on your past failures;

rather, positively utilize them to build up an effective new future hope, the change that could transform your life and that of others. It is in your power to renew yourself; this will help you uplift your authentic-self. Henceforth, renew yourself, rebuild yourself, revive yourself, promote yourself, and strengthen others. Invest time in manufacturing a new powerful self. Begin now to identify areas anddesire change within yourself in order to meet your purpose. Track down those factors that lead you into fear and deal with them. Never rely too much on people to grow; rather, encourage independent effort that could enable you to handle responsibilities. Create positive feedback and reinforcement for your efforts and accomplishments. To strengthen your confidence, self-motivating towards and monitoring of your activities are crucial. When lack of confidence affects your self-esteem, remember the statement by Jan Ferguson:

> *"I am a valuable human being with strengths and weaknesses and I will become more confident caring for myself and learning strategies to build my confidence."*

Step 1- Repeat this to yourself in your head as often as you can.

Step 2- Practice saying it aloud as often as possible.

Step 3- Look in a mirror, give yourself a smile and speak the words.

Step 4- Hold your head up, take a deep breath and say it to somebody you like" (2009).

How to Meet Good People and Get to Know Them

In an attempt to meet with the good people out there, never be afraid to make the first move. Always be the first person to initiate your relationship with them. Check them out and pick who you want to relate with because healthy relationships bring about progress. Do not sit and wait for them to come to you. Many people do wait for others to pull them out in everything. Well if you do, be assured you will remain there forever. It is your absolute duty to do it. Get acquainted with good people. When you get to know them, you learn a lot from their uniqueness and life experiences which will help you to improve. Two heads are better than one. Susan Jeffers said,

"Check out your body. Determine what you need to do to create what looks and feels healthy… then make it happen. Most of us do not "sculpt" our lives. We accept what comes our way… then we gripe about it. Many of us spend our lives waiting- waiting for the perfect mate, waiting for the perfect job, waiting for perfect friends to come along. There is no need to wait for anyone to give you anything in your life. You have the power to create what you need. Give commitment, clear goals and action; it's just a matter of time."

- Susan Jeffers
Feel The Fear And Do It
Anyway 1987, (p. 63).

Section IV: Relaxation is Needed

Relaxation is a way of loosening your mind and body to free your body from pain, stress, and bad thoughts. This keeps you in a very sober condition that helps you to sleep soundly and function well. The Scripture says, "Do not let your hearts be troubled; trust in God and trust in me" (John 14:1). Always take a deep breath, reflect, and examine yourself, asking yourself these questions: What are my greatest fears and my smaller ones? Have I allowed these fears to develop to uncontrollable anxiety and depression? What are those things that are terrorizing my physical and mental functioning? Are these fears imaginary ones or real? Are these fears man-made or self-made? How could I handle things and sort myself out from these fears? Never allow your fears to stop you attaining your goal. When you're at work, try to go to one room to relax yourself and rejuvenate your energy; it makes you fit to work. Relaxation assists you to fight your fear factors. **What is relaxation**? And how do I go about it? Relaxation helps one overcome emotional and negative stresses such as anxiety, and fear disorder. It protects you against mental ill-health; it heals your physical as well as emotional break-downs. Relaxation encourages the body's natural healing process and provides good quality sleep. As a student contesting fear, or if you are due to give a presentation next day, try to apply these techniques step by step:

1. Turn your phone off.
2. Take time out during the day and go to a quiet place to relax and meditate.

3. Wander about with an open mind, and visualize all the good things around you as you reflect on them.
4. Think about how well you have performed in the past.
5. Reflect on one of your favourite teachers, and how well you perform in her class.

    Reinforce yourself, and say, "I am going to do well tomorrow too." Give yourself a little break and walk away from that scene and purchase a delicious dish to eat. Take your favourite juice and go to a quiet place to relax, eat, and drink then go home and take a nap.
6. After the nap, take a soothing bath.
7. Play and listen to your favourite music or dance, and dance! Cool yourself.
8. Pick up your book and start preparing for your presentation for the next day.
9. Try to go to bed early in order to feel refreshed and strong the next day. Take deep breaths in and out for a while before you sleep. Do likewise in the morning before you get out of the bed. It helps a lot. As you implement these methods, you will surely feel the effect of this relaxation technique in your life.
10. Avoid relaxation drugs. If you do take them, you are endangering your system. Your relaxation mechanism prevents you from panicking and anxiety.

This measure is applicable to all walks of life. If you are a businessman, teacher, counsellor, minister, driver, engineer, pilot, etc. you must relax and have a time-out in all your tasks. Thus, you are urged to relax your mind and body when you have work to do. Form the habit of relaxation daily. Schedule a play period of 15 minutes per day. Once or twice a day, meditate for 10 to 20 minutes by repeating your favourite word or phrase. Be humorous and greet everyone you meet with a smile. Entertain yourself with your favourite music cassette or CD or VCR.

Sleep: Physiological standards for sleep are: New-borns sleep 18 to 20 hours a day, a growing child 12 to 14 hours, an adult 7 to 9 hours, and older persons 5 to 7 hours. Chronic sleep loss affects the metabolism and hormonal function of your body.

Basic Diet Plan: A diet of whole grains, fresh fruits, and vegetables, low or non-fat dairy products, and less red meat is ideal.

Move the Body: Hit the gym and exercise for about 45 minutes or more. By the time you finish reading this book, you will have circumnavigated through all the known faculties of life with an enriched package of sound phenomena of how things are made and how they work in a real world. Henceforth, in everything you do, adopt a donkey's attitude in order to succeed.

There once was a farmer whose donkey fell into a deep pit. The donkey hopelessly cried aloud for rescue but all in vain. The owner, the farmer, thought about what to do and decided to do away with the donkey. Unfortunately, he came up with the idea that the donkey was too old to live so he made up his mind to bury him alive by covering it with a heap of sand. He invited his friends to help him fill up the pit with the donkey in it. The friends took their shovels and began to fill the pit. The donkey was too smart and realized immediately what was happening and cried dreadfully. At once, he had a thought and stopped crying. Inspired by nature, he made use of the sand to rescue him. To everyone's greatest amazement, he stopped crying for a while. He then decided to make use of each shovel of sand dropped on him to free himself. He began to shake off the sand dropped on his trunk and step up bit by bit. Both the farmer and his friends were amazed to see what the donkey was doing. The farmer and his friends, out of ignorance, kept dropping sand till the donkey freed himself. In a short while, everybody, with great astonishment, saw the donkey step up over the edge of the pit and happily jump onto the ground.

Life is full of ups and downs and must bring to you a lot of difficult situations. It is left for you to use your wise discretion to tackle it. Only, be wise enough to handle it otherwise you will give up. Always devise a means to sort your problem out. Learn from the trick of getting out of the pit; shake off the sand and take a step up at a time. Each of your troubles is a roadblock or steppingstone; you cannot avoid it but can handle it, if you convert it to your advantage. Your lifestyle matters a lot. It is your obligation to decide how you are going to live your life. You can choose to make it a success or not. Watch what you eat because food can have negative and positive effects on you. If you do not eat well, it has a negative effect, so always check your diet, and change your mode of eating. If you eat well, it has a positive effect on you as well. Do as much as you can to improve the quality of your life. Do some exercises which your body can take. A well-planned fulfilling life leads to self-confidence. According to Christine Gingham:

> *"Other things you may like to consider including in your new lifestyle are activities which can positively help you live a more fulfilling life. Taking classes in communication skills, management, assertiveness, or life skills can be a real help. But so can joining in sculpture classes, for example, if that's what you've always wanted to try. Now is the time to explore all those avenues which can lead you to a more enjoyable lifestyle."*
>
> *- Christine Ingham*
> *Panic Attacks*
> *What They Are, Why They Happen and*
> *What you Can Do About Them 1993, (p. 124).*

Section V: Help Yourself to Adjust to Change and Get Organized

When you move from one job to another, from one apartment to another or from one city to another, your body's limbic system (brain section responsible for emotions) is fired by many new stimuli, so much so that much anxiety resulting from the excitement puts you in disarray. You have to get organized so that your bodily functions will become normal. We have to take charge of our destiny if we want to change. Analyse your choices, priorities, and dreams to help make decisions that can change your life forever.

If you are in a job you hate, look for another job. If your marriage is faltering, work actively together to understand and resolve the problem. If you are not the person you want to be, work harder to be different. As you strive to make meaningful changes in your life, be willing to step outside your comfort zone and get rid of the chatterbox that underrates you. If you want to make yourself more valuable in your profession, develop an area of expertise by striving to acquire expert skills. Breaking through difficult barriers will take you an awful lot of courage to attain.

Devising Your Own Strategies for Change

- Read quality books, studying to stay abreast of the developing trends in your chosen industry.
- Live with positive expectations.
- Develop a love of service.
- Recognise and work from personal strengths looking for ways to improve skills and knowledge as I do each day.
- Eat right, and exercise and follow a healthy lifestyle.
- Constantly learn and explore new ideas and work methods, using mentors, conferences and seminars to improve skills and knowledge.
- Prioritise activities at work and make choices accordingly.
- Remember your purpose and let it guide all your activities.

Section VI: Be Assertive: Passive and Aggressive

Dr. Heather Becker designed the assertive Job-Hunting survey to be used at the career Counseling Centre at the University of Texas. She said that passive or non-assertive men and women who waited to be invited for an application for a job would either be left out in the cold or end up in positions that they would not be happy with.

What Assertive People Do

1. The first step in being assertive is that before one's interview, it is a good idea to contact an employee to learn more about the company which is going to interview her regarding the company's situations. Employers want assertive, enthusiastic, knowledgeable employees, so the more you know about the company, the more you are likely to impress the potential employer.
2. The second point is to use an experienced employment counsellor who would have a better idea what type of job you are qualified for but do not let them choose jobs for you, for you know your strengths and abilities better than they do.
3. The third step is to contact the person you would be working for directly rather than applying to the personnel department, showcasing your background and ability in solving problems.
4. The fourth point is to talk to recruiters at college campuses or visit a job fair. But these situations are

used by passive people for there are many people using this methodology. Your best bet is to contact employers who are looking for assertive, aggressive people with initiative.

5. The fifth step is to check available job openings before deciding what kind of job you would like. The answer is to know your capability and look for jobs that require it, no matter how long it takes to find one.

6. Employers need assertive people who aggressively have momentum to set the wheel of action in motion. In the beginning, you need to push hard and persistently to set the wheel of growth in motion. Then each little positive push makes a little change in position. These small changes build up and the wheel of growth spins faster and faster. Finally, the momentum of this movement becomes a force all on its own. When a business is powered by momentum, all you need is less physical force to keep the "wheel" turning. Then you can focus the rest of your energy on supplying the targeted, well-planned product or service. Your momentum speeds you through the challenges of daily activity and helps you overcome those large obstacles that occasionally appear in your path.

The Process of Powering Growth Through Momentum is Explained in Five Stages

1. **Identifying Your Starting Point**: In life, it is always difficult to start a thing but the difficulty helps us to re-evaluate and understand the situation. To gain momentum in life, one needs to grow in four areas:

- **Education:** You need to read, study, and attend seminars to increase your understanding of your profession.
- **Productivity:** You need to understand the technology needed to effect a change.
- **Organization:** To be more efficient, organize the filing of your paperwork and reorganize your work.
- **Processes and Systems**: When you know which means will help you, design the processes and systems to implement your starting point.

2. **Align Your Energies with Your Life's Purpose and Position.** Align your purpose, passion and strength to cause changes. Develop a strategy to communicate to the world the story about you and your business. To systematize the strategic process, begin to implement a contact and customer management program that daily details who to telephone, how many appointments to set up, and how many personnel need to be sent out.

Put People-to-People Contact to on Your Schedule

Making the Most of Face- to-Face Contact

Some people use telephone, e-mail, and voice-mail to reach their customers but the best contact is person-to-person talk. Whether you are delivering a sales presentation, explaining a contract to a new client, conducting a doctor/patient interview, a counsellor/client meeting, delivering a report to your associates, helping a customer buy a book or holding a one-to-one meeting with your superior, your ability to perform well in face-to-face meetings is very important to your overall professional success. Each time you involve in any kind of face-to-face meeting with, say, your co-workers, you have a small lapse of time in which to deliver the most important piece of information. You want people to leave the meeting feeling well-informed and well-grounded in the topics discussed. Delivering face-to-face information effectively and accurately shows respect for associates and yourself. Television programs deliver information to us in small seven-minute durations, and by so doing, they allow us to have a short period of attentive listening and watching. It is wise to use simple tools of breaking your presentation or meeting into manageable seven-minute segments. This style of presentation helps your listeners learn more, remember more and walk away feeling better.

To Facilitate Your Self-Confidence, do the Following

- Develop a spirit of acquaintanceship with people who have a positive effect on your life.
- Increase your social activity with good people.
- Choose to meet life-empowering people.
- Talk to everyone.
- Show a sense of humour.
- Always be appreciative.
- Assist others when they need your help.
- Ask others for help when the need arises.

In life, it is important to associate with knowledgeable people who love to serve. It is advised that one be a part of a problem-solving program so that all one's shortcomings would be made even with those of the experts. You learn every day from those higher on the ladder of life. But to socialize with people, remember we are all unique and, as such, a good demeanour pays a high dividend when talking, eating, playing, working, and meeting with people. One should undertake to seek to know other people's personal problems and should endeavour to provide honest solutions according to one's capability. Be an endearing personality, lovable in all circumstances.

Here is a story to help you improve your authentic-self. One of the lists of facilitators of self-confidence above stated we should choose to meet life-empowering people. Self-empowering fellows are very helpful in all aspect of our lives. They are there to assist you in times of difficulties. They are the guiding touch-light on your dark road. Like the story of "The Old Man and The Sea," a fisherman called Santiago and his faithful little friend named Manolin. In a nutshell, the story was about life struggle. The author, Hemingway, viewed life as a continuous struggle for survival. The old man, Santiago, was a lonesome man but luckily, he had a little boy, Manolin. The boy was everything to him in times of difficulties. Santiago could go out for fishing for days without catching a fish and came back disgusted, but it would be only Manolin who would be his source of comfort. Santiago was a man of undaunted spirit. According to the author,

> *"He had a great interest in the American baseball league, and he took every available opportunity to read about it in the newspapers. It was from one of the baseball stars, Joe Di Maggio, that he took his inspiration and confidence. When he was on the sea and experienced great difficulties, he reminded himself of Di Maggio and built up his confidence, more so when he had heard Di Maggio's father was also a fisherman. Besides Di Maggio, another source of inspiration the old man had were the great lions that he had seen on an earlier trip to Africa. Whenever he slept, he dreamt of the lions and built up his confidence from their fearlessness."*
>
> J. Oti Awere
> Epe-Ara-Araromi-Ekiti
> "The Old Man and The Sea" 1985, (pp. 3-4).

One can confer the importance of role modelling here in building self-confidence. Santiago built his confidence through copycatting Di Maggio and African lions. His journey did not end here. But it continues with his little faithful friend Manolin. Here is another version of the story,

> *"Singular in his efforts in this direction is the boy, Manolin who acts as Santiago's general factotum. He acts sometimes as the old man's wife or mother by procuring food and drinks for him and keeping him company to ensure that he ate it. He is also Santiago's helper in a wide range of activities.*

> *So, when Santiago was in difficulty on the sea, he wished many times that Manolin was with him. Dependence as a theme is therefore given a wide and exhaustive examination in The Old Man and The Sea."*
>
> *J. Oti Awere*
> *Epe-Ara-Araromi-Ekiti*
> *"The Old Man And The Sea" 1985, (p. 11).*

This little narrative shows the importance of having a responsible and knowledgeable person around you as you build your self-confidence; a person who can cheer up and influence you positively. You need someone to help you because two heads are better than one.

Chapter Three

Section I: Take 100 Percent Responsibility for Your Life; Total Commitment

Develop Your Own Helping Methodologies and Core Principles

"As the dimensions of the tree are not always regulated by the size of the seed, so the consequences of things are not always proportionate to the apparent magnitude of those events that have produced them."

Colton, Familiar Quotations, and
Webster Encyclopaedia of Dictionary.

"The plant reveals what is in the seed. The seed includes all the possibilities, however, only if it receives corresponding energies from the sky" (from the Ancient Egyptian Temples Proverbs).

They say negative attitudes give rise to negative consequences and positive ones yield positive consequences. This implies that we have to start right with good intentions and plans. Check yourself, list your habits that are not working and replace them with workable habits that are positive. This is true because bad habits and their outcomes induce fear and stress in the internal environment of the body. If the body adapts to a stressful condition for long, a mental disorder appears, consequently causing a major disease. We have to avoid this situation.

> *"Taking responsibility means being aware of the multitude of choices you have in any given situation."*
>
> *Susan Jeffers 1987, (p. 63).*

Jeffers is reminding you that it is your duty to turn yourself around or remain where you are at the moment. It is your choice to say, I don't want to be a driver any longer. Today I am going to enrol in a college to acquire more skills. I am going to be a doctor of education or a medical doctor. From now on, I must maintain positive thinking and no more negativity in my thinking. I will cast out my 'chatterbox,' that inner little voice that resounds in you which tries to drive you crazy.

According to Jeffers:

1. Taking responsibility means never blaming anyone else for anything you are being, doing, having or feeling. "Never?" you say. "But this time it really is

his fault" (or her fault, or the boss fault, or my son's fault, or the economy's fault, or my mother's fault, or my father's fault, or my friend's fault!). "Really, it is!" If I missed anyone or anything, just add it to the list. Until you fully understand that you, and no one else, create what goes on in your head, you will never be in control of your life…

2. Taking responsibility means not blaming yourself. I know this sounds contradictory, but it is not. Anything that takes away your power or your pleasure makes you a victim. Don't make yourself a victim of yourself! For some, this is more difficult than not blaming others. Once you become aware that you have created so much of your unhappiness, you have a tendency to punish yourself and put yourself down. "There I am, messing up my life again. I'm hopeless. When will I ever learn?" This, again, is not taking responsibility for your experience of life. It is important to understand that you have always done the best you possibly could, given the person you were at any particular time. Now that you are learning a new way of thinking, you can begin to perceive things differently and possibly change many of your actions. There is absolutely no need to be upset with your past, present or future behaviour. It is all simply part of the learning process- the process of moving yourself from pain to power. And it takes time. You must be patient with yourself. There is never any need to be down on yourself. Nothing is your "fault." Yes, you cause your unhappiness,

but this is no reason to cast blame. You're simply on the path toward greater self-fulfilment, and it is a lengthy process of trial and error.

3. Taking responsibility means being aware of where and when you are NOT taking responsibility so that you can eventually change. For example, anger, upset, blaming others, pain, vengeance, lack of focus, self-pity, envy, helplessness, a constant state of limbo, impatience, joylessness, fatigue, intimidation, attempts to control others, obsessiveness, addictions, judgmental, disappointment, jealousy, (backbiting, hatred).

4. Taking responsibility means handling the Chatterbox. This is the little voice inside, the voice that tries to drive you crazy - and often succeeds! I'll bet some of you don't even know it's there (I was shocked when I became aware of it), but I promise you, it holds the key to all your fear. It's the voice that heralds doom, lack and losing. We're so used to its presence we often don't even notice it is talking to us. If you are not aware of your Chatterbox, it sounds something like this: 'If I call him maybe he'll think I'm too pushy, but maybe if I don't call him, he'll think I'm not interested...'

5. Taking responsibility means being aware of payoffs that keep you "stuck." Payoffs explain why we choose to perpetuate what we don't want in our lives. Once you understand payoffs, your behaviour will make much more sense to you. Payoffs mean the consequent results of actions.

6. Taking responsibility means figuring out what you want in life and acting on it. Set out goals then go out and work toward them. Figure out what kind of space you would like to live in ... then create it. It doesn't take a lot of money to create a peaceful, loving home for yourself. Look around and see who you would love to include in your circle of friends... then pick up the phone and make plans to get together. Don't sit around waiting for them to call you. Check out your body. Determine what you need to do to create what looks and feels healthy... then make it happen. Most of us do not "sculpt" our lives. We accept what comes our way... then we gripe about it. Many of us spend our lives waiting - waiting for the perfect friends to come along. There is no need to wait for anyone to give you anything in your life. You have the power to create what you need. Given commitment, clear goals and action, it's just a matter of time.
7. Taking responsibility means being aware of the multitude of choices you have in any given situation. For instance, what are you now? A trader, a driver, a dropout from school, a lazy fellow? What do you do if you are good for nothing? It is not too late for you to amend your life. As a trader, you can still pull yourself up to earn a degree in a famous university of your choice. It is in your will power to decide what you ought to be.

If you want to be a psychologist, medical doctor, academic doctor, nurse, manager, professor, pastor, a priest, a nun, etc.

if you want to be a potential fellow, or a bogus fellow, the ball is on your court. Therefore, you can drill your ball the way you want. It is your choice to drink and dance all day or remain in your bed all day. What do you prefer? Is it to make yourself a counterfeit or a successful man or woman? Or to be happy or to be sad? You have an absolute right to make a choice on what to be. You have to hold firm your core principle on how to advance in life. Making a choice is a crucial thing in your life, and if you make a good choice, you are great! If you make the wrong choice, it is up to you. Think twice before you act. If you intend to be successful, make a good choice now. If you want to be happy, trash all those things that upset you. Hence, you need to work harder on them. There are at least thirty ways to change your point of view.

Mastermind Your Way to Success

Masterminding is the gathering of **Four to Six** people for the purpose of fact-finding by racking their brains searching for ways and means to handle a problem in order to create a result that contains the most beneficial outcomes.

> *"For where two or three are gathered together in my name, there I am in the midst of them."*
> Jerusalem Bible Matthew 18:20 (p. 28).

This assertion relates that when individuals gather together to concentrate on issues, such as the acquisition of new ideas, knowledge, and a varied number of resources on solving a problem with an invocation to God Almighty, there is always an illumination that guides the way to the expected and desired solution.

This is necessary because two heads are better than one in dispelling fears and doubts that creep up when confronted by an enigma in management affairs. The mastermind is the power we muster to one another in synergy, (working together) supported by the power from the Divine. A mastermind group should include people of professional calibres from different faculties of life. The people of this group should openly bring to the table their expertise, experience, and management style in handling over-commitment, selling services too cheaply, focusing too much on triviality (worthlessness), too little delegating, too small thinking, and much complacency in personal and business life. The mastermind group, made up of people with perspectives, experiences, skills, and networks for business strategy, internet marketing, real estate, and the success strategy and the coaching strategy for wealth empowerment, should meet every two weeks to help each other for the mutual benefit for all. The ideal size of a mastermind group is five to six people and the duration of the meeting should be between one to two hours. One person is assigned the duty of regulating the time apportioned to each member to speak and taking the roll call of members.

Conducting a Mastermind Meeting

1. Open the meeting with an invocation to the Most High God to take control of the activities and to grant the members the wisdom and understanding

needed to carry on the meeting and to enlighten the members in understanding and assimilation of all the subject matter.

2. Members use the first hour to discuss their situations, opportunities, needs, challenges, and success stories since the last meeting.

3. **Negotiate for Time:** This time, a request for extra time is made since each person is entitled to 10 to 15 minutes of talk.

4. **Members Make their Requested Speeches, for Example:** "I need advice on how to raise an income of £100,000", or on a personal level, "I think my son is taking drugs." Then experts in each area begin to offer their solutions to the problems presented.

5. **Make a Commitment:** Members, under the direction of the moderator, make declarations of what they are going to work on either developing their choices from their problems or from what they heard from other members. Their choices should aim at an action leading to the completion of their goals and the overall achievement of the mastermind group.

6. **End the Meeting with Mratitude:** The meeting is ended with a prayer by the group expressing gratitude and a sense of an accomplishment of goals.

7. **Accountability:** Each member endeavours to keep on beat the project he or she has chosen to deliver at the next meeting and also ensures that other members meet their commitments.

The mastermind group deliberations help one to have a clear view of what is needed to be done in order to marshal in the process of success in a business and gain self-confidence. It is said; "By knowing, one reaches belief. By doing, one gains conviction. When you know, dare" (Proverb from the Ancient Egyptian Temples). Team-building prevents fear in each individual. By working in teams, groups as well as individuals, one achieves a lot. The wise men say, "Experience is the best teacher." The more we work in teams, the more we acquire wisdom.

Acknowledge the Totality of Your Being

To understand the totality of your being, you have to examine self in order to have a view of the essence of being. The inborn and genetic structures lead us to the original self, which in turn, as development progresses, puts on the clothing of other forms of parental care and other significant persons like loved ones, school teachers, religious preachers, cultural traditionalists, and social associates, and friends.

As Virginia Woolf writes in her novel, "Orlando", a biography is considered complete if it merely accounts **for six or seven selves (that is, full selves)** whereas a person may have as many as a thousand. William James envisions the self as:

"The sum total of all that (a man) can call his, not only his psychic powers but also his clothes, and his house, his wife, and children, his ancestors, and

friends, his reputation, and works, his land, and horses, and yacht, and bank accounts. If they wax and prosper, he feels triumphant, if they dwindle and die away, he feels downcast.
- William James
https://experimentaltheology.blogspot.
com/2008/02/theology-of-peanuts...

Thomas Bouchard of the University of Minnesota, beginning in 1997, collected pairs of separated twins from all over the world and reunited them while testing their personalities and IQs (intelligence quotient-an index of relative intelligence of a test designed to determine the intelligence of an individual score in reference to the scores of others), putting together the studies of such IQ tests of tens of thousands of individuals. The table of the test records looks like this; 100 percent correlation score meaning perfect identity, zero percent being non-compliance.

The same person tested twice	87
Identical twins reared together	86
Identical twins reared apart	76
Fraternal twins reared together	55
Biological siblings (children of same parents)	47
Parents and children living together	40
Parents and children living apart	31
Adopted children living together	0
Unrelated people living apart	0

Adopted from (pp.82-83), Genome by Matt Ridley, 2006.

The tests showed that the twins sharing the same genes, the same womb, and the same family scored almost the same amount as the same person taking the test twice. The conclusion from the studies disclosed that about half of our IQs were inherited and less than one fifth was due to the environment we shared with our family. The rest came from the womb, the school, and other outside influences. It is reckoned that the heritability of childhood IQ is about forty-five percent, whereas in late adolescence, it rises to seventy-five percent. As we grow up, we gradually express our own innate intelligence and leave behind the influences stamped on us by others. This is true as our sense of whole self-shifts as we move up or down the levels of development. Sometimes our sense of being is inflated while at other times it is too negative. We must acknowledge both sides of the equation of our life by first paying attention to the positive successes that are rich in experiences containing formulas of doing things, and succeeding in them. Sometimes, negative results have signals that indicate that things are not right. We must not ignore weak results and their purports.

Oftentimes, it is uncomfortable to face what is not working in our lives. In the long run, it might mean self-discipline, confronting somebody or something, risking not being liked, asking for what you want, demanding respect, instead of settling for a humbling relationship or quitting your job. We must not live with disquieting circumstances that do not work. Not recognizing a bad situation that needs a solution is based on fear. But when deciding on taking action on fear, it is wise to dwell on solutions that are not extreme. Normal treatments of disturbing situations may run like a discussion with your boss, counselling, scaling back your expenditures, and seeking professional help. Start with a list of what things are not working and set goals for handling them. You can start with finance, career, business, family, health, appearance, and personal growth. In each case, *choose an action and do it. Never be afraid of acting rightly.*

In psychology, a paranoid person always feels that others are out to get her, and so she throws her blame on them for her frustration and confusion. The process of this blaming attitude on others is called ***projection.*** For example, a young girl who has been fired from a job claims that it is due to the office politics rather than her incompetence in poor job performance. Another case of blaming others comes from the younger adolescent persons who strive to be on their own and live their experiences the way they want. But the parents keep worrying about the way they are doing things. More often, the adolescents and the parents clash head-on. Rebellion rules the day, as each awards blame for the inadequacy on the behaviour of the other.

This is like the case of Mr. Jacky who was sent to both secondary school and university to acquire a sound education by his parents but he decided to make a wrong choice by following uncouth/ bad-mannered people who smoked hard drugs and engaged in other hanky-panky ways of life. His relatives advised him to come out of that but he saw everybody as an enemy. At this point, everybody rejected him and then he began to accuse them of not helping him. The answer he received from his relatives is this: *"You chose that evil path and you must walk on it alone **by** yourself."* My mother used to put across this adage whenever something happened; "Use your tongue to count your teeth." In literal meaning, tell yourself the truth and stop blaming others. Accept yourself and take challenges and be responsible for your deeds and actions; as one makes his bed so he lies on it. At any rate, it is time to stop the blame game and start facing the matter squarely. The formula E + R = O means Event + Response= Outcome. This means that every result (O) has a cause (E) and is generated by the application of response (R). We can blame events (E) such as the economy, lack of money, lack of education, racism, gender bias, boss's attitude, superiors, teachers, wife's or husband's disapproval, lack of support, and our failure to deliver the expected result. But the fact of the matter is that we have to stop looking outside for the cause of our shortcoming; we have to stop the limiting factor, the failure factor from within *by creating a strategy for winning*. If the lack of money is the problem, then we need to cut down on expenses. or if lack of education is the case, we need to continuously educate ourselves and learn new skills. To dwell in ignorance, lack of awareness, fear of running risks, fear of confrontation, or disapproval, would mean limiting yourself from achieving your potential. You should have a reference goal of what you want and decide to take the risk of reaching that goal.

I always create a strategy in my life. As a result, I always strongly believe in the philosophy of when one road closes, another opens, ultimately in a better way. My late mother, Mrs. Ojukwu Monica Konye Nwadike, used to tell her children, never put all your eggs in one basket. This wise advice enabled me to believe in the application of alternatives in all my endeavours. I won't let anything that I could handle tie me down. I wrote this book – **Building Up Self-confidence,**

A Fundamental Way of Conquering Fear - for three main reasons; One is to combat the fear that erodes confidence in me and assist others to build their confidence and maintain it, respectively. When I was about to start this write-up, fear of consideration emerged, and I began to think whether I would make it a reality. I began to consider so many things, especially what the talk-down individuals would say. As I was pondering, my thought gave me a lot of discouraging reasons not to write it but knowing that *whatever you do, people must talk; for many, many men have many, many minds.* Subsequently, this adage fortified me and then I ignored those numerous negative self-thoughts and the loud voice of the chatterbox in me. I moved on to do my research and write. Bearing in mind that I am writing to contest fear in me and to help others, I said to hell with these thoughts. Then I rode on gathering my facts and immediately, I contacted one of my classmates, a person of great foresight as well as a great researcher to act as moderator for my work. Once you maintain a positive frame of mind, things will work out well for you. I know for sure that there were certain things I could have achieved in the early years of my life that fear and lack of self-confidence stopped me from achieving. For this reason, I will not allow them to recur provided I am not hurting anyone in my daily decision makings.

Again, it is not easy to turn around and do it right. It requires a determined awareness, strict discipline, skilful resourcefulness, ability, and a willingness to take risks. As well as consulting ourselves, we should ask other people about the truth of things without fear of failing. We should remind ourselves about practice, meditation, delegation, trusting, listening, asking questions, and keeping our eye on the ball in order to create a formula for scoring. The principle of self-transformation needs creativity to climb towards the desired result, monitoring and making sure that what has been planned is being implemented and each sectional process achieved.

Listen to Your Feelings- They are Trying to Tell You Something - Man, Know Thyself (Egyptian Temple Proverb)

Many people live in fear and resignation to the extent that they give up struggling for anything. But when we sleep, our minds are under the control of our inner self which knows who we are and our potential. It is right always to put our ambitions and shortcomings in prayers or meditations and then listen, watch out, and analyse eventual appearances, thoughts, and voices that emerge in relation to what we are brooding over in our minds. Your inner self can use your five senses, bodily signs or sensations to speak to you. You have to train to acquaint yourself with the subtle events taking place in you. Your inner core is imprinted with your best self and is connected with the universal mind just as we are connected to the earth through gravity and to the atmosphere through air and moisture. The nature of feelings you receive reflects the messages contained therein. Joy and euphoria mean a positive message, an urge to go forward and a sensation of fear and threat is telling you to withhold action and delay. Let me give an idea of one's desire, her dream, the apparition in the dream and the connection to an eventual desired result. As one of my interviewers disclosed, she left her existing job without first getting an alternative job. This condition kept her running around and looking for a new job. She attended interviews for jobs and she was successful in the interviews but her success did not translate into getting a job. One night, after her nightly prayer and meditation, she retired to sleep. In her dream, she heard the voice of one of her ancestors calling her by name and asking her to go to where she worked before to look for a job. The ancestor reminded her where to go. Then she did exactly according to the directive of her ancestor. She picked up an information directory to locate the site. She found the site and sent in her application to the manager of the office. Within a week, she was invited for an interview. At the interview, after looking at her certificates and credentials, the manager offered her the job of secretary and asked her to report to work on the following day. This is the job from which she retired early on (source from oral interview with Jean). When you are in a joyful mood or in dire need of compassion, God the Creator is also in a joyful sympathetic passion with you. If you are well-trained, and disciplined, his feelings flow as messages in different forms to you. The foregoing story bore witness to the fact that we are connected to someone outside us who is always there to help us reach our goal of self-satisfaction. We are connected to the Almighty God. Simply in physical terms, we are connected by telephones, televisions, WhatsApp and radio which give us the intelligence contained in the atmosphere. So it was that God created all things and endowed them with faculties to prosper and reach the ultimate ends. The wise man says be all ears. That is to say, **argue less and listen more.** The Egyptian proverb says:

> *"By knowing, one reaches belief. By doing, one gains conviction. When you know, dare."*
> https://therit.weebly.com/egyptian-proverbs.html.

We have to be interested in the people in order to know them because accurate knowledge gives rise to precise action that yields good results. Another word of wisdom from the Egyptian archives says:

> *"The first concerning the "Secrets," all cognition comes from inside; we are therefore initiated only by ourselves but the Master gives the keys."* When self is in possession of the accurate knowledge, the truth (Maat-truth Egyptian) opens the way.

Be Grateful When You are Feeling Good and Graceful When You are Feeling Bad.

They Say Eevery Cloud has a Silver Lining (Milton)

> *"For every failure, there is an alternative course of action. You just have to find it. When you come to a roadblock, take a detour."*
> - Mary Kay Ash
> Founder of Mary Kay Cosmetics,
> By Jack Canfield
> The Success Principles 2005, (p.111).

What achievers have always learnt is that even when you cannot move forward, you can turn right or you can turn left.

The difference between the actual world and how we choose to interpret it is so vast that we often make mistakes, overact, and fill in some of the spaces with some fear of unknown mysterious ideas, like love, fear, disgust, sadness, surprise, happiness, and anger. As Daniel Goldman notes in 'Emotional Intelligence':

"The first laws and proclamations of ethics, namely the code of 282 laws of ethics of Hammurabi of Babylon (1792-1750 BCE), the ten commandments of the Hebrews through Moses around 1270 BCE, the Edicts of Emperor Ashoka of India (264-227BCE) the Egyptian 42 laws from the Book of the Great Awakening of the 42 gods of Hall of Justice from the Old Kingdom (2649-2152 BCE)- can be read as attempts to harness, subdue and domesticate emotional life."

Some problems call for watchful concern and some rejection would not result in being cast out. We tend to use emotional hammers where we need to use surgical tools. *Life experience is the best teacher but the tuition is high.* We also tend to kill a fly with a gunshot rather than with a fly-paper. No man ever became great or good except through many and great mistakes (William E. Gladstone). There are times when one feels that the end of the world has come because the basic fabric of one's life has broken down. It may be a failure in an examination, the loss of a job, divorce, the death of a loved one, a business failure, a devastating illness or your house got burnt down. But later in life, one finds that when one way closes, another one opens; that, in the midst of chaos, there is always a way out to the bright side. Just as stated below,

> **"When life hands you a lemon, squeeze it and make lemonade."**
> - W. Clement Stone

This is my personal experience based on when one road closes, another opens. I was in the USA, my nationalized country, when my Mother Superior asked me to proceed to the UK for a pro-life mission. I left everything behind and proceeded. I felt a great loss in my life as a human being. But arriving in the United Kingdom, God opened a wider door for me. I had never thought that I would be an author of this book. Producing this book empowered me ascertain my self-confidence. In any difficult situation, God is directing us to an unforeseen great future. Another point is that I could upgrade my writing about "Building self-confidence, A Fundamental Way of conquering the Fear" because of COVID – 19. Everyone knows about the outrageous breakout of COVID-19 in the year 2020 and its lockdown crisis. So, staying at home during lockdown enabled me to work on this project. While sitting at home, I had the opportunity to read and research more on some books to improve on my self-confidence and to help others to do likewise. Even though one is out of a job, it doesn't mean that one is idle. It was difficult time, but one must make use of it. In any difficult situation, one must devise a means to roll on. Confident people always find a way to control any predicaments. They never allow dilemmas to have power over them.

Another good example is an oral interview by Ben: "I want to tell a story about when one road closes, another one opens," he said. "I, Ben, was fortunate to work in Guinness Brewery (Nig.) Limited as an assistant electrical engineer, in Lagos, Nigeria and later I was sponsored to study as an engineering student at Ahmadu Bello University, Zaria, Nigeria in 1966. I was to retain my salary, my annual salary increase, job position promotion, and my right to be graded as a deputy chief engineer after graduation from the University. But all these privileges did not last long, for, in 1967, the Nigerian Civil War broke out. I was one of the Ibo students in the University earmarked to be killed by the Hausa rioters. I was living in Zaria Samaru City, not in the University hostel. As I planned to move into the University hostel, on the day of rioting, I saw some rioters surrounding my house, waiting for darkness to come down and at 8 pm, I went on my knees praying. Suddenly, my Hausa houseboy, who did my household chores, Hassan, showed up in the crowd. He told them that every day I fed the 'almejeris' (orphans), gave clothes to them, and money and I was their 'megida' (master). These rioters went away, and Hassan came to escort me to the University. When I arrived at the gate of the University, I attempted to introduce myself to the guards but they refused to allow me into the University and tried to kill me with their swords. I fought with one of them and was able to overpower him by taking away his sword. Luckily, in the nick of time, the Dean of Studies, an "Ibo" man (my tribal man) was entering the University from outside; I rushed to him to tell him of the fracas (dispute) between me and the guards. Then I was allowed to enter the University hostel.

The following morning, the University closed down and the students were asked to go home. I came down to Lagos to my job but the commotion around was too much for me to bear. Consequently, I decided to go to my hometown in Eastern Nigeria, leaving behind me all the good things that I enjoyed in the Guinness Brewery. In the East, I escaped assassination twice. However, when the Civil War ended in 1970, I went back to the brewery to resume work and I was told that someone had taken my job. I stayed in Lagos with my relatives to look for another job. One night, the spirit of my father motivated me to go out to the street to meet someone who would help me. Then, I went to the Labour and Employment Office where I had had an interview for a job as a senior works officer, to check whether there was an available opening. I was told to wait. On leaving the labour office, on the street, I met one of my brothers-in-law. He said he knew one Public Works Engineer who was recruiting workers. We both called on the engineer in his house and explained my need for a job. The engineer referred me to a Coca-Cola Engineer who was also my wartime close friend. When I met him, there was, first of all, a reminiscence over old times and then a discussion about getting a job. He took me to the Coca-Cola Chief Engineer who posted me to the Coca-Cola Bottling Plant, Kano, Nigeria as a Senior Electrical Technician. Lastly, we had the one road of the brewery closing and another road of the Coca-Cola plant opening. Wise people say "Heaven helps those who help themselves." I could infer from your story that God performs wonders for good people.

Turn Your Melo-Drama into Mellow-Drama - Make Your Emotional Play Become Maturely Wise to Maximize What You Are

> *"After that, God saw all he had made, and indeed it was very good. Evening came and morning came,"* **Genesis 1:31**
>
> The Jerusalem Bible
> Popular Edition 1974, (p. 6).

We must learn from this by appreciating what good we have done in the past so as to have optimistic confidence in confronting any problem. We have to celebrate our successes in order to be encouraged to achieve more. We must highlight our small achievements so as to learn from the successful elements of those events. Life experiences contain ingredients and formulas for tackling new ones. For instance, I reflect on how the journey of my life began. I remember when I was a housemaid for three different women. I was solely engaged in farming and petty trade in my village selling peanuts, and moi-moi. After which, I started primary education and was able to finish primary six successfully. Then I enrolled in secondary school and obtained a diploma too. Immediately after secondary education, as I was waiting for my result, I started learning typing skills with old typing machine. Once I mastered typing skills, I started working as a self-employed typist in

Orlu Town, Imo State in South-eastern Nigeria. The typing skills granted me the opportunity to secure a job at Nneji and Sons Printing Press in Orlu Town near Orlu-Owerri Road. During the weekends, I tended a tomato garden. After a while, I entered a convent. Immediately after my convent training, I had my first religious vows and was sent overseas and I found myself in the United States of America. There, I studied and obtained an Associate in Science Degree diploma in Medical Secretarial with honour roll, Dean's List. I kept on striving till I obtained a Bachelor of Science Degree in Computer Information Systems. After this, I enrolled for a Master of Science Degree in Business Administration and with academic honour roll excellency. Finally, I enrolled to study Psychology, and obtained the Doctorate of Philosophy Psychology (Ph.D.) with honour roll- Summa Cum Laude. In the USA, I worked as a social care practitioner (CNA). In the United Kingdom, I enrolled in a Counselling Skills Course at Cambridge College and obtained a diploma in counselling.' Besides this, I enrolled in early years childcare level 3 and was successful; as a result, I became a qualified childcare practitioner in the UK. I worked in this field till present combining it with my religious apostolate counselling of the vulnerable young mothers with pregnancy crises.

If I include all my achievements in life, this book will be too voluminous. I never believed that I could achieve so much. I did achieve these goals because I have a strong will called "Determination." However, I encourage you to list out as much as you can of all your achievements to uplift you and to assist you to strive higher towards your goal. One can see that in life per se, many people are reserved while others are so flamboyant that any little thing they do, the whole world must hear it. Hence, everybody is unique and that is the reason why some people would have achieved a whole lot and no one knows about it. The most important thing is to look into one's achievement (1) from birth to 20, (2) From 20 to 40 (3) from 40 to 60 years of age. By listing positive deeds within each interval, one can shake one's head and say, "I am a good guy." We can create a success graph from which we can derive a formula by plotting into the graph new values of projects we want to embark on and proceed from the developments. This helps us to build up successful earmarks that are needed for analysing a problem and predicting its solution. God created us by his words (thoughts, Hu = Divine utterance Egyptian) by saying, "Let the earth cause grass to shoot forth, vegetation bearing seeds, fruit trees yielding fruits according to their kinds." Likewise, we make good things happen by entertaining good thoughts that generate good events. By imitating God and cultivating good thoughts based on past successes, we call forth further good thoughts and events to happen.

By Contemplating (Concentrating) on Your Successful Past, it is Wise to put it like this:

1. **Areas of Achievements:** Spiritual practice - business, educational, financial, personal private life, and physical.
2. **Personal Disciplines Observed:** Faith in God, prayer vision, meditation, diet, exercise, and reading.

3. **Overcoming Obstacles like:** Eating too much, struggling to tell the truth, staying idle, drinking too much, living in lassitude (exhaustion of mind or body). We recount how effort exerted, in each case, enabled us to arrive smoothly at the success points.

Mind Your Business

Stay focused on your core genius. But what is core genius? At the basis of individuality and diversity is spiritual your personality, that which makes me - me and you – you, but life experiences can modify the basic personality to the extent where it can transform it to something else. We are all endowed with basic personalities rich in inner resources that help some to be writers, others to be actors, psychologists, preachers, dancers, and so forth. Therefore, it is wise to stick to your core personality though this can be influenced by other personalities. What is not acceptable is being a jack-of-all-trades, as one may sometimes spend useful resources on ill-fated projects that one is not qualified to handle. They say one thing at a time and that done very well is a very good rule as many can tell. Many fear being wasteful by asking for help which they will pay for and which they can do by themselves or are afraid of letting go of their control of things because they fear that others working for them may not comply with their specifications the way they want things done. All the same, to avoid crowding everything into one hand, it is productive to delegate some well-designed tasks to others. By so doing, one's innate ability to do things is spread to others by allowing them to do the finishing touches. A business runs smoothly and progressively when it is headed by a well-coordinated and creative organizer who has a good store of ideas and foresight and can formulate strategies for everyone's emancipation and business growth. Our success, however, depends on having a team of skilled personalities which is capable of translating the ideal formulations into tractable (amenable to reason), appreciable productions. This applies to all aspects of the goals you are embarking on. ***Contact people who know better than you know.*** Two heads are better than one. The wise man says, "success is based on team effort." We learn from others to improve. A tree does not make a forest. Hence, do not think that you know it all.

Section II: Release the Brakes Avoid Fencing Yourself in at Times

Before we let loose our control on our cautionary caprices, it is worthwhile to examine the subject matter with clear attentive tools for spotlighting the value points, the difficult tasks, and the desired end results. It is not only good to keep the door open but also wise to be able to predict the outcome of the events involved to assess what we need to know and do in order to proceed with self-awareness and self-reliance. These two qualities, coupled with faith in the Universal Creator, are necessary for engaging in adventures that are challenging. Our senses, when attuned to their unique lifestyles, perceive only what they need to survive. Given the right note, they make us bellow without understanding why. We have brains that respond very speedily and indiscriminately to any threat, real, imaginary, subtle or polite. When one sees a fruit one has seen before one recognizes the colour, shape and location. This helps us to recollect our ability to reflect on ourselves by touring our past. This is self-awareness. How many things that exist are we really aware of? To feel secure and be sure to step forward, one must have self-awareness based on a rich repertoire of eventful past events as stated by the Egyptian saying of wisdom: "By knowing, one reaches belief, by doing one gains conviction. When you know, dare." Self-awareness relies on self-reliance which in turn, thrives on things, associates, follows a line and returns to the first thought with additional insight from its travel, putting all together, re-evaluating all and then moving on to a new vista of horizon. This means, from our inborn nature, we always feel threatened by change because it always heralds uncertainty and failure. But our life with its success also grows immensely on change as we boldly strive across valleys and gullies of obstacles to reach our destined targets. As we have been used to laying a stranglehold on things we believe in, which yield dividends, we often fear a novelty which ushers in new skills, new rules and new customs. Mild novelties have noticeable peculiarities that can be handled but complex ones have profound intricacies of hardness to unravel. Our elders say, "You can shed tears for a small atrocity, but you have no tears, no ability to cry, for a devastatingly complex one." To dare forward would require strength of character, accurate knowledge of things and experience replete with capabilities to visualize the constructs of projects.

Maturity in how to discern what is from what is not is a prerequisite for making a jump into a decision without reins.

This means that to get out of one's comfort zone, one has to have a reassuring objective and a predictably measurable result before getting on board with a project. For it is said, "Think before you act." But self-pity and self-blame would stop one from exploring the untraveled way of life and daring to win the gold. Goal-setting must be the yardstick for breaking the roadblocks which deter us from achieving in any venture. After assessing and reassessing the details of what it takes to achieve a career, it is time to step out, doing one bit at a time. We must be keen on observing changes and new developments, so as to have a strong footing on the project. Caution, not fear, is the watchword to guide us through the unknown territory of an adventure. We must not fence ourselves in and remain static; rather, we must advance with confidence and faith in breaking new grounds in order to be progressive.

Be Open to What Is

Ignore Negative Thoughts After Introspection

According to Weiner Heisenberg, a German physicist (one who knows the workings of matter, energy, forces, and motion of the universe) who postulated the principle of uncertainty, that nothing ever stays the same since what we perceive from time to time is a rough estimate of what really is, nothing really is certain because everything is undergoing changes every moment. An Indian saying asserts that you cannot cross the same water in a river twice for since the water is always flowing, you cross each stretch only once, not twice.

A man went out to find an average man. He ended up finding no average man because all the parts of the body of all people did not measure up to the appropriate sizes required for particular heights. Some short people have long arms and so on. Gauss Carl Fredrick (German Mathematician/Physicist/astronomer) drew a curve and found it hard to locate a reliable average point, for the average is represented by a group of points in this case.

In an Igboland folk-story, "otukpukpo", known as a woodpecker, was very adept in pecking wood with its strong beak. Once upon a time, it prophesied that no tree would be left unattended on the day its parents would die. It happened that it had a big boil in its beak on the day its parents died and so it could not peck a tree. It is said that if wishes were horses, men could ride. You can never tell the day from the look of the morning. Very much so it is not always easy to locate what is so as to be open to it. What is, is what has been averaged from a multitude of would-be's that have been generalized to represent the truth. What is advised is to look for the truth and when one finds it, one should stick to it. Jesus said to his disciples, "If you remain in my word, you are really my disciple and you will know the truth and the truth will set you free, says the Lord," (John 8:31-). The word here means a principle that encompasses certain accepted facts that have been tested and found efficacious (capable of producing desired results). Thus, all we can do is to learn as much as we can from the truly successful people, the most renowned motivational masters in the fields (like management skills, sales, and marketing strategies, industrial business, and entrepreneurship.) This leads to accurate knowledge of what is, for acting with half knowledge creates fear, doubt, and stress. This is important, as our elders say, "The earthworm has no tool but its head for penetrating the soil because it has the power, authority, and know-how for doing so." Another Christian maxim says:

> **"Keep on then seeking first the kingdom and his righteousness and all these things will be added to you."**
> *From the Holy Scriptures (Matthew 6:33).*

You must first seek to find the right source to proceed to reach the goal. If we want to harvest a good mango fruit, we must know how to plant a good seed and grow it. When you learn the right way to succeed, stick to it; it will help you uphold your self-confidence.

Be Aware of Yourself: When You Know Yourself, You're in Control of Confidence

The preconscious, conscious, and unconscious minds combine to give the notion of self-positioned on impulses, moods, and memories. The best way to understand a thing is to remove it from its context; then break it into its many parts until one unearths the underlying principle. A successful man stands out from the crowd with exceptional excellence but self is also really a compound me made up of the self and the other selves. As Confucians (followers of Confucius-Chinese first Teacher and Master born 551 BCE) stated:

> *"When you see a man of worth, think of how you may emulate him. When you see one who is unworthy, examine your own character".* I put it, *"there can be no me in isolation... I am a totality of roles I live in relation to specific others."*

Though many traits are hard-wired by our genes, they are not fixed for there is an inter-play of peers, culture, human nature, and individual hereditary package (which include gender, life in the womb, accidents, ethnicity, and family traits) that contribute hugely to what we are. In modern life, emotional reactions from depression, stress, tough cultures (cultures in which the valued social goals are only for the elite few members but unavailable to everyone else), and fears are the foremost causes of diseases. Conscious deep relaxation is the way to bring relief to the ailing mind. There are people who are trying to live good lives but are overburdened by the hereditary flaws, faults committed, bad habits formed, unfortunate environments, and other adverse circumstances. These fall short of reaching their normal psychic maturity/cosmic consciousness. For these persons and others who seek cosmic conscious awareness for solving problems and psychic stability, it is required to have alpha wave training. From the Ancient Egyptian Temples the saying goes like this:

> *"All is within yourself; know your most inward self and look for what corresponds with it in nature."*

Smiling Uplifts Self-Confidence Smile at Strangers; Look into Their Eyes and Say "Hello."

Write Your Five Most Stubborn Positions and See if You can Soften Them

To be secure, people tend to say to others, "Mind your own business" but they are open only when in the company of acquaintances. In a broad sense, psychologically, we are advised to feel comfortable and relaxed when among all people, to reach out to any stranger with good eye contact and say "Hello." Though, sometimes, it is wise to wait for others to initiate the contact because of the fear of being rejected or being insecure. We are encouraged to be approachable to others because it is natural to be friendly to others. But the general rule is to be open so that you can reach people who may need us and people whom we need. Being approachable, is one of the ultimate ways of establishing one's self-confidence. In the Holy Scriptures (Hebrew 13:2), it has been stated thus:

> *"Continue to love each other like brothers, and remember always to welcome strangers, for by doing this, some people have entertained angels without knowing it" Hebrews 13:2.*
> The Jerusalem Bible
> Popular Edition 1974, (p. 292).

More so, Jesus admonished his apostles saying to them,

> *"When you are entering the house, greet the household and if the house is deserving let the peace*

you wish it come upon it but if it is not deserving let the peace from you return upon you. Whenever anyone does not take you in or listen to your words, on-going out of that house or that city, shake the dust off your feet." Mathew 10:12-14
The Jerusalem Bible
Popular Edition (p. 17).

Here a word is enough for the wise. We now know we must be open to people, not with fear of rejection or apprehension or insecurity but with confidence and honest intention to do a good turn. Let us take into consideration the five steps suggested by the Psychologists' Book of Self-Tests by Louis Janda Ph.D., letting you to feel comfortable and relaxed when around other people.

1. In the first two weeks, smile and say "hello" to strangers that you make eye contact with in friendly situations like college classes, at work, on the elevator, with the cashier on the counter or customers with you in the line at the bank.
2. During the second two-week duration, practice your small-talk skills (self-talk or heart-talk). When in a queue with other customers, turn around and say, "Oh what a beautiful day today." At the gas station, ask the station cashier how she has been. There are exceptions who will snub you, but many people will respond to your friendliness.
3. In the third step of your self-treatment of shyness, give other people compliments for everyone likes to

be pampered or flattered. Tell your classmate that you appreciate her comments. Tell your co-worker how you like his tie.
4. In the fourth step, start to make invitations to people. Ask your classmate to go to lunch with you. It is time to make friends though not everyone will accept your offer. Remember *"Nothing Ventured, Nothing Gained."*
5. The last step is for you to join good group clubs, something like assertiveness training groups or a book club. Your concern about sensitive people will fade away as you assume positive active roles among other people.

In a heart-talk meeting: You can meet a parent whose complaint is her child's report card with C's, a salesperson planning to sell a car or a CEO Chief Executive Officer) overseeing the merger of two companies. The people speak about their needs and wants, hopes and dreams, fears and concerns, hurts and pains in a constructive non-judgmental way, and feelings that block teamwork, synergy, creativity, and intuition which are vital to the productivity and success of any venture, are openly expressed and cleared. Another technique of openness is about assertiveness training. How assertive are you and how do you express yourself? In a perfectly acceptable or extremely ambitious, hard-driving, self-centred way? To be assertive is to be socially appropriate in the self-expression of your feelings. There are clinical psychologists like Spencer A. Rathus who developed Rathus Assertiveness Schedule in his Behaviour Therapy. In item 15 of the schedule he states, "If a close and respected relative were annoying me, I would smother my feelings rather than express my annoyance." The answer is to be polite not to openly express all feelings towards people who are far off. It is nice to be acceptable and tactful by keeping our thoughts to ourselves. Again, we are advised to be appreciative of other people. According to a certain management study, 46 percent of employees leaving a company do so because they feel unappreciated; 61 percent said they felt bosses did not value their importance as people; 88 percent said they did not receive acknowledgement for the work they had done. All these point to the power of appreciation. I am going to give you four examples of the art of appreciation.

Here is an example of an oral interview by Ben as an Assistant Electrical Engineer in one of the popular in Nigeria. He is in charge of the power control room and all the blueprint electrical circuit drawings. It happened one day that one of his colleagues, Katuka, an electrical engineering foreman, worked on a control panel of a boiler that supplied steam and hot water to the company. He offset the starting probes that made the boiler start burning fuel oil that heated the water. Each time the boiler started, it caused a lot of smoke and unburnt fuel to escape and therefore it could not boil water. The electrical engineer and the chief engineer were called in to see what was happening. They tried to start the boiler, but the boiler did not start. It generated a large amount of smoke. At this point, they decided to ask Ben if he had any idea. He observed that when the boiler started, there was no spark in the control box. He then rushed for the drawing of the panel and showed them that the starting probes were offset and that the probes needed to be set at 38 degrees for the proper action to take place. Katuka denied that this was the case. Then Ben opened the panel and there it was, the probes were pushed apart. He undertook to clean the probes because they were dirty and smoky. He used a gauge to set the probes at 38. He then showed the position of the probes in the drawing and how the probes worked. The chief engineer said he wanted to find out who was right, Ben or Katuka? As the chief engineer pressed the start button, the spark came on and the boiler started to function very well. Then the engineers met and gave a job termination notice to Katuka and summoned Ben for a discussion on his further educational training in one of the famous Universities in Nigeria to do a three-year electrical engineering course. This is the story of knowledge of one's job, hard work and the corresponding consequent appreciation. Based on this story, you can see that some pave their ways through others' mistakes. Also, established in this story one could see fear in action. If Katuka wasn't afraid and shy, he would have asked his co-worker to assist him at that time he saw that the starter was not functioning well. He would have saved him from running into trouble and losing his job. Therefore, always ask and you will receive.

Another example of the art of appreciation of a worker's importance was when Nurse Alice was a director in a group home in the USA. Her manager appreciated every job she did. In effect, Nurse Alice put more effort into her duties. As a reward, her manager increased her salary and granted her an opportunity to acquire more experience in her nursing career. She was given a scholarship to further her program in nursing management. One can see here that one good turn deserves another. Alice was not the only nurse in that institution but as a result of her good efforts, she was recognized, rewarded, and appreciated by her boss. Appropriately, let us aim to attract the favour of others wherever we may be. The wise saying goes, "With team effort, we successfully achieve our goals." Let your motto be win-win.

Another example: Mollie had the opportunity to travel overseas for mission work and to study, not because she was a genius or an intellectual, but as a result of her hard work and being a resilient individual, focused, obedient, humble, loyal, patient, and respectful to authority. She was also a lady with foresight. These features qualified her to find herself working overseas. Being in the States, she got more considerations through her hard work and academic performances. After her missionary activities, she studied and graduated. She was assigned as manager of her institution to manage the affairs of their international business. Since her efforts were appreciated, she felt more motivated and became very enthusiastic and more open to working effectively.

Another illustration is about two ladies who sought employment. One was given a full-time job and the other a part-time job. The lady with a full-time job lost her job as a result of non-compliant behaviour. Then the lady with the part-time job was asked to replace the full-time lady because she was hardworking, punctual, and loyal to the management. Appreciation does not come by itself, but you must do something to obtain it. One good turn deserves another. Good performance gains good results and good rewards. Every year, a management consulting firm conducts a survey on 200 companies on what motivates employees. This is the result: 10 ways to really motivate an employee.

Employees	Supervisors
Appreciation	Good wages
Feeling "in" on things (Sympathetic)	Job security
Understanding Attitude	Promotion Opportunities
Job Security	Good Working Conditions
Good Wages	Interesting Work
Interesting Work	Loyalty from Management
Promotion Opportunities	Tactful Discipline
Loyalty from Management	Appreciation
Good Working Conditions	Understanding Attitude
Tactful Discipline	Feeling "in" on things (Sympathetic).

Appearing first on the employees' list is appreciation. This appreciation has three forms, namely, auditory, visual and kinaesthetic. In the auditory form, persons want to hear it. In the visual form, people want to see it, and in the kinaesthetic form (feeling perception), they need to feel it like a pat on the back or a hug. It could be the tone of the voice and words or it could be the tenderness of a touch. It is advisable for a person in authority to apply the three ways of communicating love to those who are being governed by telling them, showing them something and giving them a loving touch on the back.

Develop Your Compassion – Be Willing to Learn from Friends and Family

In order to become a fully liberated and developed personality, one must do away with all past anchors of past hurts, past unfulfilled dreams, past anger, and past fear. To be compassionate is to sympathize with others in their suffering and to be merciful when aggrieved and touched by the needs of the afflicted people. Shakespeare describes mercy like this:

> *"The quality of mercy is not strain'd: it droppeth, as the gentle rain from heaven upon the place beneath; it is twice bless'd; it blesseth him that gives, and him that takes: 'Tis mightiest in the mightiest; it becomes the throned monarch better than his crown,"*
>
> *- Shakespearian Famous Quotes.*
> *https://www.bing.com/videos/search?q*

To Develop the Attribute of Compassion One Needs to

Do the Total Truth Process

1. At the start, you feel anger and resentment. I am angry. I am fed up with you.
2. You feel hurt: it hurts me, I feel disappointed.
3. Fear comes on you. I was afraid of you because of what you did.

4. Then remorse, regret, and accountability turned me round. I am sorry for what happened. I could have known better.
5. Reparation: All I ever wanted was to be nice.
6. Love, compassion, forgiveness, and appreciation: I forgive you for what happened. I appreciate you. I love you. Thank you for talking to me this way.

The Process (Steps) for Forgiveness

Acknowledge your anger and resentment.
Acknowledge the hurt and the pain experienced.
Acknowledge the fears and the misgivings entailed.
Own up to any wrong part you played.
Acknowledge what you were asking for that you did not get.
Let bygones be bygones and forgive the person.
Then do this affirmation technique; "I release myself from all the demands and judgments that have kept me limited. I allow myself to go free, to live in joy and love and peace. I allow myself to create fulfilling relationships, to have success in my life, to experience pleasures, to know that I am worthy and deserve to have what I want. In that process, I release all others from any demands and expectations I have placed on them."

Make Peace with Imperfection

To start with, our bodies have aeons of times of changes that contain mistakes made during cell divisions. Those mistakes make us vulnerable to diseases and so they make us imperfect. It thus becomes natural to accommodate any frailty that falls to our lot. It is said that chromosome 4 is responsible for our fate. In chromosome 4 lies a gene that causes Huntington's Disease. There are four other neurological diseases that result from chromosome 4. It is said that there is a word in the middle of a gene that is repeated several times. so much so that there is a stuttering repetition in the function of the gene. This is responsible for the dementia and bizarre involuntary movements of a patient afflicted with Huntington's disease. There are many instances of this. The DNA (deoxyribonucleic acid) during duplication repeats itself in some cases, thousands and thousands of times and so there are some miscounts and mismatches, though there are repair mechanisms that take care of these mishaps. No amount of good living, good medicines, healthy food, loving families, or great riches can alter them. Huntington's disease strikes between age 30 and 50 years. However, we must live with it peacefully (pp. 55-64) Human Genome by Matt Ridley. John 1:1 says, *"In the beginning the Word was and the Word was with God and the Word was God." (John 1:18), "No man has seen God at any time, the only begotten God who is in the bosom with Father is the one that has explained him."* The lesson here is that the Universe was created out of imperfect inequality and therefore it is natural to be imperfect. Many people succumb to fear and agony when they are diagnosed with incurable diseases. As said earlier, it is possible to be afflicted with one of the mishaps of this life. One must be amenable to the whole idea that life is imperfect. There was a story of a person who was diagnosed with a terminal disease and was told she had a few years to live. She went on taking medicines, doing exercises, thinking positively, and taking good care of herself, and kept her faith alive. The good news was that she lived beyond the prediction and what is more, she lived long enough to achieve all performances in normal human circumstances. Her faith in God created a good molecule in her which **shut off the emotion of fear**. You can be at peace with imperfection too. Remember, cowards die many times before their deaths. Be brave and think positively in order to gain self-confidence.

Section III: Act As If

Resist the Urge to Criticize and Watch it Get Comfortable not Knowing

Nagging or pecking at others breeds conflicts and conflicts create discord and stress which are emotionally disquieting. One needs to be careful not to be restless and fearful, just because one is ambitious. Life must be lived with a daring aptitude and zest. Let us examine *"Act As If"* in two contexts. In one aspect, one must act just as if one has attained a goal and is consuming it. Another aspect is to baulk at the seriousness of having a misfortune and organize for a redress to nullify the bad effect. *If you have the image of a catastrophe in your mind, you would be subject to fear and fear will numb your ability to inspire yourself.* To succeed, you must think, talk, and do things that are uplifting so that you can change to a new reality that is forthright. You must use your internal psychological thermostat (electrical regulator) to monitor the world and your level of performance and to regulate and redirect you to your desired goal. When you set a goal or you are out to perform a job, behave as if you are fully in charge and dispense your capability in a more inspiring and resourceful way. That builds up self-confidence that is convincingly reassuring to the higher authorities.

Be Aware Life is Not Fair

If Someone Throws You a Ball, You Do Not Have to Catch It

The natural elements, though they act very intelligently and efficaciously, are vulnerable to mistakes and errors. When you are in the worldly system, expect surprises. They were empowered to do what they do by the Lord God Almighty. In the book of Genesis 1:20, God went on to say: *"Let the waters bring forth a swarm of living souls." (Genesis 1:24) "And God went on to say: Let the earth put forth living souls according to their kinds."* These are just examples. Each system is enabled to act automatically on its own. The rain, sunshine, thunder, hurricane, and others have their seasons and activities. All you need is accurate knowledge of things and their eventual behaviour. Nothing is to be taken for granted. Anytime you fall out of sequence in observing the rules of the game, you are sure the consequence will be forthcoming. All it boils down to is like scouts say, "Be prepared." Do not be scared. Elisabeth Kubler-Ross, M.D., psychiatrist and author of the classic 'On Death and Dying', says:

> *"I believe each of us is born with a life purpose. Identifying, acknowledging, and honouring this purpose is perhaps the most important action*

successful people take. They take the time to understand what they are here to do and then they pursue that with passion and enthusiasm."
- *Elisabeth Kubler-Ross, MD.*

Everything has a reason why behind its action and that includes us. The way to have the least number of errors in life is to discover your life purpose, *what you are good at.* List out two or more of your unique personal qualities, such as your mathematical ingenuity, enthusiasm, and inventiveness and list out your methods of enjoying them and expressing these qualities when interacting with others. Practice your qualities the way the world sees them favourably. All smoke without fire is not good. You must put your light on the mountain so that people can see it. You must be effectual and prepared before you start a journey, otherwise, there will be mistakes and headaches and fears on the way. Life must never be approached with levity and mediocrity because it is elusive. It must be consumed with expertise in order to escape its errors.

Search for Truth In Other Opinions and Try to Understand the Statement

What is being said here is that one should never jump to conclusions; one should give a fair hearing to every case. Discussions are not supposed to have winners or losers; they require participants who are expressing their opinions in a socially acceptable manner. In anything we do, we need relationships with friends, family, staff, bosses, the board of directors, customers, partners, associates, audiences, students, teachers, and others. Do not be afraid of shyness or social anxiety. How are we going to associate together? What are the rules and guidelines for the relationship? Marshall Thurber of Money and You Program of Accelerated Business School for Entrepreneurs, San Diego, California, put up the following guidelines as the rules of engagement: Be willing to support our purpose, values, rules, and goals. Speak with good purpose; no making people wrong. If you disagree or do not understand, ask clarifying questions. Make only agreements you are willing and intend to keep. If you cannot keep an agreement, communicate as soon as **practical** to the appropriate person. When something is not working, first look to the system for correction and then propose a system-based solution to the person who is responsible for it. Be responsible. No blaming, no defending, no justifying, and no shaming. Another way to search for truth is to have what is called **heart talk**. To get to the heart of the matter in discussions, it is required to hear what is coming from other hearts. Cliff Durfee, the originator of the Heart Talk Method in a regular meeting at home, in the office or in the town meeting, suggests that a Heart Talk creates a safe, non-judgmental way of allowing people to express opinions that generate teamwork synergy (putting energy together), creativity and intuition.

The Results from Heart Talk

- Enhanced listening skills.
- Constructive expression of opinions.
- Improved conflict resolution skills.
- Improved abilities to accept other viewpoints.

Development of Mutual Respect and Understanding

Creates a sense of communication unity and bonding. Do not compromise your integrity, deal with truth and nothing but truth will set you free.

Have a Heart Talk

A family of eleven individuals had a squabble. The individuals fell out and could not function together anymore after a disagreement on how to continue doing what they had been doing. They normally contributed some amounts of money towards the reconstruction of a wrecked house, farming and paying for a lawyer's service fee in a land case. They used their father's easy chair as an object to pass round and the head of the family chaired the gathering while his deputy recorded what everybody said. One complained he had no money to contribute. Another said his family problems drained his pocket. Another said that the family head was not allowing him to talk. But he was over-ruled because he tended to dominate talks and when his opinion was disallowed, he would feel upset. Others were too poor to contribute.

Results of Heart Talk

1. Agreement that the family integrity should be upheld no matter what.
2. A token amount of money should be contributed to show appreciation.

3. There should be a togetherness dinner and prayer for unity.
4. Love of each other and love of family progress should be a priority.
5. Everyone was free to voice his opinion.
6. There was an amicable ending of the meeting. Everyone went home confidently.

Become a Less Aggressive Driver

We are advised to take it easy in a peaceful way in whatever situation we are in; (Psalm 37:7-9) "Keep silent before God and wait longingly for him. Do not show yourself heated up at anyone making his way successfully. At the man carrying out his ideas, let anger alone and leave rage. Do not show yourself heated up only to do evil. For evildoers themselves will be cut off. But those hoping in God are the ones that will possess the earth." My people are equally admonished to cultivate a humble, discerning, and sagacious attitude in dealing with people when in a challenging situation as follows; one who hurries too much in order to be early in doing the day's chores is always late. One who eats food in haste always bites his tongue. One who rushes unwittingly always falls into a trap. A dog that pursues a lion is risking his life. If you run very fast to reach the target, the one walking slowly and steadily will eventually reach the same target. The one chasing an innocent person is the one that must fall and get hurt. One who is hard-hearted dies earlier than one who has offended the gods. There is one Ibo story that runs like this. One day, the *Tortoise* and the **Dog** challenged each other in a race; the tortoise, a slow-moving animal, claimed it would beat the dog, a fast-running animal in a race. The dog looked down on the tortoise and they decided on a date and a target for the race. On the appointed day, the tortoise, being a smart creature, cooked the dog's food and left it on the side of the road leading to the target. They both took off. The dog ran very fast. Suddenly, the dog came to the food left by the roadside. The dog sat down to eat, feeling comfortable that he was ahead of the tortoise. After finishing the food, the dog went on to have a rest and dozed off. The tortoise walked up to the point and saw the dog fast asleep. The tortoise craftily passed by and reached the target time before the dog. When the dog woke up, it ran very fast but was late because the tortoise was already there at the target. What is the lesson here? All haste without proper discernment makes a clever person a simpleton (fool). Stephen R. Covey The 7 Habits of Highly Effective People wrote in the foreword:

"One of the most profound learnings of my life is this: "If you want to achieve your highest aspirations and overcome your greatest challenges, identify, and apply the principle or natural law that governs the results you seek. How we apply a principle will vary greatly and will be determined by our unique strengths, talents, and creativity, but, ultimately, success in any endeavours is always derived from acting in harmony with the principles to which the success is tied."

Stephen R. Cover
"The 7Habits Of Highly Effective People
Powerful Lessons in Personal hange 1989, (p. 7).

I believe that the tortoise applied this natural law and it earned him smart success. He also applied a wonderful strategy to reach his objective. Moreover, the dog was not focused; he had a divided mind and he was easily distracted. In all your endeavours, try to handle one thing at a time. One after the other and moment by moment and with a good strategy, you get your way successfully. It is not a question of being intelligent but being smart and creative as well as being strategic.

Practice Being In the "Eye of the Storm"

Living a life without preparing for it is miserable. Here, it is meant that you assume the sole responsibility of all ventures in which you engage. You must have trained for most events that you operate and must have the will and experience to endure. You must then have the flexibility to adjust and adapt to changes. You must have the operation squarely on your shoulders. You must have an advisor who is your eyes in everything and also:

"Roll Upon God Your Way and Rely
Upon Him and He Himself Will Act," (Psalm 37:5).

You must also have a go-between who does your wishes. You must not be afraid of innovation (neophobia) or be intimidated by the intensity of a tragedy (photophobia). Here is the story of the *tortoise* and the *lion* to illustrate an experience and sagacity needed in an engagement. One day, the lion told the animals that he was sick. For this reason, many unwise animals went to visit the lion to console him. It happened that this was a plot by the lion to have an easy meal of the foolish animals. The animals that went to the lion never returned. Consequently, their footprints went into the lion's den but there were no footprints coming back. The tortoise came to the entry point of the lion's den and saw the footprints of those going in but did not see the footprints of those coming out. At that moment, the tortoise, the craftiest and wisest of all animals, declined to go in and sent word to the lion that he would come to see him when those who had gone in came back. At this point, the lion knew he had been detected. Being in the eye of the storm will afford you the ability to assess the enormity of a thing and give it its appropriate attention. If you fear the storm, you will never know what a thrill it is. The tortoise used his wonderful intuition to detect the lion's dubious trick. It is not a question of swim or drown; neither is it to swallow the bait and the hook; it is precision-manoeuvring of deliberations to detect the tumultuous centre of an event and give it its corresponding treatment. From the psychological point of view, the tortoise was in danger and he was forced to make a drastic decision to free himself from the impending danger. An experience in a concentration camp, goes thus:

> *"Then he began, "You pig, I have been watching you the whole time! I'll teach you to work, yet! Wait till you dig dirt with your teeth - you'll die like an animal! In days I'll finish you off! You've never done a stroke of work in your life. What were you, swine? A businessman?" This is a reply to this nasty naïve*

> *comment: "I was past caring. But I had to take his threat of killing me seriously, so I straightened up and looked him directly in the eye. "I was a doctor!" "I bet you got a lot of money out of people." "As it happens, I did most of my work for no money at all, in clinics for the poor." But now I had said too much. He threw himself on me and knocked me down, shouting like a madman. I could no longer remember what he shouted. "I want to show with this apparently trivial story that there are moments when indignation can rouse even a seemingly hardened prisoner –indignation not about cruelty or pain, but about the insult connected with it."*
>
> *Viktor E. Frankl*
> *Man, Search for Meaning 1963, (pp.38-39).*

One can observe that even in the eyes of a storm, this fellow still upheld his confidence and challenged the situation without minding. Don't let fear inhibit you from rising in a justified manner; rather, fish it out with a big fishing net and fry it alive. So, certain situations can make you rise, move, and act. It is only a stone or a corpse that remains still. My advice to you is to rise, move, and act in a cordial way as I did to succeed even when the going was very tough.

Once upon a time, a certain man named Nwabueze wanted to get married, though he had no money. According to tradition of Iboland, he went to his brother to get advice on how to get engaged to a girl. His family chose a girl, named Adaeze, in the next village. The girl was humble, hardworking, and obedient to her parents. He disclosed that he had a relative of the girl, Elunwa, to be his go-between in the marriage affair. Elunwa, therefore, organized the first meeting between the two families (that of the girl and that of the man). Palm wine, about 16 gallons, kola nuts, and an initial bride's price or token were given by Nwabueze's family to the girl's family. They all made an offering with a basket of fruits signifying the number of children she would bear. The man was then engaged to her. She was then the wife of the man. From that day, he would be sending palm wine to the family of the girl for 1-3 years, depending on the age of the girl. In the second year of his tending the girl, she became mature. He was informed by the parents. Nwabueze then programmed to finalize the marriage requirements. He had not enough money to pay for the bride price and to perform the fat room ceremony (traditional wedding ceremony). His people took him to a moneylender who gave him all the money that he needed. The two families met again and settled the bride price and agreed on a date to start the fat room ceremony. During the fat room period, which lasted for two weeks, he had to feed his girl, the girl's friend, and her attendants with costly food delicacies according to her demands. After two weeks' fattening, she would be escorted to the local river, Mgbede, to pay her homage to the river goddess and ask for her blessing. The following day she would go to the marketplace to show herself to the people. In the night she would be taken home to her husband's house. In the same night, the elders of her husband's family would come and offer a sacrifice at the family's shrine to the ancestors for her to bear many children. Now, Nwabueze started paying the money to the moneylender. Within a year, his wife gave birth to a baby boy whom the father named "Akubike" (wealth is strength). This man had all it took to endure, to borrow money and to strive to pay back the money but had also to enjoy his wife and son. He had to weather the storm of what it took to exist as a man. He received advice to succeed. As one wise saying goes, "One who does not have an adviser always goes astray." He was helped by the go-between for the right action at the right time. In his next venture, he would be successful because he obtained an adviser who gave expert advice, the go-between to whom he could delegate functions to be performed and the moneylender, a financier, for resources needed for the execution of the procedures. The lesson from this short story is, do not be afraid, because the fearless person paves her way. If you fall in a pit and raise up one of your hands, people around will help to lift you up. But if you keep your hands down, no one will attempt to risk bending down to pull you up as a result of being afraid of falling into the ditch with you. Always be smart, never shy away but be docile in order to succeed. A shy woman delivers a dead child. Therefore, be firm and keep striving until you become confident.

Section IV: Acting, Being More Confident, Achieve Your Full Potential

Many people think they must obtain their confidence before they ever perform. No, you perform before you get it. As you perform, you feel it around you. Whenever you act as if you're confident, you will feel tremendous change in you and those around will acknowledge a new change in you. Always bear in mind that 'action breeds confidence.' Take a typical example from the new-born baby who was born without initial knowledge yet, as time goes by, he or she gradually learns how to move her limbs, how to pick up things and how to move about, etc. This baby is exhibiting full self-trust. Most often, the baby fails and sometimes, she gets hurt, yet keeps on striving. If she fails to continue when she is hurt, she will not grow. As a result, build your self-confidence through trying and failing as President Abraham Lincoln USA did until he succeeded. You will make a difference when you act. As the little baby develops with ingrained self-confidence, so should your effort to increase your confidence. Take a step every moment to enhance your confidence. Change your old way of thinking and visualizing things. Adopt a new strategy daily. One of my English teachers urged us to learn new words each day to improve our vocabulary. More so, you ought to build your self-worth by doing and by using new techniques. Apply the technique of repetition. When you do it over and over, you become more confident. Tell yourself that you are doing well. Praise yourself because how you rate yourself matters a lot. It uplifts your spirit. Negative words have a psychological effect on you and could depress and cripple your self-confidence. Use what the famous authors call 'the power phrase' to encourage your efforts. Say to yourself, I know I am doing well. This kind of word to you is uplifting. You may not know it yourself; I tell you, it has an enormous psychological impact on you.

Act, Get Rid of Negative Posture
How Do You Project Your Body Language?
Fill Your Life with Love

One of the people you must pay heed to is yourself, for it is said, *"You must love your neighbour as yourself"* (Matthew 22:39). You must establish a high level of love, dignity, respect, diligence, cleanliness, care, and thoughtfulness. For it is not easy to give to others what you do not give to yourself. Benjamin Franklin said:

> **"It is hard for an empty bag to stand upright."**
> **www.goodreads.com>663...**

Self-respect is attractive although some sloppy people may term such an attitude as arrogance. You must create high integrity and keep it always. It then follows that you must treat others in the same way as yourself. What is love?

> *"Love is long-suffering and kind. Love is not jealous; it does not brag; it does not get puffed up; it does not behave indecently; it does not look for its own interest; it does not become provoked. It does not keep account of the injury. It does not rejoice over unrighteousness but rejoices with truth. It bears all things; believes all things; hopes all things; endures all things and love never fails."* (1 Corinthians 13:48).

To love, you must cultivate the noble attributes of wholeheartedness and uprightness. There is a story about a man who put established a business in order to help others. He set up a cassava tuber-grating machine for those who made "garri" flour. He advertised the business in the village. Thus, many customers brought their cassava tubers to be grated. The customers were so many that the machine operators were kept on the job all day. The production was profitable. The man's enemy told the government that he had not licensed his business. For this reason, he was ordered by the government to stop production. As a result of this disappointment, he decided to learn how to do agro-business by going back to school. This time, after graduating from the school, he bought machines that prepared the soil, applied fertilizer, and planted the crops. This business also failed because his workers were dishonest and corrupt. He decided to recruit new workers and train them by orientating them towards business diligence and honest behaviour in a business etiquette seminar. They signed an undertaking of their method of business operation. This time, he had everything right and was progressive. He became patient, undaunted, diligent, resolute, and with business acumen or insight, he put up a successful action that resulted in a profitable venture. He was fearless and successful.

Moral Lesson: Whenever you are doing a right thing, no diabolical action or power could stop you because the Lord is the stronghold of the oppressed. So never mind and keep thriving. Whenever you are doing right, be consistent, persistent, and persevering till a good result is achieved.

Keep Asking What is Important
Choose What to Fight Wisely

To live well, one needs preparation because life is evolving and keeps on getting more informed and complicated every day; life-long learning is envisaged. One needs to discern and pick up information regarding relevant pieces of business skills, sales skills, negotiating skills, and successful business practices in success rallies, conferences, and seminars. Aiming at what is competent and suitable requires being armed with the knowledge of management skills, sales, and marketing strategies, communication (connectivity by air and land), and other business facilities by either going back to school or listening daily to programs from audio CDs and audiotapes. If you are under fear and stress, you need to have this tape which teaches audio technology that has claimed to alter brainwave patterns resulting in positive mental and emotional changes to the listener. The audio cassette program is called Holosync Centerpointe tapes developed by Bill Harris of Centerpointe Research Institute (call 1-800-945-2741 or www.Centerpointe.com). Allen Koss, a successful Hollywood television producer, was once in a dire situation in which he lost the edge for creativity, ate more food to soothe the pain coming from the anxiety, stress and vicious cycle of the resulting events. He gained a lot of weight. However, while perusing a copy of Psychology Today, he came across a publication about the Holosync audiotapes. He reached out and procured the tape. He used the tape and picked up his motivational energy and became productive once again. We are advised to listen to Fred Pryor Seminar/Career Track (9757 Metcalf Avenue, Overland Park. KS 66212, phone 1-800-780-8476; www.pryor.com), recorded sources on personal development and business development. We are also advised to listen to audio-programs, on maximum confidence, self-esteem, and peak performance, and A 30-Day Journey from Where You Are to Where You Want to Be at www.jackcanfield.com. Define your purpose in life and organize to achieve it. Do not panic. Put fear behind you otherwise, you will never prosper.

When Trying to Be Helpful, Focus on Little Things

Think of something good and set aside quiet times for meditation and prayer. When planning for a project, it is good to be simple and cost-effective. Aim higher in your expected achievement but start off by dealing with little specifics that compose the main body plan of the enterprise. One thing at a time will accumulate in time to a mountain of desirable results. A man named Obieze was frustrated and angry because he was living in another man's house where he was treated like an unwanted stranger. He set out to build a house in the village of Umunna. He got a designer to give him a plan and what materials he needed to put it up. He set off to collect the materials. He obtained bamboo trunks, palm fronds, and palm leaves and made mats out of them. He went to the forest and procured tree trunks, some without forked branches for beams and a ridge and others with forked branches for supporting pillars. When all the materials had been collected, he hired native house building experts who constructed the roofs with the palm mats, palm fronds, and bamboo trunks. They then lifted the palm mat-thatched roofs and set them in position. The house was to be completed by putting up the enclosing four walls made up of clay bricks. Obieze went on to make clay blocks and once again hired native bricklayers to put up the walls. In time, before the rainy season set in, he moved into the house and celebrated his achievement. Frustration, anger, and stress stirred him up from feeling complacent in another man's house and made him determined to be a man in his own house. Like the author of this book, a condition aroused and motivated me to begin to read and write. Most importantly, these conditions enabled me to achieve a great deal in life especially gaining my self-confidence. I never dreamt of studying up to a doctorate level, but challenges and conditions led me to educate myself to that level. Conditions and challenges again led me to write this book. Accordingly, I wish you to be fearless when you need to act justly; it is just and right to act aright. Remember, those who trust in the Lord are like Mount Zion; unshakable, standing forever (Psalm 125:1).

Be the First One to Act Loving and Reach Out – Be a Better Listener

It is said that all learning affects the brain, accentuating, modifying, and influencing the birth of personality. Good mothering, talk therapy, religion, cognitive behavioural therapy, and teachers as observed by neurologist Martha Denckla, help the brain grow dendrites and make connections to other nerve units. Thus, caresses and cuddling incite arousal of love which triggers the cuddle chemical oxytocin. This chemical makes you feel calmer and behave better. We adjust ourselves to each person we interact with. As a result, we have a flexible self. If inflexibility of self-fixations or compulsions becomes the order of the day, then the situations will be unhealthy, and socially unacceptable. Thus, in a relationship with others, when ill-temper and ill-will prevail, the way to obtain resolution and harmony is to use love as an overture in introducing issues. Though they are inflexible and stiffly opposed to kind words, yet good-naturedness has an appealing force that disarms aggression and rancour. Extend an amicable hand to the warring faction and be all ears in gathering facts and opinions about the contention. But being the first to extend a welcoming hand is not to say that one is weak and permissive or easily yielding to the other's opinion. The way to settle issues of controversy is to obtain **the middle-of-the-road attitude of "live and let live."** One time, the two villages of Umuagu and Umuelu were fighting for a marketplace to be stationed in their territories. A group of elders were empowered to find a resolution to this matter. After studying the locations approved by the villagers, the elders concluded to locate the marketplace on the borderline between the two villages. But the market location finally moved to the village that was commercially inclined and conducive. Both parties to the dispute rejoiced and thanked the chiefs who were the judges.

Imagine You Are Like Everyone Else – Be Punctual Always

In order to boost your self-confidence, form the habit of being punctual. Plan ahead of time and always be punctual. Once you are always, punctual, others would regard you as a reliable individual and would trust you with certain responsibilities. The most important thing is that, you are affirming your authentic self-confidence. As you continuously building yourself-confidence, you must to embrace the twelve habits of punctuality as follows:

1. ***"Make Being Prompt a Priority:*** Form the habit of putting behind you anything that would restrain you being in time. So, let promptness be your motto.
2. *Know Why You want to be Punctual:* For instance, I the author always want to be in time to enable myself to settle down to avoid nervousness. Then organize myself before the event or the job time and to be seen as a responsible and a good time management etc.
3. *Track How Long Tasks Take:* Be organized, make your list and know how long a task takes you to complete.
4. *Use a timer:* Timer would assist you know how long it takes you to finish a task.
5. *Be Ruthless with Your To Do List.:* It is better to say 'no' to something you don't have time for than it is to say 'yes' and then be an hour late.
6. *Be Prepared to be on Time*: Get your things ready before hand.
7. *Give Your Self a Time Cushion:* Always give yourself extract time to avoid being late.
8. *Be Prepared to Wait:* Better to be in time than to be late. It is not a waste of time to be early.
9. *Change Your Thoughts about Being Early:* Maintain positive thoughts for punctual; it is part of being

organized and good time management skills. I love being punctual always. It upsets me for being late.

10. ***Always Leave on Time:*** Always motivate yourself to leave home in time. Just hit the door and drive off or catch your bus.

11. ***Set Up Reminders:*** I love setting reminder on my phone. It is good to form this habit because it helps a lot. You will mis your appointments. So set your reminder at least an hour ahead or the time be early for your appointment.

12. ***Practice the Day Before.":*** This is very crucial for confidence builders; whenever you have essential events as examination, talk, interview, or presentation, practice before hand and most important, do rehearsal.

But we are also unique and different and there is something else we do not understand. We have become aesthetic and have strong ardent desires for happiness in all systems. When in a congregation of people, we should not feel stage-fright or fidget. Depending on what part we play, we should summon up the courage to do our utmost. In Matthew 10:16-17, Jesus said:

> ***"Look, I am sending you forth as sheep amidst of wolves; therefore, prove yourselves cautious as serpents and yet innocent as doves. Be on your guard against men."***

We are now to examine the manner of modesty in handling oneself in association with others. In arranging your choices, priorities, and dreams with respect to the following, let us consider our dealings with:

Faith and spiritual activities.
Family personalities.
Friends involvement and people.
Personal proclivities (inclinations).
Health issues.
Profession (vocational.)
Money and financial activities.
Recreation.

You are to observe certain success demeanours that befit the operative occasions. How to put yourself across with powerful words, phrases, body language, and communication techniques to other people without displaying fear is a matter of preparation for the occasion. In order to avoid sending a wrong message to the audience, one must avoid the following actions: Swinging legs, tapping feet or being fidgety. These actions show you are nervous and lack self-confidence.

- **Crossed Arms:** Crossed arms indicate insecurity.
- **Twirling the Hair or Making Aimless Hand Gestures, Playing with Your Hair**: Also indicates insecurity.
- **Lack of Eye Contact:** This shows you are not focusing on the audience or you are not factual or to be believed.
- **Biting or Licking Your Lips:** This also indicates you are nervous.

- **Open Palms/Closed Palms:** Open palm gestures suggest openness and willingness to help and closed fist suggests lack of authority.
- **Touching the Mouth, Nose, or Chin:** Shows insincerity.
- **Frowning Face:** Shows aggressiveness, antagonism and provocation. There are many simple ways to show that you are relaxed, confident, and successful in handling issues.

Sending Signals of Self-Confidence

To behave as a leader, you must handle yourself as a leader. You must walk like a leader, dress like a leader and talk like a leader and feel self-contented. Make an effective entrance by greeting the client and giving the impression that you are glad to meet with the client. Stand up straight and walk upright proudly. One way of communicating a good body language is to walk straight and tall even though you may not be a tall person. Be a strong presence. First and foremost, maintain good eye contact with others by smiling always. They "hear" your eye contact; they "hear" your smile and they "hear" your total body language. Communicate with relaxed energy. Deliver your message with excitement. Listen actively. Lean forward and watch the person speaking to you. Dress with respect and in a professional fashion in an august way. You must stay connected through networking and describe your profession in a vivid style.

Just Lean into It – Take a Plunge

Sometimes, you must take a plunge notwithstanding whether you are prepared for what is coming on. It is something like going out to fish. You do not know whether you are going to catch fish or not, but the experience is always at the back of your mind. Let us study what happened when a lion planned to eat a sheep's young ones. The lion begged a sheep to allow one of her young ones to babysit her young one. The sheep agreed but told the lion to wait for her in the night. Then the sheep summoned all her young ones to locate who was astute (*judicious)* enough to out-manoeuvre the lion and to escape if the lion tried to kill and eat her up. She located **Nwaebuleako** (the smartest among the sheep's children and the youngest among them) who said that he was so alert that he would know before the lion even thought to kill him. However, the mother sheep sent him to the lion. The lion planned to kill **Nwaebuleako** in the night by causing him to sleep on the left-hand side which was the lion's powerful hand. **Nwaebuleako** devised his own strategy by putting the lion's baby on the left-hand side. In the middle of the night, the lion woke up and suddenly and quickly grabbed the one sleeping on the left-hand side, killed it, and started to eat it. There and then, the lion discovered that it was her baby that she killed. She became angry and started searching for **Nwaebuleako**. By that time, **Nwaebuleako** had already slipped away and had run home. **Nwaebuleako** played a smart role here. It is good to be smart when you are in a danger zone; if not, you cannot sort yourself out and escape from the danger. The lesson here is that the dealing with a lion is scary and fearful but the sheep, honest and harmless, decided anyway to take the plunge. She, however, depended on her experience even when dealing with the lion, a formidable and fierce animal. Again, look before you leap. Also never think you cannot do it; yes, you can. Never look down on anybody because no one is insignificant. Besides, if you are the kind of person that people have an ill notion of and look down on, show them your ability; that you can do what others do to succeed and your ardent effort to succeed depends on your ability and willingness. I call it *"surprise-surprise."* Surprise them; do not be afraid. Show them that a short man can equally get things from the top as biblical David did to Goliath. However, I am not asking you to do as David did; rather show them that you are able by paving your way successfully on your life career. Also, let them know that a slow-running stream always runs deeper than the fast-running stream. ***Nwaebuleako is an ultimate strategist.*** The mother lion planned to kill the child of the sheep and ended up killing its own child. Never plan evil against another person because the repercussion may come back to you.

Section V: Experience Your Fear and Act Anyway; Replace the Physical Sensations Fear Brings

We must remember and say what William Shakespeare said a long time ago about when we are confronted by fearful obstacles. He said to the ghost of a murdered king gaping at him:

> *"There is no speculation in those eyes; it is the eye of childhood that fears a painted devil."*
> *- William Shakespeare*

Concentrate on the feelings of courage, boldness, fortitude, confidence, and joy. You can chant the words repeatedly until you feel emboldened to face any obstacle. When you are obsessed by images, sounds, and sights, or threatening incidences, remember to say, "Not for me and mine." In this instance, we are encouraged to embark on a venture without having got the prerequisites needed for the procurement of the desired goal. For instance, a lady desired to go overseas for higher education, but she did not have the financial resources and the facilities for going overseas. First, she started to apply for admission to foreign universities. She obtained admission to two universities but the money for the expenses involved was not there. She tried to secure a national scholarship. This also failed. She tried to involve the company where she was an employee, but the answer was not what she desired, an overseas education. She kept writing to the universities for the university scholarship overseas. One university offered her the university cooperative scholarship, but she had to pay for her passage to the foreign country. Again, money problems stood in her way. She managed to borrow money to purchase a ticket for her journey. When she arrived at her destination airport, she found out she had a long way to go to reach her host. The airline authorities made the host pay for her journey to her house. Finally, she was overseas, but her education plan was disrupted because her host made her abandon her original plan. She had to start to work and earn some money. Then she had to apply for admission to another university. At every stage, her ambition faced a roadblock. But since she had plunged into this venture, there was no going back. She had to overcome the problems with great determination and endurance. She had to over-ride all challenging situations to reach her goal. She obtained her undergraduate matriculation and was heading for the Masters graduate course. Within a short space of time, she got her master's degree and got a good job as well. It had been an arduous venture with good results. The woman's determination made this possible. We sometimes must take off unprepared and un-equipped but with the readiness to face challenges; success becomes our reward in the end.

When You Triumph in the Face of Fear, Confidence Sets In

It is said that in every cloud, there is a silver lining. Nothing is entirely bad. During the Nigeria-Biafra civil war, a man was called upon to get ready to go to the war front. Every day, news of fierce fighting and many casualties arrived in the military camp. Everyone who had been selected to go to the war front panicked in fear of what was going to happen. One of the men selected to go to war, every night, went on his knees praying. One day, he had a vision that he would be saved. At long last, the appointed day for departure arrived. As he was preparing to go on board an army truck ready to convey soldiers to the war front, he was recalled by the captain of the army garrison. He was told his office wanted him back. He had been conscripted into the army. He was not a regular soldier. He oversaw the electrical generator in the Biafra radio/television broadcasting station. The soldiers seized him on his way to the bank. Following the request by his station, he was released. At last, he remembered the whole episode and thanked God for his mercy. Always backup your dilemma with prayer because prayer saves one from danger.

I remember my triumph at displaying my graduate pictures and the American flag on my wall to rejoice and to reflect on the ups and downs I went through to achieve those precious goals. The American flag reminds me what I went through to become an American citizen and all my efforts towards success. I feel good whenever I see these images. Like when the Igbos achieve their goals, they celebrate it by shouting hip-hip-hip hurrah three times. I also say hip-hip each time I look behind. I look behind and reflect on all the odds I went through and my achievements. Then I raise my right hand and say hip-hip-hurrah! You yourself can say it. Do not be afraid to raise your right hand and say **hip-hip hurrah!** You must uplift yourself before anybody does that for you. Hence,

> *"There is power and strength in every voice! Let yours be heard! "Let nothing that you ever go through silence your voice. Your voice is your power; find ways to express it."*
> - *Margaret Dureke*
> *Words and Phrases of Wisdom*
> *For Spiritual and Emotional Upliftment 2002,*
> *(p.17).*

Scale Down the Risk

The tortoise said, *"Slow and steady wins the race."* In Mathew 6:22-23, it is said: *"The lamp of the body is the eye.* If then your eye is bright, your whole body will be bright but if your eye is **weak,** your whole body will be dark." Our elders say, "The snail, with its slimy soft muscular foot, glides over rough surfaces without being hurt." If your fear is real and the feared object must be surmounted, the easy way is to reach the height in small gradual steps of action. The spider wanted to have a meal of other insects, big and small, but it had no power to catch them. As a result, it spun a cobweb which it laced with a sticky wax. It then hid itself waiting to see its victim. No sooner had it finished its cobweb, than a fly came along and was caught by the sticky cobweb. Immediately, the spider sprang into action and put more wax on the visiting fly, thereby disabling and entrapping the fly. It then set out to enjoy its meal. For this reason, we should not be frightened by the enormity of a task but should approach with caution, nibbling at it a little bit at a time.

Section VI: Reject Rejection - Just Say Next

Always know who you are and what you want. You will then know when your enviable values have been discredited by an unwarranted rash judgment and even if the judgment is true, you should feel that you have laboured honestly and should be rewarded accordingly. **Do not accept a "No" as an answer**. Beware of the callous wolf. If the judgment is accurate, take it as an opportunity to improve and acquire more proficiency.

Do not be cowed or shy away in fear and dismay. Little by little, you will conquer the fortress of your fear and of its discouraging strategy. Rona, a 43-year-old lady, went to school to register for the courses she intended to study, and she was told her credits were below the requirement. She was told to do a preparatory course for six months before she could register for any course. She undertook to do the course and succeeded in graduating from the course in three months. She then registered for the full undergraduate courses. After this, she sought where she would be gainfully employed. But her distractors or 'talk-down individuals' continued to tell her that she would not make it because of her financial constraints. The spirit kept telling her to keep moving on and keep away from those 'road-blockers' who told her that she would not succeed. Being a positive individual, she did not yield. Although, it was not rosy all the way, yet each stage came up with its respective merits and demerits and at last, the desired goal was achieved. She earned her Bachelor's degree in science and did not end there. She kept on striving till she completed her studies to Doctorate level. Then she was employed in a hospital setting. Rona refused to be deterred and kept striving to the next stage and eventually accomplished her target.

One can see that Rona was a determined person and that was why she never succumbed to intimidation. Today she is a successful woman. Therefore, Rona is worthy of emulation. In 1970, one of my townsmen, who was a teacher and an altar boy, just after morning mass spoke to a group of my friends and me, as we were talking about learning. He said to us, "Do not shy away from learning even from little children." Even though the person you are learning from is mocking you, don't mind; just get his or her wisdom as that is the most important thing. On another occasion, one of my indigenous religious sisters said to me, "whenever you need something, be patient till you get what you need." She added that many people fail to succeed as a result of being impatient and afraid. And so, cultivate patience when you're struggling to achieve your ambition. Never mind what people say or think about you for all human beings have psychological "weaknesses." One of the famous authors called it psychological "cracks." And he said:

"We all have Psychological "cracks." The only difference is that some manage to cover them up cleverly, while others do not." All of us have psychological cracks, cracks in the "basement" that is, at the biological level, cracks at the level of our passions, cracks at the intellectual level. None of us is exempt from such difficulties. The consequences of original sin create these cracks, this brokenness.."
Marie-Dominique Philippe
Wherever He Goes" 2002, (p. 170-171).

Never allow the 'road-blockers' to ruin your career. Always follow the wise and positive individuals who have positive influences on your confidence-building.

"Positive minds produce positive lives. Negative minds produce negative lives. Positive thoughts are always full of faith and hope. Negative thoughts are

always full of fear and doubt." "...It shall be done for you as you have believed..."
- Joyce Meyer
Quotes: positive minds produce positive lives
https://www.azquotes.com/quote/735420

When there is fear or danger, do not mind. Just brave it out and say to yourself, "I will move forward no matter what happens. Believe me, it will work for you as you desire. As you move on, be mindful of whom you associate with. If you are weak, never mingle with a weak person but a strong one, otherwise, two of you will fall into a deep pit. Remember, some friends are enemies of progress. They will pamper and flatter you as if they love your progress but behind you, they are nought but wish you failure. I would have not been what I am today if I had listened to such fellows when I wanted to join the religious order. A lot of these 'distractors' kept on discouraging me. They found me unintelligent and lukewarm. Really, they instilled fear in me but I ignored them. It was only my mother that fortified and encouraged me to go ahead. Right now, I am religious as well as a highly educated person. If I had allowed fear to get hold of me, I would not have made it. The same thing happened when I was enrolling for a graduate course. I was faced with financial constraints, yet I did not quit. Fear gripped me and I thought of calling it quits but the spirit of ultimate confidence emerged and I never quit. Today I am a graduate with the highest honour. You can do it; never quit. If you dare quit, never blame anybody but yourself. Whatever you do, beware of the 'road-blockers' and avoid them. Most importantly, it is what you believe that works for you. Know what you want and go for it. Work harder and then tell yourself, "Even though I should walk in the valley of darkness, no evil should I fear (Psalm 23:4). Once you make the right choice, do not be afraid. Uplift your spirit and move on. Never have two minds as you pursue your career; act as if you have achieved it. Rather be focused and be courageous. If you dare to make mistakes along the way, learn from them and keep thriving. From our mistakes, we learn. Be mindful of ups and downs on your journey towards success. Many people are scared of mistakes, failure, and disappointments. If you are among them, do not mind. **It shall be well with you as it is well with me today.** Whatever you do, try to set your timeline to attain your objective.

In the United Kingdom, on Monday, 8th March, 2010, I began to sing this song for myself when I achieved another goal that led me into fear. The song is, 'My child, stop crying; your God is very much near to you…, Chinedum, stop crying; your God leads you, Oh! Stop crying, your God is …' In fact, this particular goal attainment is another turning point in my life. And this made me believe that when you cling to God, he will always answer and attend to your needs. With him all things are possible. With God on our side, no one can be against us (Roman 8:31). Once God says yes, no one can say no. Once more, **patience, endurance, and faithfulness** are very crucial as you pursue your aim. The intelligent ones say, "Endurance is a mighty power and patience gives many good things." Once you have these three virtues, you will prosper. Be responsible. "Responsibility is often defined as our response to God's ability. To be responsible is to respond to the opportunities that God has placed in front of you. Always guard against fear. It is your sole duty to commit yourself towards realisation of your career. Never allow or accept any defeat. Oblige yourself to total commitment. The glory goes to you if you succeed, and blame goes to you if you fail. I urge you to prosper and live to fulfil your desire aspiration. Avert yourself from choosing a regrettable career. What is a regrettable career? Choosing to take hard drugs, to be an armed robber, a murderer, a prostitute, etcetera; avoid them because these will get you stuck on the way. Choose a prestigious career to live a happy and buoyant life. Remember, once you are in a regrettable career, fear, stress, and depression will always knock at your door.

Section VII: Commit to Constant and Never-Ending Improvement

Improve in Small Increments that Uplift Self-Confidence

To uphold your self-confidence, you must commit to constant and never-ending improvement. Be up and doing to strengthen your self-confidence. Nowadays, everyone knows what it is to lose a job because of business failure. That is when a business is overproducing without overselling because of lesser consumption of goods. Hence, as a business diversifies operational enterprises, individual workers should also attempt to acquire other functional skills by constant learning and improvement. Every day new technologies and new products flood the market. One should make an effort to acquire new skills, improve the existing jobs and also take on additional skills should anything happen to the present jobs. This is applicable to any other aspect of life. After the Second World War when Japan's physical productive capital had been bombed to rubble, there remained a large stock of human capital comprising industrial skills, knowledge, and experience. This human capital enabled Japan to absorb and adapt foreign technologies. The Japanese purchased the rudimentary techniques of **research know-how** and changed these to their own **product know-how.** They adopted imported technology and developed it into their own indigenous technology. They approached this matter in two basic ways; (1) their **R and D (Research and Development)** modified and perfected imported technologies and (2) the production engineering followed through by designing the machinery according to the new improved techniques, thus creating a new equipment set-up. Thus they upgraded the original industrial structures by advancing more technologically the intricate industrial fabrics by internationalization of native industrial operations. Subsequently, they had high **R and D** resources, scientific, and engineering skills, entrepreneurial, management talents, and venture capital. They aimed at mass production and mass consumption at low cost coupled with accommodating company union's characteristics by introducing employment for life which meant that workers put in their best productivity because they no longer had the fear of losing their jobs. They established incremental developments which created new products annually. This is commitment at large but individuals can do the same by upgrading their job status. **The wise men say, bloom wherever you are planted.** The more effort you make, the more you discover and improve your confidence. Commitment is a key to achieving confidence because the more you are committed, the more confident you are.

In any problem, there must be a solution. One can guarantee how the Japanese quickly resolved their economic problem after the Second World War. That is how it should be in all aspects of life. This is a typical example of what wise people do in the thick of a difficult situation. Do not stop or drop off out of fear whenever you have challenges. Rather, strive harder and find an alternative solution to actualize your goal. There is always an alternative out there; it is left for you to figure it out by researching and contacting those who know how. You do not need to be a genius to be a great thinker or problem solver. It is an in-built grace in us if only you are able to recognize your own. My mother used to tell me this; "My child, you don't stay in a place to watch a masquerade." "Or you cannot fold your hands and sit down for your problem to resolve itself; rather, you have to get up and search for a solution; thus, you have to try other genuine ways to sort out your problem." For this reason, always explore other sources to resolve your problem. Do not give up and never be a quitter because quitters are the losers. Here is a story and words of advice for any confidence-seeker. According to The Greatest Salesman in The World:

"I will persist until I succeed.

In the Orient, young bulls are tested for the fight arena in a certain manner. Each is brought to the ring and allowed to attack a picador who pricks them with a lance. The bravery of each bull is then rated with care according to the number of times he demonstrates his willingness to charge in spite of the sting of the blade. Henceforth will I recognize that each day, I am tested by life in like manner. If I persist, if I continue to try, if I continue to charge forward, I will succeed.

I will persist until I succeed.

"I was not delivered into this world into defeat, nor does failure course in my veins. I am not a sheep waiting to be prodded by my shepherd. I am a lion and I refuse to talk, to walk, to sleep with the sheep. I will hear not those who weep and complain, for their disease is contagious. Let them join the sheep. The slaughterhouse of failure is not my destiny.

I will persist until I succeed.

The prizes of life are at the end of each journey, not near the beginning; and it is not given to me to know how many steps are necessary in order to reach my goal. Failure I may well still encounter at the thousandth step, yet success hides behind the next bend in the road. Never will I know how close it lies unless I turn the corner.

Always will I take another step. If that is of no avail, I will take another, and yet another. In truth, one step at a time is not too difficult.

I will persist until I succeed.

Henceforth, I will consider each day's effort as but one blow of my blade against a mighty oak. The first blow may cause not a tremor in the wood, nor the second, nor the third. Each blow, of itself, may be trifling and seem of no consequence. Yet from childish swipes, the oak will eventually tumble. So, it will be with my efforts of today.

I will be likened to the raindrop which washes away the mountain; the ant who devours a tiger; the star which brightens the earth; the slave who builds a pyramid. I will build my castle one brick at a time for I know that small attempt, repeated, will complete any undertaking.

I will persist until I succeed.

I will never consider defeat and I will remove from my vocabulary such words and phrases as quit, cannot, unable, impossible, out of the question, improbable, failure, unworkable, hopeless, and retreat; for they are the words of fools. I will avoid despair but if this disease of the mind should infect me then I will work on in despair. I will toil and I will endure. I will ignore the obstacles at my feet and keep mine eyes on the goals above my head, for I know that where dry desert ends, green grass grows.

I will persist until I succeed.

I will remember the ancient law of averages and I will bend it to my good. I will persist with knowledge that each failure to sell will increase my chance for success at the next attempt. Each nay I hear will bring me closer to the sound of yea. Each frown I meet will only prepare me for the smile to come. Each misfortune I encounter will carry in it the seed of tomorrow's good luck.

I must have the night to appreciate the day. I must fail often to succeed only once.

I will persist until I succeed.

I will try, and try, and try again. Each obstacle I will consider as a mere detour to my goal and a challenge to my profession. I will persist and develop my skills as the mariner develops his, by learning to ride out the wrath of each storm.

I will persist until I succeed.

Henceforth, I will learn and apply another secret of those who excel in my work. When each day is ended, not regarding whether it has been a success or a failure, I will attempt to achieve one more sale. When my thoughts beckon my tired body homeward, I will resist the temptation to depart. I will try again. I will make one more attempt to close with victory, and if that fails, I will make another. Never will I allow any day to end with a failure. Thus, will I plant the seed of tomorrow's success and gain an insurmountable advantage over those who cease their labour at a prescribed time. When others cease their struggle, then mine will begin, and my harvest will be full.

I will persist until I succeed.

Nor will I allow yesterday's success to lull me into today's complacency, for this is the great foundation of failure. I will forget the happenings of the day that is gone, whether they were good or bad, and greet the new sun with confidence that this will be the best day of my life.

> **So long as there is breath in me, that long will I persist. For now, I know one of the greatest principles of success; if I persist long enough, I will win.**
>
> **I will persist.**
> **I will win."**
>
> *From the Ancient Scroll Marked III*
> *In The GREATEST SALESMAN IN THE*
> *WORLD 1968, (pp. 63-67).*

Do not be overwhelmed with fear. Always resist it and persist till you find your way. Be zealous in striving as you sing forward ever and backward never. Claim yourself as an instrument of fulfilment and achievement and always nod your head and pat your back for every accomplishment made. Once you strain harder, "Failure will never overtake you if your determination to succeed is strong enough." Attainment will be your best bet and discouragement will never have a space in your achievement. I encourage you to demonstrate high ability and willingness as you roll towards the valley of success; say to yourself "I will persist; I will win and I will be successful."

You Cannot Skip Steps

Most people are often scared by the enormity of tasks contained in projects that are drawn up for solving problems. Life has grown by consistent additional regular increments. Trees grow big by adding, every year, rings of growth called annual rings. We, as individuals, started our lives in our mothers' wombs as single cells and finally grew into bodies containing more than 100 trillion cells. However, no matter what our dreams are or how great they are, we have to begin with one step and persistently add steps without leaving out any component in order to reach the aim. Our dreams for survival contain physical and psychological components which include self-image, fears, insecurities, strengths, noble ideas, life's orientation, desire, jealousy, and love. These faculties in our lives are stages we have to pass through, add to our personality structure and grow into maturity. You see, a fruit tree starts with a farmer planting the seeds. Then the farmer has to remove the weeds to enable the seedlings to have exclusive availability of nutrients for growth. Consequently, the young plants blossom into fruition. At the end, ripe fruits appear and are harvested. My native people do say, "It takes three months to grow food crops but a lazy and fearsome person fears to engage herself in the tasks involved in food production even when the time for doing so is short. However, we should not fear the threatening nature of a project but should pay attention to the incremental steps needed for achieving the goal, just as the farmer did not skip the weeding of the unwanted grasses and yet expected to have a good harvest.

Section VIII: Be Confident in Asking for What You Need

"Ask and it will be given to you; seek, and you will find; Knock, and the door will be opened to you." Jerusalem Bible (Matthew 7:7-9). When asking for information, direction, assistance, support, money, and time that you need to fulfil your vision and to make your dream come true, you will need to be well informed so as to know when to **act, delegate, delay or ignore decisions**. Why is information necessary? It is necessary because accurate knowledge about real-world conditions, problems about real people, things, and enterprises, and about what is required for achieving a good result from a deliberation, is essential. From Jerusalem Bible (John 8:31-32), Jesus said to the Jews, "If you make my word your home, you will indeed be my disciples; you will learn the truth and the truth will make you free." Accurate knowledge from the truth is needed. Some of the truths are contained in the Beatitudes from our Lord's sermon on the mount (Matthew 5:1-17), "Happy are those that hunger and thirst for what is right: they shall be satisfied. An ideal way for asking is expressed in our Lords' prayer in the Jerusalem Bible as follows:

"So you should pray like this: 'Our Father in heaven, may your name be held holy, your kingdom come, your will be done, on earth as it is in heaven. Give us today our daily bread. And forgive us our debts as we have forgiven those who are in debt to us. And do not put us to test, but save us from the evil ones."
(Matthew 6:9-13)
From Jerusalem Bible 1974, (p. 11).

There are Four Parts to this Plea

1. Honour to the benefactor.
2. Submission and humility from the recipient to the donor.

3. What is being asked for, and
4. Pleading for mercy and protection from all unforeseen circumstances. Each section has an attendant dedication and sincerity of motive of good standing. The recipient must be of good character and the donor must be of a resourceful status with integrity and compassion, able to relieve pain and resuscitate one to a normal happy mood. There are many philosophies that govern what you're asking for and getting what you want or need in your life. Here, Mark Victor Hansen and Jack Canfield recommend that you learn t following from their book, The Aladdin Factor:

1. **Ask as If You Expect to Get It:** Ask with a positive expectation from a place you have already been given it.
2. **Assume You Can:** Believe that you can get a promotion provided you are of good standing.
3. **Ask Someone Who Can Give It to You:** Earmark who has the authority to make a decision about it.
4. **Be Clear and Specific:** Be moderate but ask for that which gives you adequate satisfaction.
5. **Ask Repeatedly:** One of the principles of success is persistent continuity of persuasion.

ASK- Ask- Ask- with Absolute Confidence

Our elders say, "Anyone who always asks questions is always guided to the correct action. Why do people ask questions and what are the right questions? When a group of people or a person wants to start a business enterprise manufacturing goods or planning service capacity, the question arises, how do I start off? Why do I/we want to start it? Where are we going to set it? When do we start? What kind of products will be needed? And who will buy the products? There are many questions and answers that must be settled before the outline of what to do shows up. Subsequently, anytime you want to set up your business, remember *Five-* **Ws' and One -H** *(Why, Where, When, What, Who, and How.* As a result, these '5 Ws' and '1 H' will always give clues on how to start off. In reality, **fearsomeness, hopelessness, and disappointment** are part of the dangers in the complex operation of putting a new product or service on the market, with the odds at least five to one against any new product.

Section IX: When Your Fear is Really a Phobia

When does fear escalate to terror?

We are all designed with the original pattern encoded in our DNA but produced under the influence of the environment and run under the control of modulating motivating chemicals, the foremost of them being dopamine. Fear is a life-saving faculty of fight-or-flight that is installed in us to forewarn us and prepare us for the right action in concert with the environment. Our five senses (eye-sight; ear-hearing; nose-smell; tongue-taste; skin-touch) monitor the environment for the right information with reference to the standard optimal information encoded in the brain. When the information coming from the outside is above or below the normal requirement for an optimal performance, fear is turned into a phobia, something hateful. Of all impressions in our memory, ninety percent come from the eyes. More so, when we subject ourselves to watching violent television shows, horror, and murder films, torture-laden films, cartoon-like violence caricatures, and such like disgusting expressions, we inundate our memories with hateful images that will first sink in and later rise in the way we express ourselves in a sudden, unexpected and disastrous way. In acquiring this hateful habit, individuals dilute the good behavioural standards encoded in us until they end up expressing themselves in panic attacks, restlessness, fleeting thoughts that are not connected, dizziness, headache, agitation, recurring episodes of sudden acute anxiety, and phobias. Take, for instance, this scary story of September 2011 in the United States of America. After 9/11, the lives of the average American men and women changed. Everybody then lived in fear. Security was tightened up. There had been distrust and suspicion in the minds of everybody. People were afraid to answer questions when someone was asking for direction. People panic as a result of fear and uncertainty. Airlines lost jobs and customers because everybody was afraid to fly. The 9/11 episode on USA soil instilled permanent fear in the minds of many people. However, the courageous ones later overcame it and began to fly again. Hence, no condition is permanent. No matter the situation, one has to move on. However, we cannot cease to travel or apply for our visas; we have to move on, come rain, come sun. Americans are now afraid and are developing phobias about the countries they see as terrorists to their country. There is nothing one can do to convince them that anybody in those countries is friendly to them. More than a thousand studies have shown that watching media violence shows has led to real violence in real people making people hate people; the younger you are the greater the influence. Take for instance the scary bible stories about the Ten Commandments of God and hellfire that instil fear in some of the Christian believers. The commandments of the Lord are meant to make us fear God and respect human beings. But some people have developed phobias and do not even want to hear about it. This picture of hell is meant to instil permanent fear and hatred of sin and hell but also, when it sticks permanently, it could lead to a stressful mood of anxiety, neurosis and phobias. In general, images of fear, horror, danger, and violence hit the right hemisphere of the brain harder than the left and those dominant in the right hemisphere are badly affected, making them susceptible to violent tendencies. Another example is that in ex-soldiers, fear has become part of them. If one has a relative who is an ex-soldier just watch him or her; just a little sound makes him panic. Progress always involves risk. You cannot steal a second base and keep your foot on the first (Frederick Wilcox).

No Sweat, No Sweet

This is a story of farming in the Igboland in South-eastern (Nigeria) because farming is a labour-intensive occupation that scares indolent people who are unwilling to suffer for the good fruits of hard labour. On a Monday morning in the early part of February, young men sharpen their machetes and get ready to go to the bush to clear it for farming. Women and grown-up children join in the bush-clearing exercise. It takes about one month to clear the bush and a few weeks more are allowed for the cleared bush to dry up. At the end of March, the dry leaves and trees are set on fire. At this point, the arrival of the first rain is expected. When the rains come, planting of the crops starts in earnest.

After all the planting has been done, the weeding period sets in. Different kinds of grass and the cut trees grow back among the crops. They have to be removed. Weeding takes three stages; (1). Removing the weeds and trees that have grown back (2). Hoes - tilling the soil to open it up for nutrients to reach the crops; (3). Using native trowel-like sheet metal scoops that the farmer uses to collect all the weeds together in random heaps, thus keeping the entire farm clean. By this time, heavy rains have started and it is difficult to work in the rain. But diligent, hopeful people go on laboriously to do their farming to ensure a good harvest. Yams are staked; maize is watched for loppers, earworms, corn borers and aphids which must be destroyed. Early harvesting of leafy vegetables can be done. In May, maize is ready for harvest. This means that three months' labour is what it takes to feed well, or starve in the case of a lazy man. They say in Latin "Labour omnia vincit"- This means that labour overcomes everything. During the months of May, June, and July, when the rains are heavy, the sloths hide inside their houses while the enduring and energetic ones in their rain-proof suits go to the farms and tend to the crops. The weeds and the pests have to be nipped in the bud to ensure maximum growth and yield. During the growth period, fertilizer is applied.

In August and September, the first harvest of yams takes place while the yams are still in growing conditions. Care is taken when cutting away the yam tubers not to harm the fibrous roots because after the tubers have been removed, the dug holes are closed back and the yam crops go on growing new leaves and putting out new tubers for the final harvesting. Again, fertilizer is applied for the second time. In October, yams grow bigger. November is the final yam harvest month. The celebration of the new yam festival is done in September and the final yam festival is celebrated in December. Before these festivals, the farmers have offered sacrifices to their forefathers with the new yams. Meanwhile, the Christians give thanks to God Almighty in their various churches. After all the crops have been harvested, cassava is left in the farm to mature for two years before harvesting. There is a special celebration by young girls who have previously and collectively joined their aunts and sisters in crop cultivation during the intensive farming season in some communities in Igboland. After the final harvesting, the girls gather in groups, fetch firewood and carry it to their aunts and sisters. This ceremony is called "Ibuje nku"- carrying firewood to the elder sisters. The girls go to the farms to weed them then feast on the delicacies offered to them by their host sisters and aunts. They receive entertainment and gifts and stay with the hosts for "Izunato" eight days. It is said by Wordsworth "Oh blessed retirement, the glory is mine; How happy is he who reigns in shades like this a youth of labour with age of ease." Smollett said, "Glory is the fair child of peril." **No sweat, no**

sweet. Subsequently, one must work hard to maintain his/her confidence in all aspects of life.

You have to Act Confidently Until You Attain Confidence

To maintain your self-confidence, you should act confidently. How do I feel confident? 'How you present yourself affects your confidence and affects how other people perceive you.' For this reason, do the following,

1. Look smart by dressing smart.
2. Walk upright and smile at people.
3. Sit upright and listen attentively.
4. Always exhibit a pleasant image of self.
5. Avoid slovenliness of self; it devalues your self-confidence.
6. Act as if you're changing your old thoughts, words, body language, and your habit of eating, style of dressing, to create a new you.
7. Act as if you're living confidently now.
8. Form a habit of learning new ideas every day.

Section X : The Challenge

High Intention-Low Attachment

According to Alberto Salazar, "If you want to achieve a high goal, you are going to have to take some chances." This is shown by the story below. A boy named Paul suddenly became sick with bad eyesight which threatened to make him blind. He had had a smallpox attack which affected his eyes. He was referred to the Sudan Interior Missionary Eye Clinic, Kano, Nigeria for treatment. He was promised a cure for his bad eyesight but he had the challenge of having no money. A relative helped him to go from Enugu to Kano, Nigeria. He arrived at Kano and was received by the Missionary establishment. He stayed in the hospital until he recovered his sight. He came home and went to Lagos, Nigeria to start going to school. His brothers helped him and he studied for two years in the college. Paul obtained a certificate that enabled him to secure a job in a bank where he then worked and later retired. His son also obtained a university education and secured a lucrative job in the same bank as his father. Paul was in need with the challenge of going blind, but, with the help of his good relatives, he had the chance of seeing again and a whole world of goodness opened up for him. The Missionary Clinic doctors treated him for free. **Taking chances means success**. If Paul was afraid, he would not have succeeded.

Joyce Mayer also inspired us with this injunction, "Don't Give Up! No matter how bad the condition of your life and you, don't give up! Regain the territory the devil has stolen from you. If necessary, regain it one inch at a time, always leaning on God's grace and not on your own ability to get desired results."

Another story of challenge goes like this. There was a family of a man known as Nzeike who had two wives, and each woman had two boys. The eldest son, Uzochi, graduated from a college and was preparing to go to a university. His father refused to allow him to go to university, saying he would rather be paying attention to the education of the children of the other woman. So Uzochi invited his senior uncle Ugonna to come and advise his father. When the appointed day arrived, other members of the family gathered in Nzeike's house to discuss his son's university education. When Nzeike insisted that his refusal was categorically unchallengeable, other members of the family decided to put up a plan for a fundraising campaign. They asked Uzochi to obtain admission to a university and the expenses for the first two semesters. The members of the family organized a send-off, a musical entertainment party in which dialogue, dancing, songs, and humour were combined to entertain the invited dignitaries who were expected to donate good amounts of money. The event was successful. The money was raised for Uzochi and paid for the two semesters at the university. Then the organizing group went further to seek a scholarship facility for Uzochi. In the university, Uzochi applied for the award of the university scholarship. He passed the test set for the selection of those who would receive the scholarship awards. As a result, Uzochi obtained the university scholarship for his professional study in Counseling Psychology. Immediately after he graduated from the university, he found work as a counsellor in a hospital. Shortly after, he was made a supervisor of his department. This is an episode of a challenge that gave birth to a chance which resulted in happy events. Take the challenge by the horns, and never fear it.

Another example is about the author. I arrived in the USA as a missionary and after a while, my visa expired. I did not even know what this meant but later I was told. Because of this predicament, fear engulfed me and I did not know what to do. I met someone who directed me on how to resolve the matter. The person I was directed to meet was unkind and mean. I lost every hope but did not quit. I took challenges and chances till I ratified my status. Moreover, challenges followed me all through my stay in the USA, both financially and otherwise. But one thing is certain, I never one day succumbed; rather, all these difficult situations enlightened, empowered, and led me to challenges and tremendous success. One of my friends who knew about my woes and fears called me die-hard when she learnt about my success. You can do the same; never yield. When my mother was alive, each time we went to the farm, and we, the children, tried to be lazy, she would put this proverb across to us;"Uzo di ogologo atukwasa ya ukwu odinkenke" -meaning if we hurry and put in more effort, the work will be finished as early as possible. For this reason, be up and doing till you accomplish the task. Never focus on your past failure, but rather let your focal point be on your progressive effort.

Be Willing to Pay the Price

Once you set a goal, you must do everything humanly possible to achieve it.

Be up and doing to achieve it. How do you achieve it? You achieve by:

1. Planning well.
2. Developing confidence.
3. Being optimistic.

4. Being focused.
5. Devoting your time to achieving it.
6. Doing a lot of research to learn how others succeeded.
7. Amending where you fail to get it right.

Section XI: Practice – Practice - Practice
How to Deal with Obstacles

We are to start with maxims that give enlightenment on how to face life.

> *"Our greatest glory consists not in never falling but in rising every time we fall."*
> *Oliver Goldsmith*
> https://quoteinvestigator.com/2014/05/27/rising

A Japanese proverb states: *"Fall down seven times, get up eight times."* A wise Igbo man also states: "A man falls eight times, rises up nine times."

Obstacles in Life are Created by the Following:

1. Doing things without first learning how they are and how they work.
2. By developmental psychological suppression of endeavours of an emerging mind of a child by muting its autonomy so much that it makes the child have a life-long sense of fear and self-doubt.
3. By natural phenomenon such as being born blind or having a devastating crippling accident.

Every stage in life has its attendant ability and disability. Good preparedness in a stage means good rewards without rancour but ill-preparedness yields a sad result that spells malcontent and disconcerted fear. Each time one has the ambition to inculcate the good qualities of methods of operation into one's life, there is always an obstacle rearing its head to stop the aspiration. In every aspect of an encounter one has to have an enduring and humble mind not only to do the positive work in growing up but also to have an equal force to combat the ensuing repulsive energy. Whenever success is attained, energy has been spent on both positive and negative aspects of a task. Let us consider what we need to do with respect to the following good attributes of life. The ancient people promulgated certain truths and how to achieve them. The book of Proverbs 1:1 says, "for one to know wisdom and discipline, to discern the sayings of understanding, to receive the discipline that gives insight, righteousness, judgment, and uprightness to give to the inexperienced ones shrewdness to a young man knowledge, and thinking ability." (Ephesians 6:11). "Put on the complete suit (uniform) of Armor from God that you may be able to stand firm against the machinations of the devil." In the ancient Egyptian Mysteries, the Neophyte (a convert) was required to manifest the following attributes:

1. Control of thought (thoughts give rise to words, words to actions).
2. Control of actions or justice (unswerving righteousness of thought and action).
3. Steadfastness of purpose or fortitude.

4. Identity with spiritual life, or higher ideals (temperance which is an attribute attained when the individual has gained conquest over the passionate nature).
5. Evidence of having a mission in life.
6. Evidence of a call to spiritual orders of the priesthood in the mysteries; the combination of which was equivalent to prudence or a deep insight and graveness that befitted the faculty of seership (priesthood).
7. Freedom from resentment, when under the experience of persecution and wrong (courage).
8. Confidence in the power of master as teacher.
9. Confidence in one's ability to learn (Fidelity).
10. Readiness or preparedness for initiation.

A fat woman wants to be an athlete. Her fatness is an obstacle. She has to trim down to an acceptable level by going on an adequate prescribed diet program for doing so. She then has to take to the gymnasium for physical exercise. Then she is ready to train to be an athlete in any contest of strength. Let us look at food hazards as obstacles in eating. For instance, if one wants to eat cassava fufu, she has first to peel away the inedible bark of the cassava tubers. The cleaned tubers are then put in water and allowed to remain in water for five days to ferment. By so doing, the hazardous poison contained in the tubers is dissolved away. The fermented tubers are now soft and are sifted to separate the fibrous part from the pulp. The pulp is cooked twice and pounded twice to produce cassava fufu. There is always this process of refinement of a raw material for procuring a finer required part in every engagement in life. The obstacle has to be removed. Obstacles jeopardize and obstruct the road to success in any event and horrify those who are ambitious to succeed.

Cope with the Inevitable

William James, a Philosopher stated:

> *"Acceptance of what has happened is the first step to overcoming the consequences of any misfortune." Along the road of life, there are shocks and jolts and we have to bend like the willow and absorb them in order to live longer and enjoy a smoother lifetime. We can turn over a new leaf by reading a Mother Goose rhyme: "For every ailment under the sun, there is a remedy or there is none. If there be one, try to find it; if there be none, never mind it."*

Source: https://www.quotes.net/images/1913.png

Do not Get Even with Your Enemy

Do not Get Even with 'Energy Vampires'

Jesus said, (Matthew 5:43-44) "You have heard that it was said, you must love your neighbour and hate your enemy. However, I say to you: continue to love your enemies." This statement is for spiritual as well as for psychological health because when you hate your enemies, your resentment has power over your sleep, your appetites, your blood pressure, your health and happiness, and can create chronic hypertension and heart trouble. That statement by Jesus is teaching us how to keep away from having high blood pressure, heart attacks, depression, stomach ulcers, and other emotional ailments. *Physicians say that a fit of anger and fearful panic can kill a man with a weak heart.* When Jesus was preaching that we should forgive our enemies "Seventy times seven", He was actually talking about a business cooperative attitude. For example, an attorney in Sweden had no money and needed a job badly. He could speak and write several languages. For this reason, he applied for a job position as a correspondent for some firms doing business in importing and exporting commodities. Most of the firms replied saying they had no need for his service. But one man in a firm wrote to the attorney saying the attorney was wrong and foolish and that he did not need a person like him because he could not write good Swedish and made a lot of mistakes. In return, the attorney, infuriated, thought of retaliating by paying the man from the firm back in the same way. Then the attorney changed his mind saying maybe he made real mistakes. The attorney wrote to the firm saying:

"It was kind of you to go to the trouble of writing to me. I am sorry I was mistaken about your firm being a leader in this business field. I am sorry and ashamed of myself. I will study Swedish language more diligently to correct my mistakes. I thank you for helping me on the road to self-improvement."
A few days later, the attorney received a letter from the firm telling him he had obtained the job. You see how "a soft answer turned away wrath"? The attorney just applied the right cooperative

principle of tolerance in a job. Be mindful of the energy vampires (people who are pessimistic and negative will drag you down.) These people could drain you and make you feel discontented. 'They are those people that often complain a great deal, use you and do not give anything positive back, or who make themselves feel good at your expense'
by Litvinoff (2004).

Always endeavour to associate with those who would enhance and value your life. 'Energy vampires' have negative ideas. Avoid them completely. The Psalmist calls them 'bigotry and evil people.' He asks you to avoid bigots as those will influence you negatively.

The Power of Positive Thoughts

The right choice of positive thoughts will put us on the highroad to solving all problems. The Roman emperor, Marcus Aurelius (161-180 AD) once said in eight words: "Our life is what our thoughts make it." If we think happy thoughts, we will be happy. If we think miserable thoughts, we will be miserable. If we think fear thoughts, we will be fearful. If we think sickly thoughts, we will be ill. If we think failure, we will fail. I do agree and believe in what Marcus Aurelius said. I use myself here as an example; as a USA student, I always maintained positive thinking about my education; I always empowered myself, come rain, come sun, come snow, etc. that I must make it a huge success and I did. What you believe works for you. Believe in yourself and it will work for you too.

Marc Woods, a former British swimmer, who competed at five Paralympic Games, winning 12 medals, believed and it worked for him. Therefore, "let Marc's courage, commitment and unwavering determination help you find the strength to go out and achieve your ambitions too."

The Psychology of Power of Thoughts

A famous British Psychiatrist, J.A. Hadfield asked three men to submit themselves to test the power of mental suggestion on strength, which was measured by gripping a dynamometer (instrument for measuring force.) He told them to grip the dynamometer with all their strength three times. The first time he tested them under normal conditions, their average grip registered 101 pounds. The second time he tested them under hypnotized conditions telling them they were very weak, their grip was 29 pounds. Finally, in the third round, under hypnosis, he told them they were very strong and their grip made an average of 142 pounds. In the third time when their minds were filled with positive thoughts of strength, they increased their physical powers by forty-one percent. Such is the amazing power of positive mental attitude.

The Psychology of Power of Positive Thoughts of Mind

Mary Baker Eddy, the Founder of Christian Science, was walking downtown in Lynn, Massachusetts one cold day. Mary slipped and fell on the icy pavement and was knocked unconscious. Her spine was so severely damaged that she was convulsed with spasms and the doctor said she would die. But lying on what was supposed to be her death bed, Mary Baker Eddy opened her Bible and was led by divine guidance to read these words from Matthew 9:2:

> *"And behold, they brought to him a man sick of palsy, lying on a bed and Jesus said unto the sick of palsy, Son, be of good cheer, thy sins be forgiven thee. Arise, take up thy bed and go unto thine house." And he arose and departed to his house. These words of Jesus, she declared, produced within her such a strength of faith, such a surge of healing power that she, "immediately got out of bed and walked." "That experience," Mrs. Eddy declared, "was the falling apple that led me to the discovery of how to be well myself and how to make others so. I gained the scientific certainty that all causation was mean and every effect a mental phenomenon."*
> - Dale Carnegie
> *How to Stop worrying and Start Living 1985, (P. 117).*

How to Get Rid of an Inferiority Complex

If you are shy and afraid to appear and talk to an audience, you must identify the cause of your shyness. What most people do is to first improve their appearance so as to make themselves proud. You must also train in public speaking, phonetics, and the right vocabulary. Finally, you must prepare yourself and rehearse giving that speech about a hundred times, talking alone in an empty room. You must also try to be nice and social. If you are shy (lalophobia and anthropophobia-fear of speaking before people), that social ineptitude of yours makes you nervous because if you say something stupid, people will disapprove of you, then you can say to yourself that if people do not have a good reaction, it is no big deal.

Here are Five Steps to Improve Your Social Anxiety or Shyness

1. For the first two weeks, if you are taking college classes, smile and say hello to students who are entering the classroom with you. At work, smile and say hello to people who get on the elevator with you. Do the same thing with the cashier when you buy gas or foodstuffs. Be the first to initiate contact.
2. For the second two weeks, speak nicely to people when you are waiting in line at the supermarket, remarking how beautiful the day is. There will be exceptions of people who dislike that but most people will respond to your friendliness and openness. As you go on, you will notice how much nicer the world is becoming.
3. In the third step, offer people compliments and also pat them on the back, saying to your classmate, you appreciate his/her viewpoint. Show people that you like them.
4. Reach out to friends by extending invitations or asking a co-worker to have lunch with you. You are now getting to know people who like you.

5. Here, you are to face your fear (social anxiety). You are to join a club (assertiveness training program club or a book discussion club). You are to make a comment in every club meeting, so, you have to prepare and rehearse your comment before a mirror in a room. You may feel nervous the first time you appear and speak to people but as time goes on you will be comfortable around people.

Another Magic Formula for Fighting Worry Situations is to do Three Things

1. Try to analyse the worry situation fearlessly and honestly and figure out what is the worst that can possibly happen as a result of the problem escalating.
2. After finding this out, reconcile yourself to accepting it.
3. Then, calmly devote your time and energy to trying to do something fearlessly by improving upon the worst which you have already accepted psychologically. You can seek expert advice on how to proceed. That is how problems spur people to innovation. Do not get downhearted. Forge on to a new horizon.

On 7th April 2010, young man aged 30 approached me where I was handing out leaflets as I was counselling and approaching girls going in for abortion. This young man came to me and took a leaflet then went through it and returned it to me. Then I asked him to take it home to his girl. He said no, that he had no woman and added that he was heartbroken. He then left. My heart melted and all my attention was on him as he was dragging himself along hopelessly. If you had seen him, you would believe he was really hopeless and heartbroken. I was wondering what could become of his fate. Thus, do not find yourself in that kind of hopeless situation but try to shake your obstacle off and roll on. In any despair, refer to this quotation from the Holy Bible:

> *"Happiness: Do not abandon yourself to sorrow; do not torment yourself with brooding. Gladness of heart is life to a man, joy is what gives him length of days. Beguile your cares, console your heart, chase sorrow away, and it is no use to anybody. Jealousy and anger shorten your days, and worry brings premature old age. A genial heart makes a good trencherman, one who benefits from his food."*
> (Ecclesiasticus 30:21-27)
> From Jerusalem Bible 1974, (p. 939).

This will encourage and fortify you as you walk through an obstacle. An obstacle is what we encounter every moment but sometimes, out of ignorance, we fail to recognize it. Soon, we see ourselves messing up. For instance, one of my relatives recognized his own earlier and fought it early enough. This young man had wanted to be a priest. As soon as he thought about this, an obstacle emerged. The obstacle was this vernacular language problem. He could speak English fluently but he did not know how to speak his native language which was one of the compulsory subjects in the seminary in Igboland of Eastern (Nigeria). However, he did not quit his Divine call; rather, he made an alternative choice by enrolling in the Western side of the country where the English language was in vogue. This young relative of mine made a brilliant decision in fighting obstacles and fear. If you are responsible, obstacles cannot inhibit you from achieving your potential career. Therefore, never let fear and obstacles take away your dream goal; rather, always try your utmost to thrive; you could make it happen. Then, always have an alternative solution to attaining your ultimate ambition.

Section XII: Exceeding Expectations

Exceeding expectations is written in natural expressions. You cannot move your car until you accelerate the speed by adding more force. Every calibration or calculation in nature has a plus (+) or a minus (-) above or below the normal standard. Take, for instance, your body temperature. It is calibrated with cues (signals of information) from the environment at 98.6" F plus (+) or minus (-) 0.5, reaching its zenith (highest point) in the afternoon and its base (lowest point) in the morning. Let us listen to these biblical statements for further clarification of the facts. (James 2:13) "For the one that does not practice mercy will have his/her judgment without mercy. Mercy exults triumphantly over judgment," (teaching forgiveness and endurance). (Matthew 7:13-14), "Go in through the narrow gate because broad and spacious is the road leading off to destruction and many are the ones going in through it, whereas narrow is the gate and cramped, the road leading off into life and few are the ones finding it." Here we must endeavour to succeed with pain and hardship in our daily pursuit of happiness with a persistent struggle. (Matthew 5:41), "And if someone under authority impresses you into service for a mile, go with him two miles." In our regular daily duty, we are expected to go an extra mile by keeping the environment clean and arranging things in order to be pleasing to all people. (Matthew 5:20), "For I say to you that if your righteousness does not abound more than that of scribes and Pharisees, you will by no means enter into the Kingdom of the heavens." (Matthew 23:1-3), "Then Jesus spoke to the crowds and his disciples saying, "The Scribes and the Pharisees have seated themselves in the seat of Moses. Therefore, all things they tell you, do and observe but do not do according to their deed, for they say but do not perform." Here we are advised to exceed the righteousness of teachers for our experience is the best teacher. For "whereas narrow is the gate and cramped the road leading off into life" is another way of saying "by sweating, one earns sweetness. Hard work pays high dividends and does not hurt.

A medical student was worried about passing the final examination, worried about what to do, where to go, how to set up a practice, how to make a living. While reading a book, he came across a passage from Thomas Carlyle (from Famous Quotations, Author on Action and Cheerfulness in Doing More Work), "Our main business is not to see what lies dimly at a distance but to do what lies clearly at hand." This means that the best effort to prepare for tomorrow is to concentrate with all your intelligence, all your enthusiasm, on doing today's work diligently well. Jesus said in Mathew. 6:34), "Never be anxious about the next day for the next day will have its own anxieties. Sufficient for each day is its own badness." Never procrastinate (postpone) till tomorrow what you can do today. Our Lord's Prayer says, "Give us this day our daily bread." We are to plan for tomorrow in our time schedule but we are to execute perfectly the ordeals of today in their entirety. What emotional factors cause fatigue, psychological troubles, boredom, resentment, a feeling of not being appreciated, a feeling of futility, hurry, anxiety, worry - they exhaust a sedentary (sitting) worker, make him/her susceptible to colds, reduce his/her output, and give him/her a nervous headache. Unpreparedness and lack of dedication in one's call in life generate these fearful anxieties when a person is giving a poor performance in a job. Here is a story of a man devoted to his job. The man secured a job but his manager did not want him and tried to induce him to commit an offence. For this reason, he made out a work schedule by which he had to start to work at 6 o'clock in the morning when there was no bus to bring him to work. The worker then made an arrangement with a fellow worker to bring him to work every morning at 5.30 am. This fellow worker failed him because he failed to show up at the place where they had agreed to meet. Then, the worker managed to escape being late to work by hiring a taxicab driver to take him to work. He as well agreed with the taxicab driver to meet him at a restaurant from where he could be taken to work every morning at 5.30 am at the charge of five dollars. The worker had to leave his home at 3.00 am and travelled by bus to a certain point from where he had to walk to the restaurant every morning. The senior manager of the business was told that the worker spent a lot of money every morning riding in a taxicab. As a result, the senior manager asked the worker if that statement was right. After ascertaining the fact, the senior manager told the worker to get receipts for all his taxicab fare payments from the taxicab driver and submit them to his office for reimbursement. The worker was very glad but his manager was disappointed and enraged. The worker spent a lot of money for his transportation to work but at last, his devotion to his job paid off for him. He received the best-worker award for the year in both souvenir and cash bonus. The worker received financial rewards for the extra duties he did after the regular work hours by overhauling the water treatment system and sanitizing the filling machine. The worker had a personal transformation by becoming self-confident, self-reliant, and influential among the workers. Another worker had a problem in her work station each time she had her 30-minute break because the worker who came to relieve her at her post was careless. For this reason, she decided not to take a break anymore. She was reprimanded for not taking breaks because she was required by the federal law to take the 30-minute break during working hours, but she accepted the reprimand record anyway rather than having trouble in her work post. Later on, she was recognized for her dedication and attitude towards her job and was paid for 30 minutes overtime every day. This is a woman who was conscious of her good record and good work and determined to keep them so. One can infer that the actions of these workers from the passage were as a result of endurance. Their endurance earned them good rewards, which proves the saying of the wise man that one good turn deserves another.

Also, endurance is a mighty power and patience gives many good things. Teachers sometimes give bonus questions in examinations to find out students who can excel above the standard marks. Bonus questions carry high marks and if you train to answer bonus questions, you are bound to stand above and beyond any student in the class.

In the Greek Marathon war with the Persians (present-day Iran), the Greeks defeated the Persians. Being enthusiastic, one soldier volunteered to convey the news of their victory home to Athens by running through the rough Greek countryside. He ran nonstop until he reached home and said, "We have won!" and after that, he collapsed and died. This is how running a marathon race (about 26 miles) in the Olympic games started. The runner was a man of talent and exertion and endurance who exceeded man's capability. Today, a medal (victor ludorum-master of games) symbolizing the best performance at the Olympic games is awarded to an athlete who wins four first places in four track and field events. To exceed expectations, you must run the marathon race of life to win the golden fleece of life. Jesse Owens, an African-American, obtained this medal in the 1936 Olympics in Berlin, Germany contrary to Hitler's belief that a German was destined to win the medal. Also, endurance, determination, and strength of character will encourage one to pursue one's goals in life with extra zeal till the ultimate victory is won. I truly believe this because this kind of action earned me my huge academic success. Honestly speaking, I was extremely over-zealous and aggressive over it as a result of circumstances and again, I strongly believe that every disappointment is a blessing so disappointment and undermining granted me wonderful achievement in life. Therefore, never lose hope; rather go for it and hit the road to win the marathon race of life to win the golden fleece of life. I won my own academic medal; I wish for you to win your own medal. This is a big challenge to you, so do it. Never be afraid; you can do it okay. (John 15:13) Jesus said, "No one has love greater than this that someone should surrender his soul on behalf of his friends." Again it is said in 1Corinthians 13:2-7-8. "And if I have the gift of prophesying and am acquainted with all the sacred secrets and all knowledge and if I have all the faith so as to transplant mountains but do not have love, I am nothing. It bears all things, believes all things, hopes all things, and endures all things; love never fails." Here we are told that to really do a thing, we must love it and to love a thing, we must give it more than it requires with all our whole heart, all our whole soul, and all our whole mind, for there is no greater love than this that someone should surrender his soul on behalf of others. Love blesses the receiver and the giver. Love never fails.

Section XIII: Time Schedule in Planning as You Search for Self-Confidence that Dismantles Your Fear

History of Man by Daniel J. Boorstin 1983 Ed. Random House New York Joanna Baillie; It is said, that if you do not organize your time, you may likely waste time and panic and worry because you are tired when enough work has not been done. As a result, it is necessary to redefine time and make sure each hour has something allocated to it and work and relaxation go hand in hand. Hence, one should have a unique planning system that structures time into three occasions, principally one for work, one for relaxation, and one for sleep.

Actually, a normal man has five workdays and two days off every week. He has to specify what he would be doing when not engaged in a job in order to avoid being exposed to wanton thoughts or distracting occasions with undesirable people who would mislead him by words or actions which in turn would lead to disappointing and frustrating results. It is said if you do not use time, time will use you. In other words, time waits for no one and is on schedule. You must plan for some recreational breathing-time activities that turn the mind away from serious engagements and towards refreshing and relaxing pastimes. My suggestion is this; specify for every day, the work time, rest time, including time for preparing a presentation, and the sleep time. Some people break up their sleep time into naps of two hours when they are fully occupied with tasks that must be finished on time. In case you are always fearful when dealing with people, you must make time from your rest to sit down and practice your public speaking. By so doing, you pre-plan your public appearance and rehearse the procedure before acting. It is not good to jump into a show unprepared. Everything needs time to mature, hence, we must carve out time for getting ready for any event. An occasional piecemeal time devoted to doing a thing in time yields an enormous amount of good works; that is, as you regularly attend to things, things gradually get organized to maturity. Farmers do this very often. They have to tend to the crops in the farm; sometimes they are looking for pests, sometimes they are training the yam vines, some other times they do weeding and some of the time they check for mature maize. When crops become ripe, they organize for the celebration of the new yam festival. You see, each occasion has a function allocated to it. If time is wasted in not paying attention to the task at hand, there will be no time for celebration. A student must be nimble-witted in using his/her time in reading up and mastering the problems in his classwork by studying the worked-out examples of the works of professional people in each subject and by **modelling and prototyping** after them. And then, from the experience gained, she has to build up her own designs. This involvement needs time and planning and serious attachment. Then the student can relax with classical music and playing computer games. All work and no play make Jack a dull boy. A housewife prepares the kids in the morning and sends them to school on time. In the home, she must tidy up and cook food for the family. She brings the children home and gets everyone fed at dinnertime. She checks the children's homework and encourages them to do it. When they are in bed, she must relax and have some rest to obtain energy for the next activity. So the day comes and goes. An artisan self-employed carpenter wakes up in the morning, praises his God and goes off to his workshop. He has three orders of cushioned chairs to be made. He has two apprentices. He allots parts of the chairs to the apprentices and gets on with his own portion of the job. Everyone is busy. Man must eat. Steadily and laboriously sweating, they begin to assemble the chairs. By the evening, enough work has been done. They must return home and come back the next day. The man must make time for his meal, relaxation, and socialization. His wife takes care of his children. Then, he has urgency in his hands for he must get the chairs ready in time for payment to be made. He is curiously anxious for his time and his money. Time must be well managed. The wasting of time is not allowed. Be conscious of your time. As you make the right choice of a goal and manage your time well, success is right there at your door. This is the secret of my own success in life. I thought of a goal, and I made a choice of my dream goal. I timed myself, I strove harder and harder, and successfully I realized my heart's desire. That is the reason why I am a Religious person, a graduate, a Doctor of Philosophy/Psychology and that is the reason why I was able to assemble this book. I set out with my goal pursuit at the age of 28 - too late; because I was late, I squeezed my time and made it on time. Thus, I have nothing to regret. One of my late mother's proverb's was, "if you agree, your God upholds you." For this reason, whatever you decide in life is what you must be; if you want to be a successful fellow, a college dropout, a street boy, or girl, you must be that. The choice and the power are in your hands. Therefore, make your choice and blame nobody. As you make your bed, so you lie on it. An executive general manager must rack his brain when looking for solutions to business problems; he has the business news weekly magazine and reports of business progress to read. He has to make phone calls for information. Production output. Time is hectic. His timely coordination of all these aspects brings to him successful achievement which in turn, mellow into rewards of money and honour. At intervals, he must have naps for cooling down and reinvigoration. Each event must be timed in order to avoid frustration and unsuccessful deliberation. Dr. Walter B. Cannon stated,

> *"Most people have the idea that the heart is working all the time. As a matter of fact, there is a definite rest period after each contraction. When beating at a moderate rate of seventy pulses per minute, the heart is actually working only nine hours out of the twenty-four. In the aggregate, its rest periods total a full fifteen hours per day. Here, look at what the heart does every minute. Your heart pumps enough blood through your body every day to fill a railway tank car. It exerts enough energy every twenty-four hours to shovel twenty tons of coal onto a platform three feet high. This is a Divine design of time. See how the heart is timed. If it falls out of this arrangement, there must be chaos that gives rise to panic and fear."*
>
> *by Dale Carnegie*
> *How to Stop Worrying and Start Living (1985).*

During World War Two, Winston Churchill (British Prime Minister) in his early seventies was able to work sixteen hours a day. How did he do it? He worked in bed each morning until eleven o'clock, reading reports, dictating orders, making telephone calls, and holding important conferences. After lunch, he went to bed again and slept for an hour. In the evening, he went to bed once more and slept for two hours before having dinner at eight. He did not cure fatigue and worry and fear but he prevented them by resting frequently and working ably fresh and fit. Then it is advised as a rule: "Do the very best you can; and then put up your old umbrella and keep the rain of criticism from running down the back of your neck."

Here is another study on the timing of a physical worker who can do more work if he takes more time out for rest. Frederick Winslow Taylor, working as a scientific management engineer with the Bethlehem Steel Company, observed that labouring men loaded 12 ½ tons of pig iron (smelted iron) per man each day on freight cars and were exhausted at noon. He made a scientific study of all the fatigue factors involved and declared that these men should be able to load 47 tons of pig iron per day instead of 12 ½ tons. They should be able to do four times as much work as they were doing and not be exhausted. As a result, Taylor chose one Mr. Schmidt who was required to work by the stopwatch. Schmidt was told by the man who stood over him with a watch: "Now pick up the pig iron and walk----Now sit down and rest---Now walk---Now rest." What happened at the end? Schmidt was able to carry 47 tons of pig iron each day without getting fatigued better than the man who carried 12 ½ tons of pig iron each day with fatigue. Schmidt worked for 26 minutes out of the hour and rested for 34 minutes. He rested more than he worked and yet he did four times as much work as the others. And so do what the Army does - ,take frequent rests and also do what your heart does – rest before you get tired and you will add one hour a day to your life-span. Save time by planning your life engagements.

Section XIV: Education Schedule for Under-Achievement and Under-Privileged Students from 2 Years - 40 Years Instils Confidence into Under-Privileged

Under-achievers and under-privileged people suffer from a lack of self-confidence a lot. Therefore, we have to plan an educational schedule for them. It is said, "The proper study of mankind is man."-(Pope, Alexander). Also, Proverbs from the Ancient Egyptian Temples states: "If you are searching for a Neter (Egyptian god), observe Nature. Man know thyself and thou shalt know the gods. The body is the house of God that is why it is said, "Man know thyself." The above statements tell us that to teach a child well, we must use natural things, events, and reasoning to introduce to the child how things are made and how they work to prevent him from being afraid of learning. The human body is a model of everything God made and must be used in teaching numbers, letters, words, signs, functions, things, events, and activities. "Natural models and demonstrations are most impressive on the mind and lead from the known to the unknown very reasonably." (1983) Famous Quotes Webster's Encyclopedia of Dictionary 1983 by John Gage Allee. In teaching numbers 1 to 10, the ten fingers and ten toes should be used. Also, twenty Kobo should be introduced to be used in counting. In teaching ABCD, models "A" as in apple (sample or a picture shown), "B" as in Ball (a ball or a picture of ball shown), "C" as in Car (a car or a picture of a car shown) and so on should be used. In fact, the items should, as much as possible, be physically shown. Most household items are welcome. In mathematics, addition, subtraction, division, and multiplication should be taught by using pennies - withdrawing (subtraction), putting on more (addition), counting (multiplication), and sharing (division). The pictures of things and word-building with letters should go hand in hand. The child's name should be used first in teaching the names of people and things.

Here is a case study of how to run a school system for the "Almejeri" Children" in Northern Nigeria. The Almejeris are children without parents who roam about in the streets begging for anything - food, clothing, and money for their sustenance. They collect in groups under a leader (megida-master) who feeds them and assigns duties to them. The Government has created special schools for them. It is said they number up to four million in Northern Nigeria. They should be provided first of all with an area in the dormitories, which provides normal family conditions in which other children grow up. There are three groups of them - the young ones, the grown-ups, and the maimed (disfigured) ones. Thus, there are three programs to be designed for them; namely: A program for wholesome young ones (2-7 years), a program for wholesome grown-ups (5-18 years) and a program for the maimed (disfigured) ones (all ages). Since in teaching kids the Direct Instruction method is used, it is necessary to provide family models of things (food, clothes, utensils), activities, (washing dishes, clothes, cooking, yard-cleaning, sanitary cleaning, bathing, playing, studying, eating, sleeping, praying, greeting, and attitude towards others). This general teaching should apply to all. But those who have lost their limbs, eyes, or ears should be especially helped with whatever facility is needed for their comfort and comport. Names of everything, activities, and events should be exemplified with models of things, films, and CD demonstrations. There should be well-equipped workshops, laboratories, and showrooms. The adolescent ones should do both academic class-work and professional studies such carpentry, tailoring, electrical practices, agricultural activities (farming, food processing, and packaging), computer training and repairing of machines. They should be able to formulate designs for changing native cultural technological practices into mechanized industrial structures. For example, they can be taught to design a mashing machine for pounding yam fufu or cassava fufu instead of using our present native mortar and pestle. Local drinks like kaikai (illicit gin), burkutu, tuwo, and pito can be analysed and refined by developing processes for removing the undesirable components and adding some desirable palatable materials to make them more enjoyable. Our native palm oil is good oil, rich in nutrients, especially vitamin A. Students should learn how to process it by separating the vitamin A and the fatty butter from liquid oil and how to reduce the high free fatty acid (FFA) to 3% (free fatty acid-substance that makes palm oil sour - oga ukputu) level and how to keep the oil storable. Our children should be taught how to create indigenous industrial technology for our native cultural products according to international technological standards. Our cultural practices are of sound technology but they have got to be mechanized and standardized. As for the handicapped Almejeris, special attention should be paid to their infirmities to enhance their mobility and capability in doing things. For all, the "Direct Instruction Program" is there to help them develop. Also, students should be taught how to handle food products like tuwo, pito, burkutu, and yam flour by quantifying them in small customer sizes and specifying the nutrients which are contained according to internationally recommended dietary practice.

Psychological Developmental Processes of Age Groups

0-2 Years - Sensorimotor: Evaluation of abilities necessary to construct and reconstruct objects, for example, toys, pictures, colours, and drawings depicting knowledge of things should be used by the child.

2-7 **Years – Pre-conceptual:** Consolidation of symbolic functions – ability to represent things as they are by acquiring language for naming things, writing, grammar, spelling rules communication skills, vocabulary skills, mathematical and scientific foundations.

7-11 Years - Concrete Operation: Child should be able to do mathematical addition, subtraction, division, multiplication, reading comprehension in which the meanings of words is matched against the real words, ability to represent in drawing the features of an object reflecting how they are used.

12-15 Years - Formal Operations: Allow adolescents to think about their thoughts, to construct ideals, and to reason realistically about the consequent result of an event. Formal operations enable young people to reason about false presentation of truths. That is to say, to defend and debate on a proposition even though it is wrong. Formal operational thoughts help in understanding metaphors – that is, figures of speech. After adolescence, mental growth is set with a gradual increase in wisdom.

15-21 and 22-40 Years - At this point, if a person has fear of learning or is worrying about any problems, he/she should do what Rudyard Kipling suggested here: "I keep six honest serving-men (they taught me all I knew); Their names are *What and Why and When and How and Where and Who*." The basic truth is that we must equip ourselves to deal with different kinds of problems by learning three basic steps of problem analysis:

1. Get the facts
2. Analyse the facts
3. Arrive at a decision, then act on a decision.

The Summary of This

1. Write down precisely all facts (pros and cons) about what the worry, fear, or problem is.
2. Write down what can be done about it depending on the facts so collected.
3. Make a decision on what to do choosing the best factual solution to the problem.
4. Start at once to carry out the decision.

Here is an Almejeri's Problem: He has outgrown the early stages of rudimentary education in basic faculties of learning. He wants something to do.

His Capabilities: He can learn a trade/occupation. He is physically and mentally fit. He can enrol in a vocational trade school to specialize in a machine maintenance scheme. He can learn how to repair and maintain different machines.

Details of Machine Maintenance Scheme

i. Establish servicing periods of machines depending on the number of hours of usage.
ii. **What to Check:** oil leakage, water, sound of machine, appearance, and conditions of environment.
iii. **Service Practice**: Dismantle machine and label the parts for easy reassembly. Clean parts with the authorized cleaning agent. Check bearings and re-grease. Examine parts for wear and replace.

Reassemble parts and test machine for good operation. Prepare a bill for the maintenance cost and return machine to the owner after the payment of the maintenance cost has been made. Keep logistical records for all transactions and keep an account of all payments. The Almejeri is now a technical businessman with a large equipped workshop handling electric motors, generators, and electronic equipment. He was financed by the government which trained him.

Now Let Us Look at the Direct Instruction Program and all it Entails

Creating Caring School and Classroom Communities for all Students by Daniel Solomon, Eric Schap, Marilyn

Watson, and Victor Battistich. Students cannot be expected to develop commitments to social values such as justice, tolerance, love and respect for others in a vacuum; they must be able to see and experience these values in action in their daily lives in the school. They must see their school community committed to fulfilling their basic needs such as needs for belonging to a supportive social school, for feeling competent, for being self-directing and for obtaining clearly directed exemplified guidance from competent teachers.

The Highlights of the Child Development Project (CDP)

The Child Development Project (CDP) makes teachers promote children's pro-social development and their internalized commitment to learning: their kindness and considerate concern for others, interpersonal awareness, and understanding, ability and inclination to balance their needs with the needs of others, as well as their core motivation and attainment of higher-level academic skills. There are three major components of the CDP in administering, pro-social development, cooperative learning, developmental discipline, and a literature-based and values-oriented approach to learning instruction.

- Cooperative learning emphasis.
- Extensive interaction among group members.
- Collaboration towards group goals.
- Division of labour among group members.
- Use of reason and explanation in presentation.

- Explicit consideration and discussion of values relevant to group activity.
- Use of meaningful and interesting assignments that benefit the group members; for example, a group can undertake to dismantle a blending machine, clean, and reassemble it with collaboration from members and under teacher's guidance.
- Use of intrinsic incentives (explanation and discussion of important and relevant aspects of the activity) rather than extrinsic incentives (rewards, points, threats, punishments).

Developmental Discipline

Emphasizes the interaction between teachers, students and aides about the welfare of the entire community and members and encourages students to take active roles in classroom governance and maintaining classroom rules. Teachers endorse interpersonal knowledge, respect and concern by using classroom activities that expressly focus on these values. Teachers underline the importance of discipline to academic activities with warmth and supportiveness necessary for handling students who are low-achieving and from low socioeconomic-status families.

- Use of literature and value
- Orientation to promote reading, thinking, and
- Caring.

The literature-based program is to help students become more skilled in reading and reading books that are tailored to promote social values. Folk stories that teach the noble attributes of man, like morality, honesty, sincerity etc., should be applied to help them develop. Also, application of rewards should be given when such virtues are realized among them. Examples of models who have expressed these virtues and how they are glorified should be the consistent components of such literature. Books that teach the youth how to prepare for the modern workplace values are sponsored. According to the Secretary of Labour's Commission on Achieving Necessary Skills by Deborah Whetzel (SCANS) (1992), schools should prepare the students to be imbued with workplace foundation basic skills- academic and behavioural characteristics so as to be competent in the jobs.

Foundation Skills

1. **Basic Skills:** Reading, writing, speaking, listening, and knowing arithmetic, and mathematical concepts.
2. **Thinking Skills:** Reasoning, making decisions, thinking creatively, solving problems, seeing things in the mind's eye, and knowing how to learn.
3. **Personal Qualities:** Responsibility, self-esteem, sociability, self-confidence, integrity, and honesty.

Models of Instructions Recommended for the Best Educational Practices for the Best Desired Student Outcome Developed by W. Huitt (Feb. 2000).

Elements of Effective Instruction

"The Madeline Hunter Model" by Dr. Madeline Hunter

Some basic lesson presentation elements, according to Madeline Hunter's method, are explained below

1. **Teaching to an Objective**
    1. Objectives
    2. Set (hook)
    3. Standards /expectations
    4. Teaching

    Input
    - Modelling/demonstration
    - Direction-giving
    - Checking for understanding
    5. Guided Practice
    6. Closure
    7. Independent practice.

2. **Behavioural Objective Format**
    Students will demonstrate their (knowledge, understanding, skills etc) of /to (concept, skills etc) by activity performed to meet the lesson objective according to standard. Example: Each student will demonstrate achievement of the skill of addition of whole numbers by adding columns of figures with paper and pencil correctly nine out of ten times individually in class.

3. **Four-Step Instructional Process**
    1. Watch how I do it (modelling)
    2. You help me do it (or we do it together)

3. I will watch you do it or praise, prompt, and leave (guided practice)
4. You do it alone (independent practice)

4. **Motivation Tricks**
   1. Feeling Tone
   2. Reward (extrinsic/intrinsic)
   3. Interest
   4. Level of concern
      - Accountability
      - Time to produce
      - Visibility
      - Predictability
   5. Knowledge of results
   6. Success

5. **Ways of Monitoring**
   - Oral individual
   - Oral together
   - Visual answers; example - showing of hands
   - Written
   - Task performance
   - Group Sampling.

6. **Questioning Guidelines**
   - Place signal (get their attention), then ask questions.
   - Ask question before designating the person to answer.
   - Do not repeat nor rephrase the student's response. May ask for agreement by class or for others to respond.
   - Ask question then wait for 50 percent of hands (or "bright eyes" knowing looks).

- Never ask a question of a student who you know cannot answer.
- If the student is confused or cannot answer, calmly repeat the same question or give a direct clue.

7. **Retention Reinforcement**
   1. Meaning/understanding (the most effective way to learn).
   2. Degree of original learning. Learn it well the first time (and do not practice it wrong).
   3. Feeling tone (positive or negative will work but negative has some undesirable side effects).
   4. Transfer (emphasizes similarities for positive transfer and differences where there might be an incorrect transfer).
   5. Schedule of Practice (mass the practice at first time, and then create a regular following Schedule).

8. **Creating Directions**
   - Break down into parts/steps.
   - Give only three at a time, one if the behaviour is new.
   - Delay giving instructions until just before the activity.
   - Give directions in the correct sequence.
   - Plan dignified help for those who do not tune in (no put-downs).
   - Give directions visually as well as orally (visual representation of the task).

9. **Giving Directions**
   1. Give the planned directions (creation above).
   2. Check the students' understanding ("Any questions?" - Does not check understanding).

3. Have a student model the behaviour (on the board or orally).
4. If needed, remediate and recheck (it is essential that students do not practice errors).

Direct Instruction - a Transactional Model - Developed by W. Huitt (September 2001).
GCE = General Certificate of Education

Research-Based Classroom Modifications for Improving Student Engaged Time and for Leader's Guide for Student Engaged Time.

WASC = West African School Certificate

Let me cite here three more examples of the effect of time schedule in our lives. Time is like a two-edged sword; if you handle it well, it will pay you; if you fail to handle it well, it will mess you up. In all my activities, I am always conscious of time accordingly, I the author, never even one time played with my time once I had an important goal to achieve. I do not take lightly anyone usurping my time. I am always aggressive with time. I knew I was too late in achieving my life goal so since I was aware of it, I scheduled myself and maintained it. I knew I started in primary school very late and there was a huge setback on my progress in life. But I did not give up hope. I struggled and entered secondary school and after it, while waiting for my result, I enrolled in learning old typewriting skills. My WASC result was not so wonderful, so I enrolled for my GCE and I combined typing and GCE classes. As God willed it, I secured a job in a printing press with my typing skills. Later, I became self-employed and worked for a while till I entered a convent. In the convent, I maintained my time consciousness that enabled me to cope with the guiding principles of convent life. As I maintained my time schedule, I was sent to complete my paper at "ToTo" in the Northern part of Nigeria and I went and challenged it and cleared my papers. I was due for profession and after profession; I was sent to the USA for missionary work and to study. In the USA it was not that easy but I moved along with the time. I enrolled in an Associate degree program, then, after finishing it, I never wasted any time and enrolled in a Bachelor's degree program, then a Master's degree program, and finally, a Doctorate degree program. Today, I am the first Doctor of Philosophy/Psychology in my congregation, The Holy Family Sisters of the Needy (HFSN). Hence, as I was engaged in these programs, I tried to make ends meet by working to sustain myself and the poor. If you agree, your God will consent to it. I was able to challenge the time to reach self-actualization even though I was too late into education. Time is always flexible; if you want to make use of it properly it is there for you. It will work with you and if you want to waste it, it will equally allow you to do so. Time as we know it has no choice to serve you as you want it. For this reason, I implore you to make proper use of your time. No matter how far behind you are, you will still meet the time and even pass it.

Another example was a young boy who chose to waste his time and every other person's time. This young man was brought up in a middle-class family and had a golden opportunity to go to school up to university level.

Unfortunately, he made a wrong choice on the way. He was able to finish his secondary education. He obtained admission to a University and there he popped his head up and began to follow the bad boys. He started chasing girls and using his tuition fees to attend to his girls. Each time he came home and demanded money, the parents kept giving it to him until they realized his tricks. Once they stopped showering money onto him, he turned around and joined a courtesan group where he thought he would make quick money. In every ramification, he became a dropout. Then he began to roam the streets chasing girls, picking pockets, smoking Indian hemp, and even engaging in killing vulnerable elderly people for rituals, yet he gained no headway. This young man misused his time and the time of his parents. He became frustrated and then ended up hopelessly ruined forever. The young man was a failure. You cannot have your cake and eat it.

Time, they said, waits for no one. Do not blame anyone for your wrong choice and time wastage. This is also another example about a young girl whose parents were very poor. Later, her mother became a widow and life became worse for them. They could hardly find money to buy food. However, the child, knowing the importance of education, approached one of her aunts who was wealthy. She begged her to sponsor her in the Technical College. The aunt agreed and started sponsoring her tuition in Technical College. The young girl being aware of her background, made proper use of her time and studied hard in the school. Today she is a skilful electrician and is earning a huge salary. She is now the bread-winner of her family. As I mentioned above, the way you handle your time is how you are going to have it. Time never deceives; it serves everybody equally. Do not be afraid to use your time adequately. Even though you have already wasted your time, you can still turn it around and make amends. Remember, even if the world ends today, time never ends. Time is always there working round the clock with our Creator serving those who make proper use of it. I encourage you to be meticulous about your usage of time. Strive hard, devote time and prevail.

Section XV: Transcend Your Limiting Beliefs

Our limitation may emanate from the constitution of our minds. Some philosophers and psychologists describe people according to the ranking of their consciousness: consciousness-as-flesh people, consciousness-as-spirit people, and consciousness-as-divine people according to an Alchemy of Mind by Diane Ackerman. Consciousness, sub-consciousness, and unconsciousness according to Psychokinesis (mental energy that moves matter) by Michael H. Brown or as the mystics have it: simple consciousness (a few days after birth) self-consciousness (at 3years), cosmic consciousness (at 35 years) according to Cosmic Consciousness by Richard Maurice Bucke. The Christian Bible has it as heart, soul, mind, and strength (Mk 12:28) "Hear O Israel, the Lord our God is the one Lord, and you must love the Lord your God with all your heart, with all your soul, with your entire mind and with all your strength." The Apostle Thomas, called the twin, behaved as a consciousness-as-flesh man when he said in John 20:25, "Unless I see in his hands the print of the nails and stick my finger into the print of the nails and stick my hand into his side, I will certainly not believe." Jesus answered Thomas saying, "Put your finger here and see my hands and take your hand and stick it into my side and stop being unbelieving but become believing." Saint Augustine of Hippo, Africa, said in the fifth century, "I cannot understand all that I am." This means the mind is too narrow to contain itself. That means you are bound to disbelieve certain things because you fall short of the accurate knowledge of the things. You are born with this limiting belief. Some people are double-minded and feel nervous and fearful when they make decisions. Other people are obstinate in believing in only what they see. Seeing is believing. But faith demands that we live by faith and not by sight. Though weakness such as genetic disability, disoriented upbringing that makes one pessimistic instead of optimistic and the loose attitude of not taking things seriously, can cast a shadow on the way one thinks and does things, it is advised that we strengthen our capabilities by positive thinking. Our minds know all things we are, but they act according to our thoughts. Thoughts have wings and generate success when they are positively driven to action by true motivations. In our private lives, our core beliefs are what make us distinct individuals; professionally and publicly, our core beliefs differentiate us from our competitors. Now let us take some time to consider and identify our core beliefs. The questions are: Are you reasonably argumentative with credible facts based on accurate knowledge or are you erratically argumentative with obstinacy as your key credibility? Are you a good listener? Are you good in mathematics and science? Are you a creative thinker? Are you caring? Are you a willing volunteer for school or charitable activities? In your professional life, are you the team leader, the delegator or the visionary who believes in destiny? Now take time to list your important strengths and core beliefs. To differentiate yourself, you can expand your strengths and improve your professional skills by listening, researching, learning new techniques, and setting up an application of those things learnt. These questions help you to visualize your purpose in life, your dreams about that purpose and the way to approach the realization of this purpose. At the close of this exercise, you will have accomplished the following:

- You have identified your passions about your purpose.
- You have evaluated the important choices you have made.
- You have set your priorities.
- You have examined your dreams and illusions and have learnt an exercise for using your dreams to paint the canvas of your life.
- You have realized your important strengths and core beliefs.
- You have determined the unique skills by which you can excel as a professional.

Now that you have created a facility for believing in your abilities, you no longer criticize yourself, saying it is because I am ugly, fat, or disorganized that things are not working as I planned. Harsh criticism does not motivate or nurture most people. Change with growth occurs through encouragement and kind persuasion. People tend to live up to the expectations of others when truth is reflected in the power of the message we give. We can achieve more when we have a fundamental belief in our abilities. When you start to change your limiting attitude, you always feel clumsy, embarrassed, inadequate, and panicky (fearful) but as time wears on you become familiar with the new order. If you believe you can do something, you surely can but if you tell yourself that the task is simply beyond your scope, then you fail. **You must affirm** that you can do it. It takes a change of heart to affect a good result. Lasting change is a life-long process of growing. When you grow, you are doing more than just changing behaviours - you are nurturing stronger beliefs, different attitudes, richer desires, and deeper convictions. When some aspect of your life is out of step with your goals, dreams, and purpose, you can make the decision to change. Your decision to change gives you permission to dream, to imagine and to believe you can be different. When the decision to change launches you on your path to life-long development, the following forces will propel you along that path and toward the fulfilment of your purpose.

- Appreciation for things that matter.
- Acceptance of the power of your mind.
- Investment in your passion.
- Replenishment of your energy.
- Belief in your hopes and dreams.
- Celebration of victories and success.
- Commitment to continual growth.

Unlocking the power of these tools can press you forward to initiate change in your life and to walk down the path of that change with conviction and commitment. These ideas will help you shift your focus from past false starts at meaningful change to stepping out confidently on your own personal journey of growth and development.

Pursuing the Things that Matter

How many people have been stuck in situations they disliked? How many times have we wanted to be different, but we felt trapped by our circumstances? Now is the time to decide what we want out of life and then to start actions to realize the target. The most important thing is to recognize and pursue the things that matter most to you in life. Decisions should be about spiritual development, success with family and friends, health, and business. They should receive your attention, time, energy, and effort. Unleashing the power of your mind, your brain knows who you are, and your immune system knows who you are not and so your mind has all the knowledge to guide you towards your goals. The wise man says, "If you can believe it, you can achieve it." Jesus said, "If only you have faith and do not doubt, not only will you do what I did to the fig tree but also if you say to this mountain, "Be lifted up and cast into the sea," it will happen" (Matthew 21:21). If we feed our brains (mind) violence, pettiness, hopelessness, negativity, greed, and despair, our lives will unfold accordingly. Putting future positive expectations in your conscious and subconscious mind will put the wheels of change in motion and make the expectations a reality.

According to John Maxwell's audio series entitled: How to Make Personal Changes (Seven Minute Difference by Allyson Lewis (2006), there are six stages to go through to change thought into reality:

1. **Thought:** Think about who you want to become, what direction will take you there and what sacrifice you might make to get there.
2. **Belief:** You must believe in the direction you have chosen for your life and your ability to make the journey.
3. **Expectation:** Expectation causes our energy level to rise and release adrenaline into the system for physical activity (adrenaline-hormone that causes energy to be utilized for fight-or-flight situation). Expect the best and empower your expectations.
4. **Attitude:** Your attitude is a mighty tool for dealing with challenges. Having a positive attitude means facing every circumstance head-on and pushing through with zest, dignity, and integrity.
5. **Behaviour:** Your behaviour is an outward expression of your inward thoughts, beliefs, expectations, and attitudes. As you become more positive and proactive in these areas, your behaviour will become more precise in achieving the expected result.
6. **Your Performance:** This is your daily measuring yardstick for assessing your personal growth and development. At the end of the day, how you performed is registered in the activities and the result.

Remaining True to Your Passion

It does not matter if you are a corporate CEO (chief executive officer), a stay-at-home parent, a volunteer, a minister, a doctor or a retiree, you will not find true happiness and success in your daily life if you are not driven and guided by your passion. You need to put your money where your mouth is. You must have an ardent fervour in what you are doing and devote your whole attention to it. Your mind does the same thing, remembering all activities and putting you in a top form.

Replenishment of Your Energy

Without the opportunities to replace the energy we expend on our jobs, without allowing "air" into our lives, our productivity comes to a standstill. Air is something vital that invigorates us by restoring our energy. We replenish ourselves by getting enough rest, eating healthy food and by exercising. Rejuvenating your life is not a casually optional activity; you must do it in order to revive your spirit, heal life's bruises and sharpen your enthusiastic optimism.

New Leaves

The Igbo say, when a tree sheds its old leaves, it is preparing to set up new leaves. In nature, growth is a cycle. Think of an iroko tree (osisi oji); in the dry season, it loses all its old leaves, then waits for a while for the first rain in March to set up new leaves. You may consider "ohachi" (green vegetable used for food). It loses old leaves and makes new ones used in making soups. These new leaves blossom and gather sunlight and nutrients to help the tree grow taller, stouter (firmer) and healthier. Again, at the end of the rainy season, the iroko tree gets ready to repeat the cycle. This sort of renewal of cycles of growth and development is necessary for personal growth and development. Sometimes we can discard some old ideas and actions for new challenges, new ideas, and experiences. As trees shed old leaves, we ought to shed old practices to make way for new ones for growth in our lives. Some people's lives are full of "dead leaves", meaning old ideas, hurts, bitterness, anger, tension, fear, and stress; feelings that hold them back from using their abilities to grow, to be happy and be fulfilled. Some habits are harder to break - the continuance of the old routines that are no longer productive. We cling to long-held feelings, habits, and actions as if they are precious treasures, refusing to let go. To achieve new growth and make true advances towards our purpose, we need to be willing to shed our old leaves, remain bare for a while then blossom into new growth and life. At this point, let me enlighten you about Mahatma Gandhi's ideas of change and mind that kept him moving on during his time. He believed in faith and action. That always prompted him to quote, "What is faith worth if it is not translated into action?" As long as you have faith, effect it with action, then this will lead you to tremendous change and progress that you wish to see in your lifetime. Gandhi also empowered you and me today with his wisdom and insight; "Be the change that you wish to see in the world." Here, as you endeavour to make a change in your life that is total renovation of your frame of mind of fear into strong will, you must empower yourself and invoke the Holy Spirit to instil in you that will-power that will affect your wishes. Moreover, according to Gandhi, "Strength does not come from physical capacity. It comes from an indomitable (strong) will." This means that your will should be unconquerable, very determined, and deep-spirited, with no feeble mind." On another occasion, he said, "If we are to make progress, we must not repeat history but make new history. We must add to the inheritance left by our ancestors." Here we must make new leaves. Some people keep on recounting what made them or is making them not move forward. That is the reason why Gandhi advised us to drop those past events to create new ones that will move us forward. From this moment forward, say to yourself: **"Change" is on the way.** The two famous American politicians, John Kerry, and John Edward, during their political rallies, said, "Change was on the way..." For this reason, I advise you to believe in change and equally, make a better one.

Feeding Your Hopes and Dreams

To grow tomorrow, you must refurbish (revamp) your hopes and dreams. Do children have dreams? What is true is that children are in perfect alignment with their current gifts and skills. As parents, we must work hard to encourage our children to follow their dreams by first taking them to special lessons and classes, exposing them to and offering them every opportunity for proper development of the proper aptitude for knowledge. Then proper hopes and dreams will evolve. Many did not have this opportunity and proper hopes and dreams did not develop. When wrong dreams are followed, sometimes disappointment paves the way. The consequence is that we recognize that in the long run, we may not be able to pay our bills as an artist or as a musician. When fear of failure creeps in, you simply drop out. You need to develop the dream of being an artist and follow up by taking art classes and lessons at the community college, devoting time and energy to being totally well informed in the art of practical techniques. When you find yourself not doing well, you should rekindle enthusiasm by studying more art and attending art seminars to update yourself.

Celebration of Victories and Successes

You are urged to be proud to celebrate your successes. A student celebrates her success in her university degree, be it Bachelor, Masters or Doctorate, because she has laboured very hard in research work, the writing of term papers, reading up many works, having sleepless nights, and sustaining fear of pass-or-fail situations. As well as doing all that is required to make progress in any venture, it is also worthwhile to make time for the celebration of our successes. I am still celebrating my success every now and then. It is not an easy task to achieve one's goal. For this reason, whenever I look behind and visualize all the ordeals I went through during my missionary work and academic years in the USA, I begin to re-celebrate. As a result, I placed some of my commencement pictures on my room wall and on my computer screen; each time I look at them I feel uplifted and fulfilled, victorious, and self-actualized. Really, it was not an easy task. Never let your flag go down; always hold it up, come what may.

Commitment to Continual Growth

To maintain your self-confidence, it means extending your reach. It is like stretching your body to refresh your tiredness by stretching the muscles of hands, and feet, pulling your joints back into proper disposition, improving your breathing, heart rate, and boosting your circulation. From the therapeutic value of stretching, we can gain an insight into the important benefits of stretching our capabilities for higher goals. It is good to live our lives to the best but since we always ask for more, it is equally simple to be willing to stretch to extend our reach for continual growth. If you want to be more different tomorrow than you are today, choose to be different and start tackling the small changes that will make you different. Dig deeper, try harder and be willing to believe in your ability and you will do more. Most often, we fear and doubt our capability to attain our goals while, out there, some people see our ability to perform. For instance, E.E Cummings stated,

> *"We do not believe in ourselves until someone reveals that deep inside us is valuable, worth listening to, worthy of our trust, sacred to our touch. Once we believe in ourselves, we can risk curiosity, wonder, spontaneous delight or any experience that reveals the human spirit."*
>
> *E.E. Cummings*

> *Caroline Myss, Invisible Acts of Power*
> *Personal Choices that Create Miracles 2004,*
> *(p. 126).*

God created each person for a purpose; therefore, no created being is a waste. For this reason, you are useful in the universe, hence, it is left for you to find your lucky key to open your door to see what you have in there. You can do it and I did it to make a difference. You do not need anything great or huge to change the quality of your life. You must start as a mustard seed before you will be able to spread around. Thus, it is in your power and in your will to transform and enhance yourself.

Section XVI: Fuel Your Success with Passion and Enthusiasm

The word enthusiasm has a Greek origin. It comes from the Greek word, **enthousiazein,** meaning to be inspired by God or Spirit. When you are filled with spirit, you act like a sharp razor that cuts clean. It comes from within. Therefore, to really acquire this faculty of inspiration, one must practice meditation that links one to his cosmic consciousness. You must fuel your thinking force with energy from above. (cf. Matthew 7:7), Jesus said, "Keep on asking and it will be given; keep on seeking, and you will find; keep on knocking, and it will be opened to you." Psalm 127:1 says, "Unless God himself builds the house, it is to no avail that its builders have worked hard on it." You cannot do it alone without your Creator. He says whatever you lay your hand on and ask for help, you will obtain the fullness of its goodness. You can imagine how a simple artist became a millionaire by inspiration. He has his hands in almost everything arts. He did art designs, taught arts in the school, designed art shows, and sold CDs. He really became a Master of Arts, full of energy to do more. He was acclaimed to be a gifted person but on the contrary, he worked hard with help from above. He prayed and practiced his meditation moods which inspired many great people and observed simple austerity measures with temperance and self-discipline. Let us look at how ancient people who used cosmic consciousness and meditation fared. Somehow, we are often amazed at the spectacular edifices called the Egyptian pyramids. The most astounding of them is The First Great Pyramid of Giza, originally 478.88 feet (146 meters) in height, built by Pharaoh Khufu, in the fourth dynasty, from 2551 to 2528 BC. The Pyramid occupied an astonishing open space of 82.111 million cubic feet with some 6.5 million tons of stones each weighing between two and 16 tons. The stones were floated down the River Nile from Turah quarries to the places where they were dragged on ramps and pulled up onto scaffolds by means of mere ropes and pulleys to be placed into position on the Pyramid. Using simple methods, ancient Egyptian architects constructed the Pyramids. The modern man is wondering how primitive methods could account for structures like these such that the most modern sophisticated constructional engineering could not easily duplicate them today.

The good eyes of Pythagoras (582-507 BC), a mathematician/philosopher born around the time of Buddha and Confucius (those who used meditation to attain spiritual elation), saw the Pyramids as the products of mystical levitation. Pythagoras studied in the mystery school in Egypt and knew the secrets of meditation and mystical spiritual levitation. The purport here is that the ancient Egyptians used the power of the mind, the cosmic consciousness, to lift the heavy stones in building the Pyramids. At this point, let us go further in nature to substantiate the use of cosmic energy. The plants do not have brains, but they do a lot of thinking and a lot of work with the result of wonderful products such as all sorts of foodstuffs and chemicals (drugs). In photosynthesis, plants can cook and combine air, water, and minerals with the help of sunlight to do all that awesome work of creating foods. Plants use cosmic consciousness in doing what they do. What of animals? Large organisms like the vertebrates (man) possess massive reservoirs of nerves in the brain and do what they do by thinking and learning but the invertebrates like bacteria have little nerves and do their thinking and learning by genetic instructions directly. They (bacteria) are born knowing all they need to know for survival at once while vertebrates must learn and practice the most basic survival skills. Animals and plants do not have schools for learning but act more intelligently than humans who must think and learn. More so, it becomes necessary that we practice cosmic consciousness meditation which was used by the ancient Egyptians. To justify this fact, (cf. Matthew 6:26-29) Jesus said, "Observe intently the birds of heaven, because they do not sow seed or reap or gather into storehouses; still, your heavenly Father feeds them." "Take a lesson from the lilies of the field, how they are growing; they do not toil, nor do they spin; but I say to you that not even

Solomon in all his glory was arrayed as one of these." This admonition is acceptable because if you build the house of your life without the help of the master builder, you will be labouring in vain and there will be remorse at the end.

Section XVII: Just Say No to the Things that Would Inhibit Your Self-Confidence

Jesus said,

Just let your word Yes, mean Yes, your No, No, for what is in excess of these is from the wicked one."
(Matthew 5 vs. 37)
The Jerusalem Bible Popular Edition 1974, (p.9).

What is said here is that everyone has a core personality with core principles or policies based on the accepted norms of the system. These are based on what Jesus said that if you remain in my words you will know the truth and the truth will set you free. One should not fudge (to use dubious words to mislead); once a right principle or right action has been taken, that is it. When we think or have an emotional expression, these neurotransmitter molecules of emotions function as follows:

1. Dopamine: Main motivator and sustainer of emotions.
2. Epinephrine (adrenaline): Energy producer for emotions.
3. Norepinephrine (noradrenaline): Modulator of energy for emotions.

4. Acetylcholine: Exciter of memory of the emotional processes.
5. GABA (gamma aminobutyric acid): Inhibitor and modulator of emotional actions.
6. MAO (Monoamine oxidase): For breaking down of neurotransmitter emotional molecules after they have finished functioning.
7. Serotonin: In charge of repackaging and reuptake of emotional molecules after they have finished functioning.

They all operate in unison in the body to motivate you to say **Yes** or **No** depending on the principles or policies on which they were built and which you have made your key directors for accurate judgment. What would be your attitude on situations like dealing with people who tend *to hurt you by actions or by words of the mouth?* Shall we go on doing what they do or pursue our resolve unflinchingly (uncompromisingly) without retaliation? A person of integrity would keep his/her composure and say **No** to any despicable (dreadful) imposing behaviour. But there is a special case of relentlessly persistent perturbation that keeps on coming time and time again. This type cannot be combated with an ordinary avoidance. You must use exorcism by praying and mediating on it. You must affirm that "I think, therefore I exist" (Cogito ergo Sum-René Descartes 1596-1650 AD.) *This is to boost up your morale and make you stand up tall and say* **No** *to any undesirable disturbance.* In the book of (Revelation 12:1-17), Michael's battle with the dragon; this verse from the bible portrays a just defence. Therefore, we are liable to defend ourselves in a justified way; that is, in a nonviolent way, to push the dragon, devil, diabolical and dubious individuals out of your way. You can hum it out, use dialogue, speak, voice, talk or iron it out fearlessly without minding who but with respect and dignity. Of course, sometimes, this is done with aggressiveness because some people are more stubborn than the others. Nevertheless, I encourage you to stand by truth and justice and nothing will happen to you. Never be influenced by unjust fellows; do not mind their gifts to you but mind your right and integrity. Let your voice be heard and never shrink away. Never fear as a result of what they would say; remember, whatever you do people will still talk about you for many, many men have many, many minds. Just do the right thing- "Iji de ogu." Never be afraid because only the eye of a child fears a painted devil (William Shakespeare). Only truth will set you free and doing good and right. In Psalm 37:21-22, it is said, "But the righteous one is showing favour and making gifts. For those being blessed by him will themselves possess the earth. But those, upon whom evil is called by him, will be cut off." There is a story of a woman, Mrs. Edith Allred of Mount Airy, North Carolina. She said that as a child, she was extremely sensitive and morbidly shy because she was overweight and fat. She had an old-fashioned mother who thought it was foolish to make clothes look pretty and she dressed her accordingly. She said her mother did not let her go to any parties or have any fun. In school, she never joined other children in outside activities such as athletics. When she got married, she carried this aura of personality to her husband's family. She said, her in-laws were a straight forward and self-confident family and she tried to emulate them but all in vain. Every attempt they made to draw her out of herself drove her much further into herself. She became nervous and snappy and avoided friends. She tried to fool her husband by overacting whenever she and her husband were in a public place. What changed the situation for her was a kind remark made by her mother-in-law. The mother-in-law said that she brought up her children by insisting they should always be themselves no matter what happened. There and then, she recollected the misery that she had brought on herself by trying to fit herself into another person's mood to which she did not conform. Edith started being herself. She studied her personality, her strong points, and weak points. She learnt how to make good dresses of various colours and styles and dressed herself accordingly. Edith then reached out to make friends and joined organizations where she was frightened at first but later, she gained courage and dexterity when she was put on a program. She became happy and passed on this legacy to her own children by saying,

"No matter what happens, always be yourself."

Annoying Instances that People Face Every Day in Their Lives

1. Complete strangers can reach you by telephone, cell phone, pager, fax, regular mail, express mail, and e-mail.
2. They can e-mail and instant message you at work, at home, and on your hand-held computer.

3. If you are not there, they can leave messages on your answering machine or your voice mail. If you are there, they can interrupt you with call-waiting.
4. Everyone wants a piece of you. Your children want a ride or to borrow your car; your co-workers want your input on projects that are not your responsibility; your boss wants you to work overtime to finish a report he needs; your sister wants you to take her kids for the weekend; your child's school wants you to bake four dozen cookies for teacher appreciation day and be a driver for next week's field trip; your mother wants you to come over and fix her screen door; your best friend wants to talk about his impending divorce; a local charity wants you to head up the annual luncheon committee and your neighbour wants to borrow your van to pick up some lumber at Home Depot. Telemarketers also want you to subscribe to the local newspaper. Some telemarketers such as Comcast wants you to switch to Xfinity Triple Play; Verizon wants you to sign up for High-Speed Internet; CCI Cat Communications International wants you to switch to the National Phone Service; Global Insurance Company wants you; Healthcare Services Company wants you; Drug Prescription Company wants you. There is no end to all these requests. While we must put up honestly in doing what is right, we must also outline what must be done and what must not.

Let us look at cases of situations people faced and how they emerged victorious.

Case 1. How to Banish the Boredom that Produces Worry, Fear, and Resentment

To illustrate a case study of boredom, let us take the case of a lady, Alice, who was an executive. Alice came home one night from work, woefully exhausted and fatigued. She wanted to go to bed without having her dinner. Her mother implored her to sit down and eat something. While she was at the table, the telephone rang. It was one of her friends inviting her to a dance. Her spirit soared. She hurriedly dressed up and zoomed away to dance which lasted till 3 o'clock in the morning. When Alice returned home, she was elated and exhilarated. Was she previously really exhausted? Yes, she was because she was bored with her work and life as well. Here, she had a tonic that turned her around. Never have you continued to do what is boring and excruciating to you. Here is another illustration of the fact that your emotional attitude produces more fatigue than physical exertion. Some time ago, Dr. Joseph E. Barmack Ph.D. reported in the Archives on Psychology, his experiments showing how boredom produces fatigue. Dr. Barmack put a group of students through a series of uninteresting tests in which, he knew, they would show little interest. What was the result? The students felt tired and sleepy, complained of headache, and eyestrain, felt irritable and had some stomach upset. *Explanation:* When metabolism tests were taken of these students, the tests showed that the blood pressure of the body of the students and their consumption of oxygen decreased, meaning that they were bored but their metabolism picked up as soon as they started doing something interesting and pleasurable. You must always say **No** to anything that is boring and uninteresting.

Case 2. A Real Miracle Happened by Mrs. John Burger

She said worry completely enveloped her so much that she succumbed to fear, trouble, and nervousness. Her three children were living with her relatives, and her husband, having recently returned from the armed service, was in another city trying to establish a law practice. She felt all the insecurities and uncertainties of post-war readjustment. She threatened her husband's career, her children's happy home life and her own life. She was fearful of planning for responsible future events. One day, her mother visited her, and she reprimanded her for giving in and for allowing her nerves and mind to be jittery. She requested her to get up and fight back. She reminded her that she feared the situation instead of facing it, running away from life instead of living it. Henceforth, from that day, she started to face it. She started to care for her children, slept well, ate well, and her spirits improved. She gathered her children and joined her husband in their new home. She started to work, had plans for their new home, her children, her husband and plans for everything. She grew stronger and stronger, full of well-being and joy of living. A year later, she had a happy successful husband, a beautiful home, and three happy children. This is the lesson she learnt; "If a situation seems insurmountable, face it! Start fighting! Do not give in!"

Two Examples of Those Who Sacrificed Their Lives for Other People's

Human Social Welfare Fearlessly in order to Excel in Nonviolent Passive Resistance

In India, it is a culture to observe nonviolence as part of daily civil and spiritual practice as contained in the Vedic Scripture (Vedas-laws given by the Lord Krsna-God.) In the Vedas from Bhagavad-Gita (scriptural book meaning, **"Truth As It Is"** (p.164) the Lord said, "Intelligence, knowledge, freedom from doubt and delusion, forgiveness, truthfulness, self-control, calmness, pleasure, pain, birth, death, fear, fearlessness, nonviolence, equanimity, satisfaction, austerity, charity, fame, and infamy are created by me alone." Nonviolence is defined as generally not killing or harming the body (includes humans and animals) or actually nonviolence means not putting others in misery or distress and it is the constituent of true knowledge which embodies humility, nonviolence, tolerance, simplicity, cleanliness, steadfastness, equilibrium of the mind, devotion to the service of the Lord, self-realization, philosophical, and scientific search for the absolute truth. Let us look at the life of a renowned nonviolent, fearless Indian national leader, Mohandas Gandhi, known as Mahatma Gandhi (great soul), born in India (1896-1948). Educated in London as a lawyer, he was practising law in the apartheid (racial segregation) South Africa where he led the Indian emigrants against the racial discrimination in the form of everyone having to carry **a 'pass card'** in order to be allowed to move about freely. While in London, he identified that the Christian saying, in Mathew 5:39, "However, I say to you: Do not resist him that is wicked; but whoever slaps you on your right cheek, turn the other also to him," was like the Indian nonviolence culture. While in South Africa, he developed his principle, **"Satyagraha"** meaning **'firmness in truth'** of nonviolent protest, non-cooperation, civil disobedience, passive resistance against racial discrimination. He asked the Indian residents in South Africa to bring all of their **'Pass Cards'** to a general meeting to be burnt. He notified the apartheid South Africa Government Officials about his intention. When the cards were set on fire, one card at a time by Mahatma Gandhi, the officials went into action by beating Gandhi with their batons each time a card was dropped into the fire by Gandhi. Gandhi was wounded and arrested and brought to court. He, as a British trained lawyer, defended himself and his people. He won the case and the 'Pass Card' ordinance was waived and repealed for the Indian immigrants. Gandhi then left South Africa and went home to India. When he was in India, he organized the same nonviolent, non-cooperation, civil disobedience, and passive resistance against the British Colonial Government in India, boycotting foreign goods, schools, and law courts. He was arrested numerous times for his activities and imprisoned for two years but he continued his nonviolent, passive resistance against the British Colonial Government until 1947 when the British Parliament granted independence to India. He became the father of the Indian nation and was assassinated in 1948 by a Hindu fanatic.

Another man of no less reputation and of the same ilk as Mahatma Gandhi was Rev. Martin Luther King Jr.

(1929-1968), born in Atlanta, Georgia, United States of America. He went to India to study Gandhi's Nonviolent Principle, then came into prominence when he applied this passive resistance, civil disobedience to the social problems meted out to black people in the United States of America. The black people in the USA attended separate schools, ate in separate restaurants, rode in separate public buses or took seats in the back. King confronted his assailants by asking black people to demonstrate peacefully against all injustices and was jailed **16 times**. He continued peaceful protests against discrimination in housing, public facilities, and voting rights, and drew nationwide attention to injustices that the black people were suffering. He won the Nobel Peace Prize in 1964 for his Civil Rights Peaceful Leadership and is memorialized with a national holiday on January 17th for his ***"I Have A Dream."*** His activities led to the passing of the Civil Rights Act of 1964 and the Voting Rights Act of 1965 for freedom for all Americans. He was assassinated in 1968 by a white bigot.

Mahatma Gandhi and Rev. Martin Luther King Jr. should be your role models as we are fighting fear so whenever you are confronting any insurmountable situation, never fear; rather, stand tall and deal with it justifiably. Face it in a nonviolent way and deal with it in a nonviolent manner and be firm. This is the way of upholding one's self-confidence. Rev. King Jr., even though he was punished, imprisoned, and assassinated, had a hope and dreamt that one day his objectives would materialize, and his people would be freed, and it happened the way he dreamt it. Insofar, his efforts and hope were not in vain. Look at Barrack Obama today; he is the fulfilment of that dream; "I have a dream…" Looking at Obama, in spite of the fact that he is a black man, he feared less and rubbed shoulders with the white contenders during their political era and won. He never feared or dismayed that he was a black man or that he could not surpass the white man. He had high hopes and succeeded. He was able to make it to the White House and lived there as the first black President and number 44 of America President. Had it been that he was fearful, he would not have made that dream a reality. I need you to be fearless once you are striving for a genuine goal; only be fearful when you are pursuing an unlawful career. I advise you as you strive for your authentic goal, to deeply dedicate yourself to God as you reflect on this brilliant prayer by Caroline Myss;

> ***"God, please help me." Now, let it go. Hold in your mind and in your heart your problem or fears and pray, "I release my fears into your guiding wisdom."***
> *- Caroline Myss*
> *Invisible Acts of Power 2004, (p. 114).*

Remember, in everything we do we must seek for Divine intervention. You cannot do it by yourself. Someone above must lead and guide you. *When a lizard runs and misses its tree, children get hold of it.* You cannot do without Divine power and wisdom. Therefore, invoke God in this manner, "Lord let your wisdom be with me to help me and to work with me." Since you have God on your side, you will gain the spirit of foresight, creativity, will-power, and enlightenment. You must train yourself to be a good strategist and a responsible fellow. As soon as you have these qualities, you have conquered fear and your achievement is very much closer. Never say you do not know what to do or do not know how to do it. I tell you; you know it and how to do it and if you are in doubt, find out how to do it. "Never let the fear of what another person can do or what he or she can become determine the essential goodness of your soul. If you have a giving soul, then give. If you do not, then learn." Myss (2004). When you learn, you gain wisdom. But if you remain in your belief that you do not know how to do it, you will never know it. Caroline Myss again said,

> *"When we say, "I do not know what to do," we are rarely being truthful. We most likely do not want to do what we are sensing we need to do, but we are, quite frankly, too intuitive to get away with that excuse. We/you cannot be intuitive. The energy of it is a relentless internal voice that we can rarely misinterpret or silence. It is a power that works hand in hand with intuition to guide our actions in the right direction - the direction that will do the most good."*
>
> - Caroline Myss
> Invisible Acts of Power 2004 (p. 17).

You must believe in self, trust self, have faith, and maintain what Eastern philosophies called the seat of personal strength, healthy psychological boundaries, and self-sufficiency, the solar plexus. "This is also where we generate the ability to make decisions for ourselves, to handle crises and take risks."

You can make a difference in your life if you work hard. It is wonderful if you say to yourself, "I don't want to be rich and famous, but I want to make a difference." Once you start now seeking for answers to the important resources, you will find that the search can be very rewarding. Despite what other people may have told you, and answers they gave, you will still find the real fact through your ardent efforts. Be curious and put in more effort and there will be a more profound effect on your success

As I have been researching on this psychological fear aspect, God keeps on revealing facts and inspiring me the more. At 2.05 am on August 17, 2010, I had a series of dreams including dreams of Our Blessed Virgin Mary, Mahatma Gandhi, Rev. Dr. Martin Luther King Jr. and about my Church – Holy Trinity Cathedral Orlu-Biafra land, where we gathered for a celebration. In those dreams, each one was explained to me clearly. I woke up that morning happily, prayed, and thanked God. Hence, the dreams about Our Blessed Mother, Mahatma Gandhi, and Rev. Dr. Martin Luther King Jr. were wonderful inspirations for me to fight harder against fear. The inspirations shown to me were as follow: courage when you are pursuing genuine goals, fearlessness when you are saying the truth or asserting your thoughts, fearlessness when you are fighting against injustice. Be calm and gentle when facing difficult situations; be humble and peaceful as you are doing what is right. Never mind what people say about you or think about you, or the kind of treatment they give you, when you are acting justly. The same dreams urged me to be careful of diabolical individuals. In the same dreams, I was in my local Church at Holy Trinity

Cathedral Orlu where a group of Christian Mothers, including a visiting lady, were wearing their uniforms for a church celebration. The visiting lady was a stranger among the group because she was visiting, and some women began to discriminate against her for not being a member of their parish. When this happened, the visiting lady quietly and peacefully moved behind them to let them be in front of her. Immediately, I noticed her facial expression. I left where I was and went to her and hugged her, and she told me her story that the women were discriminating against her because she did not belong to their parish. I intervened without fearing anybody and I moved in the front of the women and sought for the (CWO) Catholic Women Organization's President and sorted it out with her. Finally, the interpretation of the dreams indicated that one should always stand tall and firm against injustice no matter where you are. Also, be strong in times of difficulties. The visiting lady walked away from trouble by showing them that she was more mature than they were in handling a crisis. She also applied the nonviolent approach like Mahatma Gandhi and Dr. Martin Luther Jr. and our Blessed Mother. Mahatma Gandhi, and Dr. Martin Luther King Jr. are role models when dealing with fear, crisis, and injustice. I feel confident when I am speaking the truth. I do not mind the effect on me as I do not exhibit partiality.

Section XVIII: Transform Your Inner Critic into Your Inner Coach

According to James Allen, author of **As A Man Thinketh**; "A man is literally what he thinks." And according to the psychological researchers, it is eighty percent (80%) negative self-pity thoughts such as - I should not have said that, they don't like me. I am never going to be able to do this; I am not a good speaker. These thoughts affect our attitude, our bodily biological functions, and our motivation to act. They make us stutter with fear, spill things, forget things easily, panic with sweat, breathe shallowly and taken to the extreme, they can even paralyze or kill us. Self-criticism is a reaction to an outside critical judgment by others and this takes place when one is not self-confident and self-supporting.

We are created and equipped with good conscience. In the beginning, according to Egyptian Cosmogony (theory about creation of the universe and its inhabitants), what was, was indescribable unutterable, incomprehensible power, alone, unique, inherent in the indefinable cosmic ocean called 'Nun.' This was before there was any complimentary existence of high and low, light, and shadow, presence and absence, life or death, heaven, or earth… (adapted from Cairo Museum N1160). God creates by projecting his thoughts and these thoughts are written in our chromosomes that contain the DNA which carries genetic information of how a man is made and maintained. The genetic information is the accurate Word of God. (Psalm 37:31) discloses, "The law of God is in his heart. But the genetic information is modified by culture, nurture, and the environment. In general, it is called conscience. According to Lawrence Kohlberg, a psychologist and philosopher, conscience defines justice as a basic and universal standard for a primary regard for the value and equality for all human beings and for reciprocity in highest human relations of equity and dignity. Egyptians call it "Ka" - your double. Biafran Ibos call it 'Agu' or 'Obi' (Echerem nobim-I think from my heart.) It advises you when you are in a good mood. So, you have a good conscience and good advice if you do not modify the word of God in you by having bad thoughts and bad habits. If you endeavour to keep to the true things and ways, you will modify your double positively so that when it comes to referencing to yourself, you will always receive good direction about how to think and how to do things. Lawrence Kohlberg, psychologist, believed that individuals acquire and refine the sense of justice through a sequence of invariant developmental stages. In 1957, while working on his dissertation at the University of Chicago, he tested the moral judgment of a group of seventy-two boys aged 10 through 16 by asking them questions involving moral dilemmas: The typical question was the issue of stealing a drug to save a dying woman. The owner of the drug was selling it for a price ten times what it cost him to make it. The woman's husband did not have the money and the seller of the drug refused to lower the price or wait for payment later. The question is what should the husband do? From the answers given by the group, Kohlberg deduced six basic types of moral judgment which corresponded to developmental stages, namely:

1. Orientation to punishment and reward and to physical and material power.
2. Hedonistic (hedonism-the doctrine that pleasure is the chief good for doing a thing) orientation with an instrumental view of human relations. The beginning of notions of reciprocity with emphasis

on exchange of favours - "You scratch my back and I will scratch yours."
3. "Good boy" orientations; seeking to maintain expectations and win approval of one's immediate group; morality defined by individual ties of relationship.
4. Orientation to authority, law, and duty, to maintaining a fixed order, whether social or religious, which is believed to be a primary value.
5. Social-contract orientation with emphasis on equality and mutual obligation with a democratically established order, for example, the morality of the American constitution.
6. Morality of individual principles of conscience which have logical understanding and universality. Highest value placed on human life, equality, and dignity.

Let us briefly look at what happens when you modify your conscience negatively by taking mind and brain-altering drugs–marijuana, alcohol, cocaine, hallucinogens (LSD) (Lysergic acid diethylamide) (hallucinogens-drugs that make the mind wander about).

Marijuana and Its Effect

- **Short-Term Effect**: *E*uphoria (exaggerated feeling of well-being,) mood elevation and pain-relieving.
- **Long-Term Effect**: *L*oss of drive and impaired learning abilities.

Alcohol and Its Effect

- **Short-Term Effect:** Reduced coordination, suppressed inhibition, slow processes.
- **Long-Term Effect:** Physical, psychological dependence, risk of brain, nerve, heart damage. Physical dependence - alcoholics have trouble sleeping, eat very little, and experience chronic restlessness. Psychological dependence - they have an inability to stop drinking, continue drinking despite harmful consequences and tolerance - the need for increasing amounts of drinks.

Cocaine

- **Short-term Effect:** Alertness, sense of power.
- **Long-term Effect:** Strong psychological dependence - see alcohol for explanation.

Hallucinogens (LSD)

- **Short-Term Effect:** Perceptual disorder.
- **Long-Term Effect:** Flashbacks, brain damage. This is what a person, a subject reported after taking a hallucinogenic (LSD). In a psychological test, the subject's perception of his body became unpleasant. His limbs seemed to be distorted or his flesh seemed to be decaying; in a mirror, his face appeared to be a mask, his smile a meaningless grimace; all human movements appeared to be mere mimicry, or everyone seemed to be dead. These experiences

were so disturbing that there was a residue of fear and depression left long after. The above-mentioned drugs erode self-confidence; therefore, one must keep away from them. You are absolutely cheating yourself by seeking for your self-confidence from the harbours; rather, you are heading to self-detriment as many have already done to themselves. Think before you leap.

- **Science**: This is a way of knowing. Before self-examination and self-analysis, it is expedient to know when and how something is true or not. Scientists have established a set of rules and methodology by which truth is verified. Rules, procedures, instrumentation, and methods of interpretation of data with reference to facts, concepts, principles, theories, and laws are formulated.

Assessment, measurement, research, and evaluation are the processes utilized in obtaining accurate knowledge of any event. Assessment refers to the comparison of data to a standard for the purpose of judging worth or quality. Collecting data (assessment), quantifying the data (measurement), making judgment (evaluation) and developing, understanding about data (research) always raises the ideas of reliability and validity. Reliability answers the question of the consistency of the information (data) collected while validity focuses on accuracy or truth. Sometimes measurements (scores on tests, recorded statements about behaviour) can be reliable (consistent) without being valid (accurate or true). At a minimum, for an instrument to be reliable, a consistent set of data must be produced each time it is used. So, you must be able to know the facts and then make a judgment that you are right; Adapted from Bill Huitt, John Hummel, and Dan Kaeck, Department of Psychology Counseling, and Guidance, Valdosta State University 2001. Principles for Using Behaviour Modification (adapted from Krumboltz J. and Krumboltz H. 1994). Changing Children's Behaviour New York Prentice Hall. This behaviour modification applies to children as well as adults (those who are drug addicts and those who always fear) when social, personal, and economic factors lead adults to addictiveness to drugs, nicotine, and alcohol (Behavioural and Educational Psychology).

To Develop a New Behaviour, these Apply

1. **Successive Approximation Principle**: To teach a child to act in a manner in which he has seldom or never behaved, reward successive steps to the final behaviour.

2. **Continuous Reinforcement Principle:** To develop a new behaviour that the child has not previously exhibited, arrange for an immediate reward after each correct performance.

3. **Negative Reinforcement Principle:** To increase a child's performance in a particular way, you may arrange for him/her to avoid or escape a mild aversive situation by improving his/her behaviour or by allowing him/her to avoid the aversive situation by behaving appropriately.

4. **To Teach a Child a New Way of Behaving:** Allow her to observe a prestigious person performing the desired behaviour.
5. **Cueing Principle:** To teach a child to remember to act at a specific time, arrange for her to receive a cue for the correct performance just before the action is expected rather than after she has performed it incorrectly.
6. **Discrimination Principle:** To teach a child to act in a way under one set of circumstances but not in another, help her to identify the cues that differentiate the circumstances and reward her only when her action is appropriate to the cues.

To Strengthen a New Behaviour

7. **Decreasing Reinforcement Principle:** To encourage a child to continue performing an established behaviour with few or no rewards gradually requires a longer period or more correct responses before a correct behaviour is rewarded.
8. **Variable Reinforcement Principle:** To improve or increase a child's performance of a certain activity, provide the child with an intermittent reward.

To maintain an Established Behaviour

9. **Substitution Principle:** To change reinforces when a previously effective reward is no longer controlling behaviour, present it just before (or as soon as

possible to) the time you present the new, hopefully, and more effective reward.

To Stop Inappropriate Behaviour

10. **Satiation Principle:** To stop a child from acting in a particular way, you may allow her to continue or insist that she continues performing the undesired act until she tires of it.
11. **Extinction Principle:** To stop a child from acting in a particular way, you may arrange conditions so that he or she receives no rewards following the undesired act.
12. **Incompatible Alternative Principle**: To stop a child from acting in a particular way, you may reward an alternative action that is inconsistent with, or cannot be performed at the same time as, the undesired act.
13. **Punishment Principle:** To stop a child from acting in a certain way, deliver an aversive stimulus immediately after the action occurs. Since punishment results in increased hostility and aggression, it should only be used infrequently and in conjunction with reinforcement.
14. **Avoidance Principle:** To teach a child to avoid a certain type of situation, simultaneously present to the child the situation to be avoided or some representation of it; (or some aversive condition or its representation).
15. **Fear Reduction Principle:** To help a child overcome her fear of a particular situation, gradually increase

> her exposure to the feared situation while she is otherwise comfortable, relaxed, secured or rewarded (Educational Psychology Interactive).

This is an example of the fear reduction principle. There was a little baby named Jacob. He used to fear one kind of Christmas decoration. One day, I, the author, cut down that decoration from where it was hanging and handed it to him, and he was scared. He cried and screamed. To remove fear from him, I put that object on my head and began to dance around him. He watched me attentively and at a point, he began to laugh and stretched out his hands for me to give it to him to play with. Henceforth, whenever this little baby boy saw me, he would stretch out his hands for me to give him that object pointing his hand to where it was. Consequently, he got rid of his fear and started playing with that object. We shall now go into the arena where conscience and good judgment go into interplay when making decisions.

Stanley Milgram, a psychologist, in his office in the Research Association of Bridgeport, developed a laboratory experiment which provided a systematic way to measure obedience. The question is that the conflict between the need to obey the relevant ruling authority and the need to follow the dictate of your conscience becomes very sharp when you are face to face with the military draft during the war. When you feel conflict, you examine the situation and then make a choice among the competing evils. You may act with a presumption in favour of obedience but reserve the possibility that you will disobey whenever obedience demands a flagrant and outrageous affront to conscience.

Here are examples of those who made such decisions. This is the story of one, Major General Smedley Butler, Commander, USA Marines, who was uniquely criticized. He said he was berated, insulted, and denounced as a snake or a fish and even cursed by experts. He said he was indifferent to criticism although, when he was young, he took it seriously when the jibes and javelins of ridiculous criticism were hurled at him. He mentioned a case of an incident when a reporter from the New York Sun attended a demonstration meeting of his adult-education classes and ridiculed him and his work. He was insulted personally and so he telephoned Gil Hodges, the Chairman of the Executive Committee of the Sun, demanding that an article be printed, stating the facts instead of ridicule. Later on, he said he was ashamed by fussing about the whole incident because half of the people who bought the paper never saw the article. Half of those who read it regarded the whole thing as an innocent joke. Half of those who gazed at it with interest forgot all about it within a week. He realized that people were not thinking about you or what was said about you but instead, they were thinking about themselves and what they were up to. He advised that if we were lied about, ridiculed, double-crossed, knifed in the back, and sold out by one of our intimate friends, we should not lose our heads in indulging in an exercise of self-pity and recrimination. He reminded us of what happened to Jesus when one of his twelve intimate disciples betrayed him for a price which would amount in our modern money to about nineteen dollars. Even one of the twelve disciples of Jesus declared he did not know Jesus three times. Why should we expect a better deal?

Eleanor Roosevelt, wife of USA 26th President Theodore Roosevelt (1901-1909), was asked how she handled an unjust criticism. She said,

"Never be bothered by what people say, as long as you know in your heart you are right. You will be damned if you do and damned if you don't anyway."
Eleanor Roosevelt

H.P Howell, who died on July 31, 1944, was a leader in American finance, chairman of the board of the Commercial National Bank and Trust Company and a director of several large corporations, when he was asked to explain the reasons for his success. He said that each weekend, he devoted Saturday evening to self-examination, review, and appraisal of his work during the week. He opened his engagement book and thought over all the interviews, discussions, and meetings during the week. He said he asked himself: "What mistakes did I make? What did I do that was right and in what way could I have improved my performance? What lessons can I learn from that experience"? Sometimes he said he was very unhappy with the weekly review because of his blunders. As time went by, these blunders had become less frequent and this self-analysis had made him stronger and more successful. H.P. Howell borrowed his ideas from Benjamin Franklin, a farmer in Maryville, Missouri and once an Ambassador to France, who did his own self-analysis every night. Franklin discovered that he had thirteen serious faults, three of which are:

(1) wasting time.

(2) stewing around over trifles.
(3) arguing and contradicting people.

Franklin realized that he had to eliminate these handicaps in order to move forward. However, he decided to do away with one of his shortcomings every day for a week and kept a record of who had won each day's fight. The next week, he would pick another bad habit and try to conquer it. He kept fighting his faults until he became one of the most beloved and influential men.

An episode took place in 1929 that created great controversy in educational circles. Educated men from all over America came to Chicago to see what was to happen. It was about a young man. A few years earlier, the man, by name, Robert Hutchins, had worked his way through Yale, acting as a waiter, a lumberjack, a tutor and a clothesline salesman. Now only eight years later, he was being inaugurated as a president of the fourth richest University in America, the University of Chicago. His age was thirty years. Incredible! The older educators shook their heads. Criticism not only rained but also poured on this "boy wonder" like a rockslide. He was this and he was that - too young, inexperienced, he was vilified; his educational ideas were not straightforward. The newspapers led the attacks. The day he was inaugurated, a friend said to the father of Robert Hutchins: "I was shocked this morning to read that newspaper editorial denouncing your son." "Yes," the elder Hutchins replied. "It was severe, but remember that no one even kicks a dead dog." Now, therefore, if we are tempted to be worried about unjust criticism, here is Rule number 1- "Remember that unjust criticism is often a disguised compliment. Remember no one ever kicks a dead dog." That is to say, people criticize illustrious men, not ineffectual men. Never be afraid to handle your task as you do; always remember that many, many men have many, many minds. Another example is about a monk who was brought up in an uneducated family as well as a low-income family. As a result of this, he was less privileged in all aspects of life. Therefore, he was looked down on by his counterparts. His colleagues always regarded him as good for nothing. They never believed that he could handle intellectual responsibility. Each time they shared responsibility, they assigned him either sweeping the floor, washing dishes, or cooking in the kitchen. Hence, he did it humbly while waiting for God's time. When he had the opportunity, he was sent to do missionary work and at the end of his mission, he obtained admission to a university and behold, he made it successfully up to doctorate level. All his colleagues, who thought that he could not make it successfully, were surprised. They could not imagine it, so it was beyond their comprehension. Hence, they then switched over to castigating him, and talking him down and saying, he was this and he was that... Well, no matter their criticism against him, what matters is that he bravely made his life a success. Then, never fear any criticism but mind your business and attend to your objective goal. Remember all that glitters is not gold. Do not be afraid because you fall among low-income families or under-privileged families. In the first letter of St. Paul to the Corinthians (1:26-31) he declared,

> *"Take yourselves, for instance, brothers, at the time when you were called: how many of you were wise in the ordinary sense of the word, how many were influential people, or came from noble families? No, it was to shame the wise that God chose what is foolish by human reckoning, and to shame what is strong that he chose what is weak by human reckoning; those whom the world thinks common and contemptible are the ones that God has chosen—those who are nothing at all to show up those who are everything."*
>
> *First Letter of Saint Paul to the Corinthians (1:26-31).*
> *From Jerusalem Bible 1974, (p. 215).*

Dear reader, always project the positive mindset that you are able, and you can do it. No one is insignificant. It is not a question of one reared in a royal family, a well-read family, or an influential family, but it is the question of inbuilt virtue, grace, and courage in you. At the end of this paragraph, say to yourself, I must uphold my self-confidence come what may. If you say yes, God affirms it. Always fear not whenever you are pursuing your career ambition and never mind what people say or think about you. Remember that psychologically, what you regard or think about yourself is what you will be. Consequently, your self-assumption reflects on your behaviour. I take myself as an example; when I realized that I was among the underprivileged group, I refused to claim it. I rejected it and worked harder to uplift myself and others. Today I believe that I am among the middle class;

there is no doubt about it. I feel I am among the middle class because I know where I was at the beginning. You must use your willpower effectively to upgrade yourself to the highest level. Always make effective decisions to uphold your self-confidence. Rank yourself high and be optimistic. Once you feel optimised, you will make a tremendous success. I urge you today to feel positive about yourself. Always reinforce yourself positively and keep pressing on to maintain self-confidence. The pursuit of life goal needs total self-accountability. You must be up and doing to make it happen. Be consistent to employ effective measures. It is your responsibility and no one else's. Make yourself famous by feeling your present situation, by thinking about it, and acting on the solution to your problem. Myself, I was always feeling bad that I was fearful. I began to think of a way out; then I acted by embracing those factors that made me fearful and dealt with them. Once you finish getting rid of your fear, you will feel animated. Furthermore, to maintain your self-confidence, always do the following:

1. Self-examination each week.
2. Review your progress.
3. Self-analysis.
4. Self-appraisal.

Section XIX: Create Successful Relationships

"Better to remain silent and be thought a fool than to speak up and remove all doubt," is your credo if you had a high score on the Psychology Negative Thought Test of the Social

Interaction Self-Statement Test. People who receive high scores on the negative side tend to be nervous and anxious in social situations by saying self-defeating things about themselves. A high score on the Positive Thoughts Portion shows people who have little anxiety in social situations, and who believe themselves to be socially adept. Their **Credo** (principle) is *"Nothing ventured, nothing gained."* "Three components of love are passion, intimacy, and commitment," says Robert Sternberg. The most successful relationships continue to maintain a healthy dose of this romantic "chemistry" called passion. In the development of intimacy, once we are attracted or interested in a person, we begin to confide in him or her and want to share all our secrets with this person. The most successful relationships maintain a high level of intimacy indefinitely. After about six months or years, we develop a sense of commitment and value the relationship so much that we will do whatever we can to maintain it provided we are not going contrary to the law. Leading a successful life is foremost, a matter of believing in your abilities; when you have that belief, you communicate it in everything you do. Remember the people you meet will take away from their dealings with you more than just the words you speak. They will also read success in the way you dress, walk, speak, and carry yourself. Our daily habits and rituals tell people who we are, but we define ourselves to ourselves by our dreams. By believing in our abilities, acknowledging our dreams, and letting go of the hundreds of negative messages we send ourselves each day, we are empowered by confidence and inner strength. Instead of letting the drumbeat of your negative illusions set the pace for your daily habits, I hope you will allow your dreams to build the strong and vibrant rhythm of a successful and well-lived life. Our purpose in life ties to our core convictions about life and work and the strengths we draw from them. Our core beliefs about our work must match our personal values. As a financial advisor, for example, you must have these core beliefs:

1. I can work with integrity.
2. I can help people create comprehensive financial strategies designed to achieve their financial dreams and goals.
3. I can help people learn.
4. I can do my work with honesty and joy and put my clients' interests first.

This is an interesting study by Albert Mehrabian, Emeritus Professor of Psychology at the University of California, Los Angeles. His research was based on interpersonal communication and, while the percentages would not accurately apply to public speaking or group presentations, the implications are clear: non-verbal cues and tone affect how our words are heard and understood. The Mehrabian reach tried to x-ray how people perceive us whenever we act, speak, or use body language. The wise man says, "action speaks louder than words." Information ones gives out by spoken words matters a lot. People do listen to your body language, vocal sound, eye contacts, facial expression, and your posture. Remember, people hear your words but they mainly listen to you through the subconscious mind. They "hear" your eye contact, they "hear" your smile, and they "hear" your overall body language. What messages are your posture, your facial expressions, and your physical energy level communicating about what you are really thinking on the inside? For this reason, whenever you are speaking with people, make sure you are communicating your pleasure at them with both your words and your body language. You want your body language to speak with excitement and your vocal quality to be upbeat and lively. Be prepared before you start talking so that you will not exhibit any fear. Unpreparedness exposes you to fear and your listeners will perceive it through your body language. This body language expression is just like what Jesus told his disciples in Mathew 7:14-23; "nothing that goes into a man from outside can make him unclean; it is the things that come out of a man that make him unclean." For this reason, be mindful of your listeners when you are speaking because they are reading your posture. Always take a deep breath before you begin to speak.

Create an Exceptional Customer Relationship

Here are Just a Few Details

- **Give your Client a Warm Greeting:** A client's first impression forms within the first few seconds of meeting you. Make it a habit to greet people quickly and graciously when they enter your office. Focus fully on your customer - when you are serving a customer or a client, you must fully focus all your attention on that person.

- **Take Time to Explain Your Product or Service**: Take time with your customers to educate them about the efficacy of your product or service. Do not rush them to make a decision. Remember, developing a strong relationship with your customer is more than simply making a sale.
- **Pay Attention to the Appearance of Your Business and Its Staff**: Everyone who works in your place of business should look like the ideal company representative; clean, smart, and eager to serve. Make sure your employees wear uniform or badges so that customers can easily spot them. Create a pleasant working atmosphere through small details; for example, soft appropriate music, good lighting, clean employee lounges or break rooms all make employees feel happier and more valuable. Such feelings contribute to improved performance, productivity, sales, and better service.
- **Demonstrate Commitment to Community Service**: Your willingness to invest money, time, and effort into improving your community, improves the community's trust in, and appreciation for, your business.
- **Promote Your Business's Image - Strategy:** In a typical grocery store, placed right at eye level in very conspicuous locations throughout the store, are items that people want rather than need. It is called "shelf-space." That is the strategy for selling impulse items and it works. Constructing a strong image is a powerful strategy you can use to catch the attention of your customers.

- **Making the Most of Face-to-Face Contact:** Deliver your information in manageable segments so that your listeners will learn more, remember more, and walk away feeling better about you and your services.

Capture the Listener's Attention with Verbal Flags

Every presentation, appointment, consultation, or retail sales encounter contains a few specific points that listeners must remember. Highlight important points for your listeners by using verbal flagging techniques such as lowering your voice and pausing and then saying, "this is one of the key points of our discussion."

Here are Other Effective Verbal Flags

- "Here is something you may want to remember."
- "You may really want to listen to this."
- "Are you ready?"
- "Put a star by this piece of information."
- "Circle this."
- "Underline this."

Use informational handouts of printed agenda with room for jotting down meeting notes. Use visual effects to drive home ideas such as photographs, charts, PowerPoint presentations, product samples. If you exceed your customers' expectations, they can recommend you to their friends, family members and co-workers.

Breaking Free of Negative Illusions

Dreams represent our passions in life and as such can push us forward. Negative illusions only serve to hold us back. It is said that the average person thinks over 400 negative thoughts about himself or herself every day. Our little brains go into action and we think, "I am not smart enough. My hair looks funny. I cannot possibly do that. I am sure they will pick someone else for the promotion. I am too fat. I am too skinny. I do not make enough money. I cannot. I should not. I am scared." 400 times we beat ourselves up with these miserable thoughts and set ourselves in fearful moods. Subconsciously, these fleeting ideas pop into our minds, destroy our self-confidence and diminish our potential. These negative illusions might as well be called lies because they simply are not true. We just never give ourselves permission to explore our wonderful gifts and talents. We need to look at ourselves from a different angle and see ourselves in a different light to banish fear. Let us count our blessings. *COUNT YOUR BLESSINGS*, we are told but it is not in our nature. We always count our problems instead. Today we are so primed to pay attention to bad news that we tend to ignore what is going on well. As soon as we solve one problem, we take the progress for granted. Every now and again, it does not hurt to take stock of just how good we have been. Start Counting Your Blessings by John Tierney, a columnist for Science Section of the New York Times, Reader's Digest February 2009: (p. 122).

1. **Free Time:** As much as we complain about being busy, the typical American has more free time than

ever - more than five hours per day, according to time surveys by the United States Census Bureau and Researchers at the University of Maryland and Penn State. In Victorian England, when life expectancy was only about 50, workers put in 60-hour weeks from age ten until they died. Today we put in 40-hour weeks. Over the course of a lifetime, you typically spend no more than 20 percent of your working hours on the job and experts say there will be even more free time in the future as life expectancy keeps on increasing and work hours keep shrinking. By 2050, in the industrialized world, it is projected that the average workweek will be just 27 hours.

2. **Peace:** Wars and terrorist attacks will always make us fear but it is remarkable to see how many of the world's 6.7 billion people now live in peace. In recent decades, despite the growth in population, the number of our casualties around the world has declined according to the Human Security Report Project from Canada's Simon Fraser University. And despite a new fear of terrorism following 9/11, terrorist casualties have been declining in recent years. Over the past century, even counting the World Wars, a person's chance of dying from war or violent civil strife, is less than 2 percent according to John Mueller, a professor of political science at Ohio State University. That means that the scourge of war is now comparable to the statistical risk of driving a car in the United States of America. That means no more fear.

3. **A Roomier American Dream:** While some people are struggling to keep their homes, most Americans still have plenty to be thankful for when they walk through the front door. In 1950, the typical new American house had one floor with 1,000 square feet, two bedrooms and one bathroom and even the bungalow was beyond many people's means. Nearly half of Americans did not own their homes and more than a third of the homes lacked complete plumbing facilities. Today more than two-thirds of Americans own their homes and the typical new house has two floors, at least three bedrooms, two and a half bathrooms and more than 22,000 square feet.

4. **The Reader's Revolution:** In 1970, barely half the people in the world were literate and many of them could afford only a few books. Middle-class people needed instalment plans to afford an encyclopedia. Local libraries offered a limited selection of books; new titles went on sale in bookstores but soon disappeared unless they were best sellers. Today, more than 80 percent of the world's people can read, and 22 percent have access to the greatest library in history. The web provides classic books and reference works and the online network of booksellers means that no book ever really goes out of print.

5. **The Horn of Plenty:** The royal dinners at Versailles (France) might have had graceful place settings but Louis XVI (the last French King 1754-1793 AD) would gaze enviously at the food in a middle-class home or restaurant today: kiwi fruit from New

Zealand, South African peppers, Thai pineapples, banana, and mango from the tropics. He might be amazed too at the way we take fresh produce, fish, and meat for granted in every season. Before, in the middle of the 20th century, the average persons in the world's poorest countries consumed less than 2,000 calories per day but today, a typical person in a poor country consumes 2700 calories daily, a nutritionally improved diet made possible by farmers growing more food at a lower cost. Food is so plentiful that in many countries the old concerns about hunger have been replaced by worries about obesity.

6. **The Modern Automobile:** Cars emit greenhouse gases (pollutants) and create maddening traffic jams. Compared with the models on the road in 1970, today's cars burn less gasoline per mile and emit 98 percent fewer pollutants. The basic Sedan today offers more comforts and safety than the luxury cars of old. The fatality rate has declined, and cars have become more reliable.

7. **Memories:** The gift of longer life has usually been accompanied by the loss of memories. Besides the new memory-improvement drugs being developed, we have got digital photos, videos, and e-mails to recall our best personal moments and the web to instantly help us remember who sang that song or which year the blizzard hit. In the past, only nobles could have scribes to write their histories. Today, we all have records of our lives to pass on to our descendants. Alfred Adler, a great psychologist, who

catered for melancholic- patients said, "You can be cured in fourteen days if you follow this prescription. Try to think every day how you can please someone." But George Bernard Shaw described a melancholic person: "A self-centred little clod (a dull, stupid person) of ailments and grievances complaining that the world would not devote itself to making him happy." Dr. Alfred Adler, in his book, What Life Should Mean to You, said, "Melancholia is like a long-continued rage and reproach against others, though for the purpose of gaining care, sympathy, and support." The real reason for this malady is lack of cooperation with others. As soon as he can connect himself with his fellow men on an equal and cooperative footing, he is cured. The most important task imposed by religion is "love thy neighbour." All that is required of a human being is that he should be a good fellow worker, a friend to all other men and a true partner in all aspects. Dr. Adler urges us to do a good deed every day. "A good deed," said the Prophet Mohammed, "is one that brings a smile of joy to the face of another." Why will doing a good deed every day produce such astounding effects on the doer? Because trying to please others will cause us to stop thinking of ourselves: the very thing that produces worry, fear, and melancholy. Mrs. William T. Moon, who operated the Moon Secretarial School in New York, banished her melancholy not in fourteen days but in one day by thinking how she could please a couple of orphans. She started off by saying that she was engulfed in a feeling of sorrow and self-pity after she lost her husband. As the Christmas holidays approached, her sadness deepened because she had never spent a Christmas alone. The day before Christmas, she left her office at three o'clock in the afternoon and started walking aimlessly up Fifth Avenue, hoping that she might banish her self-pity and melancholy and avoid going home to a lonely and empty apartment. She walked aimlessly to a bus terminal where she boarded a bus. After crossing the Hudson River, she heard the bus conductor say, "Last stop, Lady." Thus, she got off in a town she did not know. While waiting for the next bus home, she walked down a residential street where she came across a church. She heard beautiful strains of "Silent Night" from the church coming from an organist. She went in and sat down. The long-drawn rhythmic harmonic flow of the music made her fall asleep. When she awoke, she saw two small children who came in to see the Christmas tree and who were terrified to see her. She asked the little children about their mother and father. They said they had no mother and father. Here came her dream of helping two orphans. She took them round to a drugstore where they had refreshments. The two orphans gave her real happiness and self-forgetfulness which she needed. She realized how happy she had been and thanked God. The experience showed her the necessity of making other people happy in order to be happy ourselves. By giving, we receive. By helping someone and giving out love, she conquered fear, worry, sorrow, self-pity, and felt like a new person. If you want to banish worry and fear and cultivate peace and happiness, here is the lesson: "Forget yourself by becoming interested in others. Every day, do a good deed that will put a smile of joy on someone's face."

A Chinese proverb puts it thus, "A bit of fragrance always clings to the hand that gives roses." Much greater happiness! Greater satisfaction and pride in yourself! Aristotle called this kind of attitude, "enlightened selfishness." Zoroaster said, "Doing good to others is not a duty. It is a joy for it increases your own health and happiness." And Benjamin Franklin, American statesman, author, and scientist, summed it up very simply; "When you are good to others," said Franklin, "you are best to yourself." "No discovery of modern psychology," wrote Henry C. Link, director of Psychological Service Centre in New York, "is, in my opinion, so important as its scientific proof of the necessity of self-sacrifice or discipline to self-realization and happiness." Thinking of others will not only keep you from worrying about yourself; it will also help you to make a lot of friends and have a lot of fun.

Let us take the case of Mrs. Margaret Taylor Yates, one of the most popular women in the USA's Navy, a writer of novels. Her true story of what happened to her that fateful morning when the Japanese struck the USA fleet at Pearl Harbour (USA Military base in Hawaii in 1941 World War II) is interesting. Mrs. Yates had been an invalid for more than a year due to a bad heart. She spent twenty-two out of every twenty-four hours in bed. She said, "I would never have really lived again if the Japanese had not struck Pearl Harbour and jarred me out of my complacency and despair." One bomb struck so near her home that the concussion (violent shaking shock) threw her out of bed. Army trucks rushed Army and Navy wives and children to the public schools. The Red Cross workers telephoned those who had extra rooms to take in the Army and Navy wives and children and she was asked to be a clearinghouse of information about the whereabouts of the families. She discovered that her husband, Commander Robert Raleigh Yates, was safe. At first, she answered phone calls while lying down in bed. Then she answered them sitting up in bed. Finally, she got so busy, so excited, that she forgot all about her weakness and got out of bed and sat by a table. By helping others who were much worse off than she was, she forgot herself and never went back to bed except for her regular eight hours of sleep each night. It took her attention off herself and *focused it on others. It gave her something vital and healthy to live for.*

Conclusion

Building self-confidence, and conquering fear in one's life is crucial. Anybody without self-confidence is an empty vessel. Building self-confidence needs ultimate practice and firm determination as well as self-discipline. You also need an amazing support team to help you build your self-esteem. You cannot do it alone. You need checks and balances, role models to guide you. Imitate or copycat confident individuals and learn what they did to succeed. As you strive, let your motto be - **failure is not an option** to you; rather, success is your aspiration. This book is to help you achieve your full potential.

Building your self-confidence, conquering your fear, is a leading weapon to enhance self-esteem. It gives you a guide to control your mind in your daily tasks. It also assists you to dismantle fear that could undermine your ability to build your self-confidence. Since you have read through this book, all the resources to build up your confidence are available for you to use. I would like you to join me today, as soon as you finish reading this book, to roll back that stone of fear and lack of confidence on your way and say farewell to fear and welcome confidence. Bin them and cast them away: all the 'road-blockers,' bigoted evil people, radiators who are against your success.

This book will be a great inspiration to you. It edifies and directs you on how to handle fear in your life and drills you on how to build your ultimate self-confidence. It will help you to get rid of the psychological stress that piles up in you every day as a result of phobias. Also, it will assist you to check 'road-blockers,' and talk-down individuals or any other obstacles towards your aspiration. Fear would have caused me my religious vocation in two ways. One incident was when I was about to enter a novitiate; pressure was mounted on me from 'road-blockers' who would have made me quit, but I resisted. These road-blockers are real friends and relatives. All their advice and suggestions were quit, quit. I was given a prospectus then to buy my needs in order to be allowed into the novitiate, but I just left it on my bed because I was afraid to go back to the convent for no just cause. But I mustered courage and proceeded. My mother motivated me and gave me her blessings. "Chigi ga edu gi" (your God will lead you), she said. Really, God led me and is leading me. This was how my name Chinedum came about. In the USA I was subjected to fearful situations. I met with lots of obstacles such as finance, immigration, diabolical people, hostility of weather, etcetera. I was at the peak of calling it quits but God intervened. If it were not for Divine inspiration, I would have given up. But on each occasion, something pulled me back and encouraged me not to yield. In any situation, never be afraid; just trust in God and strive harder to sort it out. Never forget to say to yourself, I will resist till I free myself from fear. Sort yourself out because nobody will do it for you. It is not daddy's', mummy's, uncle's, aunt's, brother's, and sister's responsibilities; it is absolutely yours, period. There are many alternative solutions to your problems. You need to research to find those alternatives. Never allow anxiety to undermine your confidence and never give up because you will definitely make it a successful one if only you strive harder. One of my villagers said that I am not intelligent but smart. I was glad to hear that because "smartness" also enabled me to attain my highest goal in life. Whether smart or intelligent, what matters is to make it successful one. Once you are smart, you are equally intelligent because a **Mumu, or a dummy** cannot be smart or intelligent.

> *"Life ultimately means taking the responsibility to find the right answer to its problems and to fulfil the tasks which it constantly sets for each individual."*
> *"It is one's duty to make meaning into one's life "period."*
>
> -Viktor E. Frankl
> Man's Search for Meaning, 1963.

If you intend to gain self-confidence, develop a strong strategy to cope with your fear. Try to abandon anything that can lead you into worry. Avoid diabolical 'talk-down' individuals because they have diabolical influences on your progress. Another set of people you should try to avoid are negativity individuals, whose thoughts are full of negative influences. Try hard to avoid them because they are dangerous to your self-confidence. However, always cling to positive individuals because they are as treasure to the building of your self-esteem. I have never given negative people a chance; if you give them a chance, you will never make headway. Nonetheless, don't give anyone the key to your self-confidence. To build your self-worth, you need to embark with a positive attitude towards your lifestyle. You have to maintain self-integrity and self-control. My goal in writing this book is to encourage young people to start, in time, building up their confidence to enable them to fulfil their dreams. Therefore, they should hunt for those things that would enable them to achieve their life dreams. Hope is on the way if you do this. Above all, form good habits to attain your self-confidence today. Achieving your confidence is certain if you apply what you learned from this book.

Fifteen Self-Affirmations of Self-Confidence

1. I begin today to undermine my fear and enhance my confidence.
2. I am now discovering my possibilities without wasting time and I am embarking on my possibilities with positive self-talk and self-motivation.
3. I believe that no one is born insignificant, therefore, I have something very unique to offer.
4. I have ultimate power to be who I want to be; for this reason, 'I must persist until I succeed' I must never quit.
5. I quite understand that the only way to overcome fear is to do the thing one fears the most.
6. Therefore, I am striving to roll back the stone of fear that inhibits my progress.
7. I am firm, strong, and I must never give up until I get it done.

8. I am committed to constant and never-ending improvement.
9. I am to be productive without failure.
10. I must keep going even when the going gets tough; I will hang on till I get it done.
11. I am exerting more pressure to hunt down my fear.
12. I am making proper use of my time to build my confidence.
13. There is no occult compensation for fear and unsuccessfulness; resilience is the key.
14. Therefore, success is my destiny.
15. Absolute success is my destiny. This is total dedication to the affirmation of self.

You can get out of your difficult situation just by not stopping or giving up. Move ahead, shake it off, and take a step up momentarily. If you say yes, your chi (meaning God) will affirm you. This is absolutely key to success. In any situation, think smartly and positively to achieve your career. Using alternative measures is crucial in attaining your goal. When people look down on you, do not mind; rather, prove them wrong by acting great! You can see the farmer's little way of reasoning by getting rid of his donkey because of old age; but to his greatest amazement, his donkey said even though he was old and dying, he was smart as well. Then he smartly rescued himself otherwise he would have been a dead one. Accordingly, make it surprise -surprise in all your endeavours. Always remember that in life there are three obstacles to success which we must avoid in order to succeed. These are considerations, fears, and 'roadblocks.'

Considerations are those suggestions which water down your ambition to be better. Once you start thinking of embarking on a project, obstacles, considerations, and 'roadblocks,' begin to hover in your memory and whys and why nots would emerge. For instance, if you want to enter a teaching career, a question like this could come up; Am I qualified? Or is there a vacancy available? Will I be able to face the uniqueness of the students' behaviour? These are the possible questions you would often embrace. These thoughts help a wise fellow to analyse and develop strategies for the situation. But a fearful individual gives up and drops out. Are you the one? No, I am not, oh! So, never be the one; rather, seek for an alternative solution. According to Dr. Seuss,

> **"You have brains in your head. You have feet in your shoes. You can steer yourself any direction you choose."**
>
> *- Dr. Seuss*
> *It Takes A Village*
> *By Hillary Rodham Clinton 1996, (p. 146).*

This means you are responsible for your rising and falling. If you steer yourself in the right direction, you will definitely become successful in life. But if you steer yourself in the wrong direction, you will be ruined forever. Handle your aspiration well, and you will gain your confidence. Always bear in mind the Six wonderful serving men; what, why, who, when, where, and how? (a) What would I love to do in my life to lead me towards success? (b) Why do I want to do that thing? (c) Who would I consult to direct me and offer me wise advice and help? (d) When is it convenient for me to proceed towards this dream goal? (e) Where would I carry on this dream goal? and (f) How do I go about it in order to succeed? These have always been the questions of successful people. I advise you today to benchmark them in order to succeed. Benchmarking is a means of copying, imitating or modelling how others do things. You could practice this repeatedly to acquire a new skill until it becomes a part of you. You equally need to have an awesome positive team support system; that is, those who will help you build up. Here is a suggestion by Jeffers - "it is amazingly empowering to have the support of a strong, motivated and inspirational group of people." It is necessary to have this in order to succeed. I personally have a great team and they enhanced my life. Most important, always motivate yourself to do the following: Arise, undermine your fear, wake up, discover your possibilities, roll back that stone of fear which holds you back. Often remind yourself that no one is born insignificant; you are but what you want to be. Say to yourself again - "I will resist until I succeed" - never quit. Quitters are always losers. "The only way to overcome fear is to do the thing you fear the most." Then be firm, be strong, and never give up. The ball is in your court. You must kick wisely to score a huge goal that will earn you a huge championship medal - that is your success in life.

I wrote this book not because I am a genius or more intelligent than the others, but with determined effort in order to share with you my experience on the effect of fear. This is also to motivate you to combat basic psychological fear in yourselves if you are having the same problem as I did.

Fear is a psychological weakness in human nature. It is an unpleasant emotional feeling that undermines reasonable thinking. Fear always constrains one's progress. One must be aware and ready to fight it. It has both positive and negative effects on everyone. When we talk about positive fear, we mean fear of God and respect for law and ordinances. In this case, fear moderates our lives. It helps us to know when we are doing the right thing and when we are offending or going contrary to the law. A negative fear factor undermines individual abilities to perform daily activities. It makes one lag behind, while resulting in an unwillingness to perform accordingly. Fear is what we instil in ourselves, or what others implant in us. Thus, I intend to entreat you in this book to assist you to become a responsible individual. I am writing this book to help you dismantle fear that could disrupt your future progress whether it is made by you or man-made. I want you to join me today to bid farewell and rest in peace to fear. This book educates you on how to handle fear and its consequences. A famous author, Jack Canfield, in his book "The Success Principles" warned us about three obstacles that hinder ones' progress. He stated,

"It's important to understand that as soon as you set a goal, three things are going to emerge that stop most people - but not you." "If you know that these three things are part of the process, then you can treat them as what they are - just things to handle -rather than letting them stop you. These three obstacles to success are considerations, fears, and 'roadblocks.' Never allow these to stop you, because

> *"They are how you have been subconsciously stopping yourself all along."*
>
> Jack Canfield
> The Success Principles 2005, (p. 57).
> How to Get from Where You Are to Where You Want to Be.

This is how I was stopping myself in the past. I was always afraid of standing in a pulpit to read. Fear always overwhelmed me, and I would begin to have considerations and reasons for not proceeding. These considerations would always be fear of making mistakes and fear of failure, rejection from people, what people would say and think about me. After thinking this way, the next option is stepping down - that is, stopping myself. Once I stepped down, I began to feel sad, depressed, and upset. Psychologically, no one feels good when They don't do well. I hope you feel the same way. Be mindful of your fear, consideration, and 'roadblocks.' Consideration is one of the main 'roadblocks' in your progress. One has to be alert. This awful experience motivated me to embark on writing this book in order to get rid of fear in my subconscious mind and help you do the same. Fear would have stopped me from executing many of my major goals in life. Success depends on the individual's thinking; if you think positively, your mind will give you a positive result; but if you think negatively, the mind will equally issue a negative result too. I believe this because since I said no to fear, I have seen myself progressing effectively. Today, I implore you to say no to your fear. Avoid those things that will hinder you achieving your career purpose. These sorts are possible circumstances that bring obstacles to your adventure. You can overcome them if you work harder. As you read through this book, master how others succeeded. Never allow anything to be your **"stop signs."** Remodel your negative thinking into positive thinking in order to attain your goal. Success relies on positive thinking. Self-trust is another way of getting rid of fear and upholding your self-confidence. Once you trust yourself, you will overcome your fear. Self-development is always accompanied by considerations, fears, and 'roadblocks.' It is left for you to handle them to pave your way because they are potential hazards on our purpose. Finally, try to discover your sources of fear and obstacles in order to face and process them so as to achieve your goal. Always ask yourself these questions; "What are those things I am afraid of? Am I afraid of making a decision? Am I afraid of speaking publicly? Am I afraid of asserting my opinion? Am I afraid of commitment or responsibility? Am I afraid of competition? Am I afraid of being judged or criticized? Am I afraid of taking a risk? Or am I afraid of making mistakes?" You know yourself better so as you ask these questions, you answer them. Then as you proceed, think of a way out to disarm your fear. There is no medication for the cure of the fear; rather, you are the cure through positive thinking and application of positive action. Immediately you complete recognizing your fear factor, it will disappear from you and you will be freed. Just work on it.

Thank you, Jack, for your noble book - "The Success Principles", I was very delighted when I came across it and I said to myself I have found a meaning for my research.

I have found it interesting doing this research based on "Building your Self-confidence, and Conquering your Fear" because low self-esteem and fear are the chronic diseases which I have been suffering daily. Fear overwhelmed me in my teenage life. It inhibited me from the things I would love to achieve. Most often, I discontinued with what I intended to do as well as withdrawing from airing my views to avoid challenges from others. Today, I decided to fight against fear of this kind by doing research on it. I am encouraging those of you who are lucky enough to read this book to join me in fighting the war against low self-esteem and fear.

At this juncture, let me enlighten you on fear and its effects. Fear prevents one from building self-esteem, self-worth, self-reliance, and self-fulfilment. I encourage you to never allow these negative thoughts to dominate you. Try to build your confidence by ignoring fear and critics, 'roadblocks,' and unhealthy considerations. Attempt to delete them from your mindset. Another inhibitor one faces is critics: However, critics could help you define yourself and will enable you to decide whether you like that aspect of yourself or not. Critics *help one judge oneself.* According to Matthew McKay,

> *"one of the main factors that differentiate human beings from other creatures is the awareness of self and ability to form an identity and then attach a value to it. "In other words, you have the capacity to define who you are and then decide if you like that identity or not. "The problem of self-esteem is this human capacity for judgment.*

Building Up Self-Confidence

It's one thing to dislike certain colours, noises, shapes, or sensation. "But when you reject parts of yourself you greatly damage the psychological structures that literally keep you alive." McKay, said, "It seems that self-esteem grows out of your circumstances in life, and your circumstances in life are influenced strongly by your self-esteem. Self-esteem determines circumstances, this means that if you improve your self-esteem, your circumstances will improve. So just stop hating yourself, and you'll get taller. Try to learn how to create positive self-statements that will foster your self-esteem instead of undermining it. Avoid ill critics; this keeps your record of failures, but never once remind you of your strengths or accomplishments. The pathological critic is always busy undermining your self-worth every day of your life. Yet his voice is so insidious, so woven into the fabric of your thought that you never notice its divesting effect. Self-attacks always seem reasonable and justified. The carping, judging inner voice seems natural, a familiar part of you. In truth, the critic is a kind of psychological jackal who, with every attack, weakens, and breaks down any good feelings you have about yourself. The critic is always with you- judging, blaming, and finding faults...

Matthew McKay (2009).

Be mindful of chronic self-criticism. Apply positive reinforcement to reward yourself. Always bear it in mind that unhealthy self-criticism leads to fear and low self-esteem. It is better you balance your self-criticism, that is, criticize your weaknesses and evaluate your strengths. I want you to know, dear reader, that someone could put fear in you in order to make you feel bad or unbalance you. He or she does it out of envy. It is your responsibility to bin it. Fear is always out there as long as you grow.

Never allow people to let you down or make you feel inferior and stupid. Remember, not everyone was born with a silver spoon in their mouth. In an academic field, some are geniuses; some are average, and some are mediocre. Accordingly, wherever you find your talent, just bloom. It takes working harder to upgrade yourself. If you are a genius, give us your intuition, and if you are average, show us your ability etc. Always bear in mind that we are not equals and our figures are not equal either. Some are bigger and taller than others, but all are performing important duties. We are not equal in all aspects; in life, some are tall, some short, some others are white, some black, some others big, thin, some others beautiful, and some others ugly, some are wealthy, and others are poor. God made everyone unique to beautify his creation; everyone is important to one another. We should be grateful for whatever we have. Never use your talent to block others or put them down but uplift each other.

On June 10, 2009, something struck me, and I awakened and said to myself, "I must stand firm to fight against fear." And I made a deal of no win for fear. Then I began to disarm myself from fear. I must continue till I find myself freed entirely from this chronic cancer that attacks my marrow. Since I started working on this project, I have started to feel better, happier, and enthused. I was an eyewitness of fear that struck on 25th September 2010 at a gathering where some members were taking an oath to be full-fledged members of their associations. One of them could not stand in front of others to recite her promise. She was gripped with fear, sweating, her voice cracked, she was shaking, and fainting till members helped her to sit down. She was given a glass of water to cool her down. This is the active work of fear. After that experience, we met, and she narrated her life story to me explaining why she panicked. According to her, her husband was a perfectionist and always critical of any household chore she performed. As a result, this woman was fed up with the situation and suffered a nervous breakdown. To avoid him, she separated from her husband. Yet the fear and the nervous breakdown never left her. In this manner, beware, because fear could cost you your life. Always hunt down the cause of your fear and sort it out. Fear, as you know, could make you lose control of self. You better guard against it. Never look behind at your past difficult experiences because they would hold you back from moving forward. Though, St. Ignatius stated, "We use the past to provide guidance for the future." For this reason, I advise you never to dwell on your past; rather, use it as a point of contact to tackle your future involvements as I did and succeeded. Remember, your mistakes are part and parcel of life; without them, you cannot learn and grow. We all learn through our mistakes or from the mistakes of others. No one is above mistakes. Along these lines, do not be afraid of making mistakes. An American musician sings, "When you fall, we get up..." It is not taboo for one to fall but it is taboo to remain down when you fall. If you fall, get up and dust yourself off and keep moving. Always keep positive thinking towards success no matter the odds. Never sleep on your mistakes; always act quickly to fix them. As you strive to succeed, never be afraid of any difficult situation. No matter the odds, you must not fear any pressure even when there is an immense problem. Do not feel ashamed of asking questions because through them, you learn. Remember, the proof of education is to learn even from little children. No one is insignificant. Everyone is valuable in one way or the other. If one lives, one has ample opportunities and potential to improve the self. The essential thing is first to accept yourself, that is to say, total self-acceptance. As you engage in making efforts every day to enhance yourself, you will see yourself dispelling fear, worries, and anxieties. Try to instil encouragement and self-esteem into your daily life. Increase your learning every day. Endeavour to learn one new thing each day. In this way, you obtain wisdom and enlightenment. As a result, start living the life you know you crave for or deserve.

According to Anthony De Meuo, fear is the root of violence; "Ignorance and fear, ignorance caused by fear, that is where all the evil comes from, that is where your violence comes from. The person who is truly nonviolent, who is incapable of violence, is the person who is fearless. It's only when you are afraid that you become angry." Go ahead; think of the last time you were angry and search for the fear behind it. What are you afraid of? Are you afraid of making mistakes? Are you afraid of a crowd or fear of failure? Are you afraid of your opponent…? Fear will make you lose your balance; hence, you better watch it and begin now to work on it. A new driver does not look behind while driving to see how all the other cars are following her. If she does, she would surely crash out of fear. For this reason, it is advisable for you to put fear behind you. "Strong self-esteem depends on two things,

(1) learning to think in a healthy way about yourself, and
(2) having the ability to make things happen to see what you want and go for it."

A lot depends on you. If you lead the way you will surely make it. Develop positive rational thoughts of self-affirmation and responses, say to self I am carrying out this goal successfully without any inhibitions. Remove fear completely from your mind. Then demonstrate your ability and willingness to perform the goal you set. Irrational thoughts or self-defeat, these draw you miles back. Hence, avoid feeding your mind with negative images of self; rather, always try to empower yourself. Positive thinking helps a lot for growth and success. The critic is always with you, judging, blaming, finding faults etc. It is your duty to bin it and keep pressing on. Put on positive reinforcement to reward yourself. Never feel dismayed.

Unhealthy self-criticism leads you into fear; try to avoid it because it is deadly. Wish yourself forward-ever, backward -never. Never wait until someone else will pull you up; you are your boss and master of yourself. If you make mistakes, learn from it, and ride on. You make a lead then others could assist you. When agama lizard fell from a high tree, he looked right and left and nobody was there to cheer him up, so he nodded his head and cheered himself up and kept going. People can easily talk you down instead of cheering you up. In this way, cheer yourself up and keep moving on. I advise you to read the books from those great authors like *The 7 Habits of Highly Effective People - Powerful Lessons in Personal Change"*, *"In Search of Excellence"* and the rest of them to improve your self-confidence. If you are lucky enough to read these books, you may have an absolute transformation of self. They're for your self-enrichment Don't be afraid of upgrading yourself; fear inhibits your achievements. For this reason, do not be afraid, for if you are afraid, you will not attain your dream. Be firm and courageous in order to achieve your ultimate dream goal. The ball is in your court - catch it. Just start it and end it well. Practice, practice, and practice. Fuel your success with passion and enthusiasm. Create successful relationships. Be focused to achieve it. It doesn't matter how you started or where you started. Rather, what matters is where and how you end up.

Improvement

Always maintain constant self-improvement and self-assertiveness as you build your confidence. This is the way of maintaining your self-confidence. Fearless people are the ones that are full of experiences and full of the knowledge of facts of life. They are the ones who have experienced difficult times and events and successfully have maneuvered the strains and rigors that problems brought to them and have gone on to claim victory and happy results. It is not that you are a strong man or woman or that you are well equipped with weapons to fight the wars of life but that you are determined and resolute to carry on whatever comes your way in life with a thoughtful discernment of understanding the makeups of the issues at stake and appropriately calculating the corresponding remedy to effect a resounding answer to the problems. Fear helps you do all these things while, at the same time, keeps you anxiously cautious of failures and mistakes. Mistakes are most times unknown while wise executions are taking place, but, because of experiences and sober deliberations, mistakes are always spotted and dealt with accordingly. We cannot live without fear, but we cannot be scared by fear either. Since events of life in our daily schedule are fraught with all aspects of fear, we must daily look out for mistakes by carefully observing our procedures and always seeking improvements in those procedures in order to excel. For instance, a woman was appointed as a cook for making different types of soup according to planned recipes of ingredients. To improve the quality of the soup, she studied food using a manual in which several formulas of ingredients were laid out for making soups. She chose the recipes that were improvements on the ones she was using. In making soups, she applied her own new formulas. The result came out to be a marvellously delicious range of appetizingly tasteful dishes. The customers who enjoyed the soups came down with tips of money for the cook, expressing their appreciation. Here, determination to improve led to research for a good quality of soups. The result was congratulations for good works which made the cook full of self-confidence, fearlessness, and gratitude. Above all, give yourself a joyful enhancement by improving the quality of your life and, by so doing, banish fear and usher in self-confidence and self-esteem. Become the new you. Good luck.

Bibliography

1. Asimov, Isaac; George Zebrowski; and Martin H. Greenberg. Creations. New York: Crown Publishers, Inc. 1983.
2. Ackerman, Diane. The Marvel and Mystery of the Brain: Alchemy of Min. New York: Simon and Schuster, Inc. 2004.
3. American Society of Hospital Pharmacists from Detroit, Michigan, Washington DC; Baltimore, Maryland; Richmond Virginian. Medical Reference Library Prescription Drugs. New York: Facts on File, Inc. 1983.
4. Barack, Obama. Change We Can Believe In. Three Rivers Press. 2008.
5. Bucke, Maurice Richard. Cosmic Consciousness. New York: E.P. Dutton and Company, Inc. 1969.
6. Boorstin, Daniel J. The Discoverers. New York: Random House, Inc. 1983.
7. Brown, Michael H. A report on the Power of Psychokinesis-Mental Energy that moves matter. New York: Steiner Books. 1976.
8. Bricklin, Mark and Sharon Claessens. The Natural Healing Cookbook. Emmaus, Pennsylvania. Rodale Press; Inc. 1987.
9. Bhaktivedanta, A.C., His Divine Grace Swam, Prabhupada. Bhagavad-Gita, AS IT IS. New York: Bhaktivedanta Book Trust. 1976.
10. Black, Jeremy. World History Atlas. New York: Dorling Kindersley Publishing, Inc. 2004.

11. Baines, John and Jaromir Malek. The Cultural Atlas of the World - Ancient Egypt. Alexandria, Virginia: Stonehenge Press. 1991.
12. Burke, Theresa with Reardon, David C. Forbidden Grief. The Unspoken Pain of Abortion. Springfield, IL. Published by Acorn Books. 2007.
13. Butler, Gillian, Ph.D., Tony Hope, M.D. Manage Your Mind The Mental Fitness Guide. Published in the United States by Oxford University Press Inc., New York 1995, 2007.
14. Canfield, Jack. The Success Principles. New York: Harper Collins Publishers. 2007.
15. Constable, George. The Brain-How Things Work. Time-Life Books. 1990.
16. Carnegie, Dale. How To Stop Worrying and Start Living. New York Pocket Books. 1985.
17. Cooper, Thomas C. Horticulture The Magazine of American Gardening Volume Lxix Number 4 April 1991.
18. Covey, Stephen R. The 7 Habits of Highly Effective People Powerful Lessons in Personal Change. New York: Free Press London Toronto Sydney. 2004.
19. C.S. Lewis, www.goodreads.com/authoror/quotes/106006.C.S. liwis
20. Degras, L. The Yam. Published by Macmillan Press Ltd. London. 1993.
21. King, Deborah. Pride of Black British Women. London: Hansib Publishing Limited: 1995.
22. Do Bells, Inge N. Magic and Medicine of Plants, Pleasantville, New York: Reader's Digest General Books. 1990.
23. Downer, John. Weird Nature-An Astonishing Exploration of Nature's Strangest Behaviour. Buffalo, New York: Firefly Books Ltd. 2002.
24. Diop, Anta Cheikh. The African Origin of Civilization. Chicago. Illinois: Lawrence Hill Books. 1974.

25. Dureke, Margaret. Words And Phrases Of Wisdom For Spiritual and Emotional Upliftment. 2002.
26. Faelten, Sharon. The Allergy Self-Help Book, Emmaus, Pennsylvania: Rodale Press. 1983.
27. Ferguson, Jan. Perfect Confidence, Published by Random House Book. 2009.
28. Frazier, Kendrick. Solar System. Alexandria, Virginia: Time-Life Books. 1985.
29. Fleck, Henrietta. Introduction to Nutrition. New York: Macmillan Publishing Company, Inc. 1976.
30. Health January 1990 Volume 22 Number 1 Published by Family Media, Inc. New York: Brennock J. Michael 1990.
31. Holmes, Ann M. Medical Reference Library Nutrition and Vitamins. New York: Facts on File, Inc. 1982.
31. Ingham, Christine. Panic Attack. P.92-93. London: Thorson An Imprint of HarperCollins Publishers. 1993.
32. Jackson, John G. Introduction to African Civilizations New York: Kensington Publishing Corporation. 2001.
33. Jay, James M. Modern Food Microbiology. New York: D. Van Nostrand Company. 1978.
34. Joslyn, Maynard A. and J.L. Heild. Food Processing Operations Vols. 1, 2, 3. Westport, Connecticut: The Avi Publishing Company, Inc. 1976.
35. Janda, Louis. The Psychologist's Book of Self-tests. New York: The Berkley Publishing Group. 1996.
36. Jeffers, Susan. Feel The Fear And Do It Anyway. London UK: Random House Limited 1987.
37. Johnson, Peterson. Encyclopedia of Food Science. Westport, Connecticut The Avi Publishing Company, Inc. 1978.
38. J. Oti Awere Epe-Ara-Araromi-Ekiti. The Old Man And The Sea. Fatiregun Press & Publishing Limited. 1985.
39. Joyce, Meyer. Battlefield of the Mind. Publishing Company Faith Word. 2011.

40. Kramer Amihud and Bernard. A. Twigg Quality Control for Food Industry Westport, Connecticut: The Avi Publishing Company, Inc. 1974.
41. Keeton, William T. Elements of Biological Science. New York: W.W. Norton and Company. 1973.
42. Lebonsky, Rieva. Entrepreneur Magazine Volume 17 Number 12 December 1989. Irvine, California. Published by Entrepreneur, Inc. 1989.
43. Lewis, Allyson. The Seven Minute Difference-Small Steps to Big Changes. Chicago, Illinois: Kaplan Publishing. 2006.
44. Luther King Jr., Martin. The Autobiography p. 88. Printed and bound in Great Britain by Clays Ltd, St Ives plc. Sd 1998.
45. Luria, S.E. 36 Lectures in Biology, Cambridge, Massachusetts: The MIT Press (Massachusetts: Institute of Technology). 1975.
46. Lange, Dianne Partie. Health Magazine February 1990 Volume 22 Number 2. New York: Family Media, Inc.
47. Lamy, Lucie. Egyptian Mysteries. New York: Thames and Hudson. 1989.
48. Lastman, Anne R. Redeeming. Grief Abortion and its Pain. Published by Victims of Abortion, P.O. Box 253 Vermont South, 3133 Victoria. Australia. 2007.
49. Litvinoff, Sarah. The Confidence Plan. Printed and bound by Ashford Colour Press Ltd, UK 2004.
50. Mahatma, Gandhi. The Wisdom of Mahatma Gandhi Calendar. 2010.
51. Malesky, Gale and Mary Kittel. The Hormone Connection. Emmaus, Pennsylvania: Rodale, Inc. 2001.
52. Moore, James M. Plant Layout and Design. New York. Macmillam Publishing Company, Inc. 1962.
53. Marc, Woods Personal Best. West Sussex, PO 19 United Kingdom 2011

54. Mazrui Ali A. The Africans, A Triple Heritage. Boston, Massachusetts, Little Brown, and Company. 1986.
55. McGeveran, William A. The World Almanac and books of facts. New York: The World Almanac Books. 2005.
56. Merrell, David J. An Introduction to Genetics. New York: W.W. Norton and Company, Inc. 1975.
57. Myss, Caroline. Invisible Acts of Power. Printed and bound in Great Britain by Mackays of Chatham Plc, Chatham, Kent. 2004.
58. McKenna, Paul. Instant Confidence –The Power To Go For Anything You Want. Random House South Africa (PTY) LTD Published by Bantam Press. 2006.
59. Ozawa, Terutomo. Japan's Technological Challenge to the West 1950-1974 Cambridge, Massachusetts: The MIT Press. 1974.
60. Oakes, Lorna and Gahlin, Ancient Egypt. New York. Hermes House. 2002.
61. Oprah, Winfred. O The Oprah Magazine. The Best of Oprah's What I Know for Sure. 2000.
62. Og, Mandino. The Greatest Salesman in the World. New York: Published by Arrangement with Frederick Fell, Inc. 1968.
63. Piel, Jonathan. The Molecules of Life- Readings from Scientific American October 1985 Published by W.H. Freeman and Company. New York
64. Pennington Jean A. Dietary Nutrient Guide. Westport, Connecticut: The Avi Publishing Company, Inc. 1976.
65. Pelstring, Linda and Joann Huack. Food to Improve Your Health. New York. Walker and Company. 1974.
66. Pope, John A. Jr. Reader's Digest Volume 174 Number 1042 February 2009 Pleasant Ville, New York. The Reader's Digest Association, Inc. 2009.
67. Pescar, Susan C. Medical Reference Library Symptoms and Illnesses. New York: Facts on File, Inc. 1982.

68. Pinckney, Cathey and Edward R. Pinckney. Medical Reference Library-Medical Tests. New York: Facts on File, Inc. 1982.
69. Paone, Anthony J. S.J. My Daily Bread. (p. 226-227) U.S.A. Brooklyni, XXVII Febuarii 1954.
70. Ridley, Matt. Genome. New York: Harper- Collins Publishers. 2006.
71. Restak, Richard M. Receptors, New York: Bantam Books. 1994.
72. Rubinstein, Joseph. Annual Editions Readings in Psychology. Guilford, Connecticut: The Dushkin Publishing Group, Inc. 1973.
73. Rossini, Stephane. Egyptian Hieroglyphics. New York: Dover Publications, Inc. 1989.
74. Schuller, Robert H. Discover Your Possibilities. Published by Harvest House Publishers, Irvine, California. 1978.
75. Smith, C.U.M. Molecular Biology. Cambridge, Massachusetts: MIT Press. 1968.
76. Silvestre, Pierre. Cassava. London: Macmillan Education, Ltd. 1989.
77. Smith, Huston. The Religions of Man New York: Harper and Row Publishers, Inc. 1965.
78. Samuels, Mike and Benneth Halzina. Well Body, Well Earth. The Sierra Club Environmental Health Sourcebook. San Francisco, California. Sierra Club Books. 1983.
79. Steve, Miller. 7 Secrets of Confidence. Straight-talking advice on how to become more confident Headline Publishing Group A UK Company 338 Euston Road London NW1 3BH, 2010.
80. Sagan, Carl. Cosmos. New York: Random House, Inc. 1980.
81. Strudwick, Helen. The Encyclopedia of Ancient Egypt. London, UK: Amber Books, Ltd. 2008.
82. Steiner, Rudolf. Methods of Spiritual Research. New York: Multimedia Publishing Corporation. 1973.

83. Sternberg, Robert. The "Triangular love scale" from The Triangle of love: Intimacy, Passion, and Commitment by Basic Books of Harper-Collins Publishers Inc. 1988.
84. Sinnes, Cort A. Vegetables. Mount Vernon, Virginia. The American Horticultural Society. 1980.
85. The Editors of Rodale Press Inc. 20 Basics of Self-Sufficiency. Emmaus, Pennsylvania. 1980.
86. Thomas, Clayton L. Taber's Cyclopaedia Medical Dictionary pp. 2076-2079 Philadelphia, Pennsylvania: F.A. Davis Company. 1988.
87. The Complete Book of Vitamins by the editors of Prevention Magazine. Rodale Press. Emmaus, Pennsylvania. 1984.
88. The Life of Mahatma Gandhi, Louis Fischer. HarperCollins Publishers 77-85 Fulham Palace Road, Hammersmith, London W6 8JB
89. Vita Cost. Com Magazine, summer 2007, Source Code PC 777HL, PO 75, 006496. Boynton Beach, Florida
90. Robert, Anthony. The Ultimate Secrets of Total Self-Confidence. New York: The Berkley Publishing Group. 1979.
91. Frankl, Viktor E. Man's Search for Meaning: An Introduction to Logotherapy New York: Published by Arrangement with Beacon Press. 1963.
92. Rodham Clinton, Hillary. It Takes A Village. New York: Simon & Schuster Inc. Rockefeller Centre. 1996.
93. Reber, Arthur S. and Reber Emily S. The Penguin Dictionary of Psychology. London: Penguin Books Ltd. Third edition. 2001.
94. Wallace, Dan. Getting the Most from Your Garden. Emmaus, PA: Rodale Press 1980
95. Wilson, Gibson Ellen. A West African Cookbook. New York: M. Evans and Company, Inc. 1971.

About the Author

Author's Commencement Ceremonies

Rose Ann Nkechinyere Konye Nwadike is a daughter of the Ndiowerri Village Orlu in Orlu local government area of Imo State in South-Eastern Nigeria. She is the fourth among the seven surviving children of Mr. Konye Mmuegbulem John Nwadike and Mrs. Ojukwu Monica Konye Nwadike. She was born on April 18, 1958. Although she was raised in a non-Christian family, her parents allowed her to become a Catholic. As a child, she was brought up according to the

Catholic traditions. Having become fully initiated into the Catholic Community, Rose Ann, as she was named in baptism, later joined the League Girls. This is an order of young Catholic girls dedicated to following in the footsteps of the Virgin Mary, Mother of Jesus. The other groups she joined as a young girl were the Confraternity of the Christian Doctrine (CCD) which enabled her to teach Catechism to both children and adults at Holy Trinity Church Orlu, now called Holy Trinity Cathedral Parish Orlu. She taught Catechism to many children who were preparing for their holy communion and for confirmations for a long period of time. It is recorded that several of those who were filled with the faith who passed through the process have become Reverend Fathers and Religious Sisters. Among them was her nephew, Reverend Father Leonard Dim. She was also an active member of the St. Anthony of Padua Society. It was through her service with the Society that she obtained the inspiration to serve the poor and the needy. Today she continues to be highly involved as a member of the Holy Family Sisters of the Needy. Although she was highly engrossed in religious movements, she did not neglect her social life as a member of her community. In her village, she became the leader of the Umuoma Ndiowerre dance group. She was so renowned for dancing that her community likened her to her mother, one of the most talented dancers of the time, becoming famous in the town. However, Rose Ann was not only known for her dancing abilities; she was also known for her wisdom and her thoughts using many proverbs learned and handed down from her parents. Among other things which she believes and enjoys are the rich and wonderful traditions and customs of her people. This earned her the love and admiration of the then traditional ruler of Orlu, the late Igwe Patrick Achulonu, the Ezeigwe of Orlu autonomous community. She is fond of the late Ezeigwe of Orlu. She started her primary school education after the Nigeria – Biafra 1967-1970 Civil War at Practicing School 1 Orlu and completed her Primary six at Premier Primary School Amike in Orlu LGA. On the completion of primary school, she obtained her First School Leaving Certificate. She later continued her secondary education at Girls' Secondary School Ihioma Orlu LGA for the next five years. At Ihioma Girl's Secondary School, she did not forget what she learned at home; to be the best example to other students. As a reward of her good behaviour, Rose Ann was made prefect of her various classes from class one to class five. She also achieved a "Certificate of Role Model Honour," issued only to the best behaved in class. After her secondary school course, she learned how to type on old typing machines. Her typing skills, combined with hard work, enabled her to be self-employed. Soon, her typing skills opened a variety of opportunities for her to secure other jobs at Nneji and Sons Printing Press in Orlu town. As it is said, "one good turn deserves another." After one year of service at the printing press, she was nursing another great desire; this time, a desire to serve not in another printing press, but in a religious community. Soon came her time to choose her religious order. She had always known that God called her to serve Him among the poor and the needy. Thus, she left the secular life for a religious life to become who she is today -Reverend Sister Chinedum – meaning *God leads me.* Rev. Sr. Chinedum made her application to join the newly founded women's religious order by the name of The Holy Family Sisters of the Needy at Nekede Owerri Imo State, in South-Eastern Nigeria. Accepted by the Holy Family Sister of the Needy, she was trained and made her first religious commitment on 22nd of August 1990. It was in her first religious commitment that she took a new name - "Chinedum Joachim." In 1991, Sister Chinedum was sent to the United States of America for mission and studies. She achieved success in her studies and obtained an Associate Degree in Medical Secretarial Diploma with honours at Lackawanna College, Pennsylvania, USA. She also holds a Bachelor of Science in Computer Information System, Strayer University, Washington DC, USA.

Sister Chinedum return to Nigeria and made her final religious commitment on 2nd of September 1995 and went back to study in the USA, earning a Master of Science Degree in Business Administration, with excellence honours, Strayer University, Washington DC, USA. Also, at Lacrosse University, she enrolled for her Doctoral Program at the College of Behavioural Sciences and Psychology, obtaining a Doctor of Philosophy/Psychology, with honours summa cum laude. She also obtained State of Maryland Board of Nursing Assistant Certification and The District of Columbia Nursing Assistant Certification from the University of the District of Columbia, Washington DC, with a specialty in working with elderly people at the Providence Hospital, Washington DC branch of Carroll Manor. She also worked at the Institute of Psychotherapy with children with challenging behavioural issues. Being religious, Sister Chinedum has mostly worked with people with various life issues. In the

USA, she combined her spiritual life with brave work despite all odds. In the Catholics Archdiocese of Washington DC, she became involved with the Igbo Catholic community as their chaplain, teaching catechism and preparing children as well as adults for the reception of Holy Sacraments. She held the post of Assistant Coordinator of the Igbo Children Catechism group. She was best remembered as the Liturgical coordinator and directress of the adult and children Igbo Lay Readers' Association. She was also the Spiritual Director for Igbo Catholic Women's Association of Blessed Tansi, Washington DC. As a result of her faithful commitment and hard work with the Nigerian /Igbo Catholics, Sr. Chinedum was awarded an inscribed plaque in her honour. Describing Sister Chinedum in her hard work and committed life pattern would be paying a great tribute to her ever-loving parents. She learned from her parents to work before harvesting in life.

In the role of her ardent efforts, Sister Chinedum worked her way through the strict immigration lines and became a citizen of the United States of America. During her process of acquiring her citizenship, she was called upon to provide her fingerprints and asked to take a US history test exam on the same day. However, being a person who does not take chances, she has always prepared herself for all circumstances of life. True to her unsurprising nature, she took the citizenship test and scored a 100 percent. In her theology of life, she would always believe that; "with God all things are possible and with the mystery of possibilities, one can always conquer impossibilities." Sister Chinedum is also revered as one who is obedient and one who respects authority. Being an American citizen did not deter her from moving to the United

Kingdom when she was asked to be a missionary there by the Superior General of her congregation. While in Britain, Sister Chinedum took the exam for UK-Life and passed it and she secured her UK permanent resident permit. Staying in the UK was a lot of fun for her as she worked tirelessly with the Good Counsel Network Apostolate in taking care of vulnerable single young mothers, becoming their Assistant House Manager. This led her to enrol in a Module 4 Counselling Skills Course in Cambridge Opening College to enable her to help the young mothers in pregnancy crisis. Later, she left for Lancaster and embarked in New Evangelisation Ministry in Lancaster in 2015 for a few months.

One of the sister's philosophies is constant self-improvement which she always followed in achieving her fundamental goals. On the 11th of February 2013, she enrolled in the Association of Christian Counselling Membership to help those in everyday crisis as part of her mission. Sister Chinedum goes to the "Abortuary centre" (abortion clinics) weekly to counsel pregnant ladies who intend to go for an abortion. Through this mission, she has saved many babies from being aborted. She organized meetings and talked to all these vulnerable mothers at least once every month. She has also extended her spiritual activities to St. Pius X Catholic Church where she served as a Liturgical Reader and a Spiritual Directress for the Legion of Mary of Our Lady of Good Counsel Presidium. Sister Chi, as a devoted religious woman, is always keen to help the faithful wherever they need counsel.

In her former church, Saint Mary Magdalene Willesden Green, in London, she was commissioned Eucharistic Minister for the sick. Sister Chinedum worked at Windsor Primary

School with "Play With Us Child Care Provision" East Ham, Manor Way, UK for six years. She also did volunteer work at St. Joachim's Catholic Primary School, London as an assistant teacher. Presently, Chinedum works Childcare Practitioner in the UK. As a dedicated leader, she was promoted to the Leadership of her Religious Community in the UK and became the first Zonal Superior of The Holy Family Sisters of the Needy (English Zone) and the first Chair of The HFSN Board of Trustees for HFSN Charity UK as well as her community local superior. At present, she is in charge of the HFSN apostolate in London. Her belief in the mystery of possibilities leads the way to her success in life. She has always been successful in life even though she was brought up in a home where neither of her parents had a formal education. She dedicated herself to academic hard work through self-discipline. Her parents were non-Christians, yet she became the first "Reverend Sister" in her village, Ndiowerre. This is another affirmation of her philosophical belief in the "Mystery of Possibilities." There is an Igbo proverb which says, "Onye kwe chi ya kwe"- meaning, "If one agrees, one's God consents. 'With her advice, Chinedum would say; "Do not sleep; awake and work yourself up." She is dedicated to time management. She has used her time well and attributes her success in life to this. She has urged young people to plan their time well in order to be successful in life, because, for her, experience is always the best teacher.

Reverend Father Leonard O. Dim
Author's Nephew
Ordained a Catholic Priest of Palm Beach Florida, USA.
July 28, 2014.

www.ingramcontent.com/pod-product-compliance
Lightning Source LLC
Chambersburg PA
CBHW031545080526
44588CB00018B/2700